BOUNDARIES

To John,
with best wishes

Roy Wright

BOUNDARIES

A memoir

Roger Knight

with forewords by
Sir Tim Rice and Mike Brearley

J.W. McKENZIE

J.W. McKenzie Ltd
12 Soneleigh Park Road,
Ewell, Epsom, Surrey KT19 0QT
Tel 0208 393 7700

First published 2021

ISBN of standard edition: 978 0 94782142 5

ISBN of limited edition: 978 0 94782141 8

Printed and bound in Great Britain by
CPI Antony Rowe, Bumpers Way, Chippenham SN14 6LH

Contents

This memoir is dedicated to

Chris

Katie and Roy, Graeme and Meredith

Anna, Danny, Jonah, Alex and Mariella

to say I love them
and to thank them for the many wonderful
and happy memories we all have to share.

Photographs

The photographs in the picture section come from a variety of sources.

Those on the section's pages 3, 9 (top), 10 and 11 appear by permission of Getty Images, the one on page 4 from Sussex County Cricket Club, the one on page 5 from Surrey County Cricket Club and the one of Cambridge University on page 2 from Mano Ponniah. I am grateful to them all for their help.

The other photographs are from my personal collection, with special thanks to my sister Cheryl for providing the original prints of some of our childhood pictures.

Foreword

Sir Tim Rice

There have been more books written about cricket and cricketers than about any other sport, unless chess is regarded as a sport (I prefer to think of Chess as a musical). Countless cricketing biographies or autobiographies have been published, as have myriad accounts of tens of thousands of cricket matches ranging from Test matches to struggles on the village green. I have many overflowing shelves attesting to these facts – from the Bible that is Wisden to the most obscure, and probably unsung, thoughts and memories of a long-forgotten number eleven. So do we, even the most dedicated cricket bibliophile such as I, need yet another book on the subject, no matter how much we love the wonderful game?

Well, the answer is probably no, as the unoriginality or blandness of eight out of ten cricketing tomes proves – not that this fact stops me buying about six or seven of them. But if the author has an original or important tale to tell, offering a new perspective gained from an unusual personal story, then the answer is definitely yes. And Roger Knight is one such author.

Roger, I know, would be the first to concede that he was never quite in the highest cricketing rank as a player – a remarkably good one although perhaps not up there with the veterans of a hundred-plus Tests. However, very few of these cherished heroes can match Roger as a writer – and few have contributed more to cricket than he has, both on and off the field.

His story is a combination of good fortune, determination and honesty. He self-deprecatingly describes himself as a conformist, but that admission in itself is paradoxically an indication that he is not. He has always been aware of, and grateful for, his privileged position and upbringing but, more important, just as aware of the lesser advantages enjoyed by others. He has been fired by a combination of Christianity, self-awareness and humour (as his celebrated graces testify).

I got to know Roger well when I had the great honour of being MCC President in 2002. I could not have survived my year in that exalted position without the wisdom, experience, tact and friendship of Roger as the thirteenth MCC Secretary. Furthermore he was dealing with perhaps the least gifted cricketer ever to have been president. When I rather unkindly mentioned just now that Roger might not have been in the first cricketing rank, I was pushing my luck as I doubt if I would even have scraped into the tenth rank.

As with any organisation with 25,000 people to keep happy and, perhaps more relevant, dramatic changes, both political and social, continually developing in the world outside Lord's, complications would occasionally arise, but Roger during his 12 years at the helm, working with ten Presidents, steered a careful and ultimately invaluable course through sometimes choppy waters. His account of those years at the game's HQ will be an invaluable resource for future historians as well as an enthralling tale right now.

Here is an autobiography that gives readers insight into the worlds of education, amateur and professional sport, travel and humanity – fascinating because Roger has somehow simultaneously led both a conventional and unusual life, describing the advantages and challenges of both, his wife Chris and his family most assuredly his greatest champions. His book is definitely not one of the eight to be politely shelved.

Foreword

Mike Brearley

Roger's memoir describes well the life of a man with several strings to his bow. In his account he comes across (as in life) as friendly, optimistic, firm and thoughtful. He takes his responsibilities seriously, along with good humour and self-deprecation. He has had an interesting life and has usually, if not always, left the communities where he worked in a better state than when he arrived (as, he writes, he hoped to have done in his three years as headmaster of Worksop College). He enjoyed his time at Lord's as Secretary (i.e. Chief Executive) of MCC, and later as President, living through interesting times. He was running the place when MCC in 2000, against stubborn opposition, at last opened its membership doors to women. All this is clearly, modestly and positively conveyed.

I want to speak here though about only one aspect of the book, namely the realisation that dawned on me as I read it of how much he and I have had in common. Both of us have lived 'charmed lives' as he puts it in his first sentence, avoiding wars, fortunate to have had excellent educations and being enabled to have at least two careers that we loved. We have been lucky too in our families.

We were sons of schoolteachers, each going to independent, boys-only day-schools in London where our fathers taught. Both of us did well in school-approved ways – sport and work in particular – and went to Cambridge. Four years apart in age, we played professional cricket, becoming county captains, but with further (not to do with cricket) aspirations.

Psychologically, I think sport provided for us not only an opening for our spontaneity and selfhood but also a route to acceptance and respectability in a broadly public school/university tradition.

Roger writes that he and his wife Chris both tended to deal with difficulties by looking forward to the next challenge (following, as he says, John Edrich's excellent advice for batting – 'don't think about or dwell on the last ball, it's the next one that can get you out').

Writing a memoir is, of course, a matter of looking back and of reviewing how one did or didn't change. One of the most poignant passages of the book comes at the beginning, when Roger writes of having been when young: 'shy and unconfident. I never felt that I was one of the dominant personalities. I was often made captain, probably because I was more compliant than the strongest characters and kept to the rules ... I didn't want to step out of line. I was aware of boundaries at an early age. This desire to conform has always remained. Perhaps becoming a schoolmaster, a county cricket captain and the Secretary of MCC contributed to the necessity of wanting to wear the right clothes, say the right things and make the right impression.'

For much of the book, I think it is between the lines that one senses this struggle, between the shy boy, who is boosted by his roles and by his conscientious responsibility, and the man, who longs to be integrated easily among people of many different kinds and be able to let go further; to risk stepping out of line, to risk wearing the wrong clothes. One day in 1978, after Roger had read the riot act to the Surrey team, Robin Jackman, his vice-captain, thoughtfully took him aside, suggesting that his team-talks were felt by some players to be too 'schoolmasterly' – and Roger tried to address this.

I know something of these feelings. Cricket provided us with 'solutions' – not only by becoming skilful players, and later captains, but also by giving us a feeling of acceptance in the banter, humour and ordinary liveliness of team life. In those days professional cricketers came from every walk and indeed from many different cultures, countries and races. Cricket gave us a chance to relax and be more spontaneous than we might otherwise have been, on and off the field.

Preface

A Charmed Life

In many ways I have had a charmed life. I was born after the Second World War and was too young for conscription; had a supportive mother and father; was educated at a top school, having passed the 11+, and university and grew up in a large school house with thirty boarders, a competitive younger sister and a very big garden as well as having Dulwich College's playing fields and facilities close by. Later, two headmasters were prepared to allow me to teach for two terms each year, and three county cricket clubs employed me for the other five months; a wife and two children stood by me through the two time-consuming careers in education and professional sport; and, most fortunately of all, I retained good health.

At first, I was shy and unconfident. Few would have predicted what was to come. At Dulwich College Preparatory School I was able to cope academically and compete on the sporting field, but the move to Dulwich College at eleven placed me in a vast school with many more competitors and able pupils. I never struggled to get into sports teams, but I never felt that I was one of the dominant personalities. I was often made form captain, probably because I was more compliant than the stronger characters and kept to the rules. With a father teaching in the school, I didn't want to step out of line. I was aware of boundaries at an early age. This desire to conform has always remained. Perhaps becoming a schoolmaster, a county cricket captain and a Secretary of MCC contributed to the necessity of wanting to wear the right clothes, say the right things and make the right impression.

It did help that I was born in September, right at the start of the academic year, and therefore I was always one of the oldest in the year group. It also helped my confidence that I was tall and fit, blessed with good hand-eye coordination. It was success in sport that helped my self-confidence to grow. After A Levels I stayed at the College for a seventh term, to attempt a scholarship to Cambridge. I never thought that I had a chance, but I did gain a place and then decided to stay on for two more terms at Dulwich to retake and improve my German A Level grade. By this time I was nineteen and still a schoolboy, so rugby and cricket produced more success.

11

Going up to St Catharine's College, Cambridge, I soon realised that there were other modern linguists in my year who had read more, spent more time in the foreign countries and were much more able to speak the languages we were studying than I was. Again it was sport, initially rugby in the first term and then cricket in the summer, which boosted my confidence. It also made me realise how much fun team sports were. They encourage banter amongst team-mates, a sense of perspective and the need to accept as a group the ups and downs of winning and losing.

I had learned at Dulwich College that wit and humour were essential to keep a balance in life. Quick-witted South Londoners always had a ready response to lighten the mood. I think and hope that this part of my character has developed and remained a constant part of me. It may not always have been apparent to others, because I chose throughout the two careers to take my responsibilities seriously. However, I knew, as I became more confident, that I could enjoy the lighter side of situations, even though I did so often without showing it to those around me.

Standing in front of a class gave me confidence to speak publicly. Finding success in sport gave me more topics about which I felt able to speak and hold my own in conversations. Running a boarding house, an HMC independent school, a professional cricket team and a private members' club taught me about management and defined how I, personally, would lead other people and organisations.

Whether we want to or not, everyone is always moving on. When it happens, do we want to hang on to the past longingly or do we move on and embrace any future challenges? I have tended not to look back but to be ready and willing to welcome new opportunities which have arisen. From cricket combined with teaching to teaching full-time, from teaching to cricket administration, from employment to retirement, my wife Chris and I have moved on and always looked forward to the next challenge. Of course we have looked back but, as we have been determined not to regret the major decisions we have made, it has been easier to react positively to the new situations.

One of the best pieces of advice given to me by John Edrich when I was a young batsman starting out in first-class cricket was not to worry about the last ball you faced. As he said, if you're still at the crease, even if you've been beaten all ends up, it is the next ball that matters, because that's the one that can get you out. As on the cricket pitch, so in life. There is an appropriate time to learn from past mistakes, but the immediate future has to be embraced and demands concentration. We have to move on and clear our mind so that we can think positively and operate efficiently.

Through it all, I have always realised and appreciated how fortunate I have been. I am grateful to so many people, who have stood by me, advised and guided me, led me, become colleagues and friends or have been prepared to follow and support me as a leader. Above all, though, I am grateful to my close family, who have supported me as a son, husband, father and grandfather, putting up with my humour and competitive spirit. They are the people who know me best.

All individuals are inevitably influenced in some way by the background into which they are born and in which they grow up. I was encouraged at home and at school to be part of a team but to remain my own person. Perhaps that is what drew me into cricket, which requires individual skills and decision-making within a team framework. It also taught me to respect other people, whether in authority and leading, part of a peer group or those expecting to be led.

My life has been a journey through schools and through sports, especially cricket and rugby. From 1970, when I left Cambridge after four enlightening years bringing greater maturity and independence, I was a schoolmaster who played cricket in the summers. For the first fourteen of the twenty-four years that I taught in independent schools, I spent only two terms a year at the schools. In the summer I played professional cricket and, for the first five years, that entailed two separate existences, living in Eastbourne for the winter and in Bristol during the summer. When I was invited back by Surrey CCC in 1978, the emphasis changed and I became a county captain who taught in the winters.

The years from 1984 until 1993 were the time when I saw myself as a proper, full-time schoolmaster, as a housemaster at Cranleigh and then, subsequently, as headmaster of Worksop College. New opportunities arose in the years ahead, and from 1994 our family life changed completely as we moved down to London for me to work as MCC Secretary.

Part One

Twin Careers – Cricket and Teaching

1

Early Life

Family

As those who have read James Hilton's book 'Goodbye Mr Chips' will know, the novella tells the story of a beloved schoolteacher, Mr Chipping, and his long tenure at a fictional minor British boys' public boarding school. My father, David Verdon Knight or DVK, as he was known throughout the thirty-six years he taught at Dulwich College, ended his career as a popular and much-respected schoolmaster. Like Mr Chips, he was conventional in his beliefs and exercised firm discipline in the classroom.

I am not convinced, though, that his views broadened or his pedagogical manner loosened after he married Thelma Patricia Dickson. Like Katherine in the book, my mother, Pat to the vast majority of her friends, charmed the teachers and headmaster and quickly won the favour of the pupils. My father was an effective teacher who became highly regarded by students and the school's governors of the College, predominantly a boys' day school in South London.

He taught geography at Dulwich, despite his degree subject being history. At different stages of his career he ran the 1st XV rugby, the 1st XI cricket, the 1st V squash, the RAF section of the CCF, Drake (one of the College's athletic houses, which competed against the other five, all named after famous historical people), Bell House (a junior boarding house), Geography Vth (a class that was generally in need of more support academically than others at the College) and the Middle School, of which he became the Head.

His sense of humour remained that of a schoolteacher, with full use of sarcasm, puns and dry comments expressed not only orally but also in the end-of-term reviews – productions which he wrote and directed for the boys to perform. He is fondly remembered by boys at the time for resurrecting the old Corps Shout, a light-hearted review at the end of the Lent term, and interpreting 'March Airs', where he wrote parodies of songs such as Offenbach's 'Le Belle Hélène', Noel Coward's 'What happened to him' and

Gilbert and Sullivan's 'Policeman's Song'. This was his artistic side, which was also expressed in later life in his painting. On retirement he helped found and acted as Secretary for The Alleynian Sailing Society (or ASSes, as they called themselves). Forty-eight years of love and service to the same establishment, as pupil, teacher and active Old Alleynian, is rare today.

My mother was a tremendous support to him and had to cope with his Type 1 diabetes and his fluctuating blood sugar levels, which were a constant concern. Our life was dictated by regular meal times, which he needed, and plain, unsweetened English food. The other members of the common room, particularly his first house tutor, Terry Walsh, were also perpetually on the look-out for any signs of a hypo (hypoglycaemia), when they would pump him with glucose or sugar lumps.

My parents were devoted to each other. She was a marvellous foil for him in the boarding house, entertaining governors, staff, parents and boys and generally keeping the family as her top priority. She was naturally gregarious, whilst he was perfectly happy with his own company, his pipe and a book, when he was not thoroughly involved in looking after and educating other people's children.

My mother used to push the pram, with me sitting on it and my younger sister, Cheryl, lying down, from Knollys Road in SW16, down York Hill, along Lancaster Avenue and Thurlow Park Road, to the College in SE21, where my father would be taking sport after school or, even further along the same road, to the Old Alleynian Club, where he would be playing cricket at the weekend. She often pushed us back too, which entailed quite a steep climb up York Hill. The Old Alleynian Cricket Club on Dulwich Common was, during many weekends, the place where my sister and I played cricket with other children in the nets or in amongst the trees and ditches, pretending we were cowboys and Indians in the days before they were referred to as cattle herders and native Americans. There was a family atmosphere, and we all made friends with others across the age groups.

I only knew one grandparent, my father's mother. My mother's parents were no longer alive, nor was my paternal grandfather, a well-loved Streatham GP, whose junior partner became our family doctor. There was another person, whom my sister and I called Gran and my mother called Tante, who visited regularly. She had brought up my mother and was a warm kindly woman, whom I adored.

It was much easier for us all when my father became housemaster of Bell House, a mere ten minutes' walk at most from the College and close to Dulwich Village. That was in 1957, by which time I was eleven and at Dulwich College Preparatory School, and Cheryl was nine and at Sydenham High School. Long before that, though, both Cheryl and I had been encouraged by our mother to play and enjoy sports in the back garden in Streatham. It was a small patch of grass with a rockery as a backstop behind the wicket, and the ball often went over the fence and into the gardens of our neighbours. For some reason we did not refer to them as Mrs Hendry or Mrs Franklyn, but as Auntie Kudu and Auntie Laddie, after their dogs' names. They were forever throwing the ball back, and I learnt to hit straight and on the ground, so that the games did not end prematurely.

There are other memories of the early years in Streatham. There was the walk down Valley Road to stand outside the large window to watch the milk being mechanically poured into glass bottles. There was the drive to Dulwich College Preparatory School, where I was selected to play in the Under-11 cricket team and the 1st XI football team. Early competitive instincts were encouraged on Sports Day, when Ian Carpenter and I used to contest the 100 yards, and in the classroom to see which of us would come top in Latin.

DCPS had a brick swimming pool, which usually had leaves in it and was unheated, so swimming was never a priority for me until, at Dulwich College, non-swimmers had to wear an almost transparent nappy-like white pair of trunks, tied at the side. The incentive to swim ten lengths and graduate to wearing a pair of blue or black speedos was immense as I moved on to the College!

Life in Dulwich

The years in Bell House were very much my formative years. As an eleven-year-old, and up to thirteen, I played every conceivable sport in the large garden with the boarders of my own age. Baseball with a cricket stump, mini-cricket with a sawn-off bat and 'gaining ground' by kicking a rugby ball were the most popular, but athletic races and tennis also played their part.

Gaining ground was a competition between one or more players on each side, attempting to punt or drop-kick the ball into space, from where the opposition had to kick it back, and in reply trying to catch the ball, which allowed our team member to take three leaps forward before kicking. A knock forward or dropped catch led to three steps back before kicking. The winner had to land the ball behind an imaginary goal-line with a drop-kick without the opponent touching or catching it. The boarding house had an enormous expanse of grass, which was ideal for energetic youngsters.

Table tennis and snooker in the common room were always an option when it rained. Constant games of table tennis on wet days when we could not play outside must have helped my hand-eye coordination, because watching the small ball closely and timing it to make sure that it was returned with the right amount of pace and accuracy were good practice for watching a cricket ball and easing it through the gaps in the field, with timing as important as power.

There were always boys ready to compete at the various sports, and in the holidays there were local friends, boys and girls, who enjoyed the same games and competitions. My sister and I thrived in a sporting environment and both of us went on to play several sports at county level as we grew up. Looking back, I am delighted that I did not concentrate on only one sport, as is too often the case today. All of these different sports helped me to improve in my favourite sport of cricket.

As I became older than the senior members of the boarding house, who were in the 3rd Form (Year 9) at the College, the relationship changed from competitor to coach, and I started to teach the house teams cricket, rugby and how to compete. All the while I was playing in year groups and then first teams at the College.

In rugby I established myself as a fly-half, in cricket as an opening batsman and off-spinner, fortunate to have Nick Cosh as opening batting partner and scrum-half in the year above me. Nick was a fine all-round sportsman and able academic, who moved on to Cambridge University, where he was a double Blue in cricket and rugby. In the year below was Simon Dyson, another talented cricketer and scrum-half, who had been a Bell House boarder. He played first-class rugby and minor county cricket, though he was good enough to have played for a first-class county.

Dulwich College was blessed with talented sportsmen at that time. Peter Howland was captain of rugby and hockey, I was captain of cricket and squash. Peter Oosterhuis, my father's godson, was beginning to show his immense golfing ability. He went on to play on the European circuit from 1969 to 1974, winning ten tournaments and heading the Order of Merit for four consecutive seasons. He joined the PGA circuit and won the Canadian Open in 1981. He was runner-up in the Open Championship in 1974 and 1982 and later became an accomplished golf analyst on TV. Robin Linnecar was a talented cricketer, who went on to gain a Cambridge rugby Blue, and Raymond Keene was already on his way to becoming a Grand Master at chess. It was easy to see why we became competitive and, in several cases, went on successfully in sport.

There were also a number of excellent musicians and some first-rate academics. In fact, Dulwich was an outstanding school, with a large percentage of boys who had passed the eleven-plus examination, so we came from many different backgrounds and were nurtured by committed, very good teaching staff. The Dulwich Experiment, as it was called, allowed boys to receive a top-class education with funding from the local authorities. It preceded the Assisted Places Scheme and the Bursary schemes that so many independent schools now support. It opened my eyes to the breadth of opportunities in education, and I opted fully into the system. It was vastly different from the 'Great Public Schools' so attacked by their critics for being bastions only of the wealthy elite. It was a privilege to have attended with the government scheme funding and to have come under the tutelage of inspirational teachers, musicians and sportsmen.

During the holidays quite a few of the local boys and girls played tennis at the Old College Lawn Club, which was five minutes' walk away. My sister and I were there a lot. Stuart Courtney, later to become the men's British number one squash player, and Jane Barham, who became his wife and also the women's British number one squash player, were both regular tennis opponents. The Bell House garden was well used and the three hundred yard path through the woods and round the lawn was the perfect place for relay and individual races. Life was competitive and filled with ball games. Cheryl also enjoyed the same opportunities at this early age, and she went on to play county squash and hockey and, after three years at Chelsea College, Eastbourne, became a PE teacher. Our mother kept a hand bell, which she rang from the upstairs kitchen window to call us in from the garden for meals. In the garden there was a magnificent beech tree, which we all climbed, including my mother when a difficult parent was in the boarding house.

Family holidays were spent body-surfing or playing cricket on the beach in Cornwall or travelling to the South of France, where my godmother owned a villa in Théoule. It was the perfect opportunity to practise my French and relax in the Mediterranean sunshine.

My parents were keen ballroom dancers and went to Peggy Spencer's Latin American classes in Penge. It also became something that I enjoyed, spurred on by practising, in my early teens, with my mother in the kitchen.

Scottish dancing and ballroom dancing were fun and probably helped to make me more nimble and lighter on my feet for sport. In later years, when we lived in Bell House, the junior dormitory had a marvellous parquet wood floor, so beds were moved out for New Year's Eve and birthday celebration dances, accompanied by Victor Sylvester records on the radiogram, which we carried downstairs from the sitting room.

We had a dog, a light-coloured retriever, which was one of my parents' answers for easing the homesickness of some of the boarders away from home for the first time aged eight. Another was the Hornby OO model railway, which travelled right round my bedroom at waist level on trestles made by my father. Building up all the additional scenery was quite a hobby, rather more than operating the trains on the tracks. The other hobby, which I always enjoyed, was conjuring and performing card tricks and other magic. It was also popular later with our children and their friends at birthday parties. The train from Herne Hill went to Holborn, where I used to buy much of my magic equipment at Gamages.

At the College I had enjoyed singing as a treble in the chapel choir, until my voice broke, and taking part for two years in the Combined Cadet Force, the basic section and then the naval section, but modern languages and sport were definitely top of my priority list, though not really in that order. I had captained all the Dulwich College cricket teams through the years, with the exception of the Colts XI, which was coached by my father. It was the right decision to appoint another captain to avoid any potential complaints of nepotism. It was the only time in my nine years at the College that I was taught by my father. I gave up Geography, his subject as a schoolmaster, at the age of 13, so we never met in the classroom.

After A levels a lot of Dulwich boys stayed at school for the seventh term and an attempt to gain a scholarship at Oxbridge. It was a marvellous opportunity to play another term of 1st XV rugby and progress through the ranks of the England under-19 trials, where John Spencer, from Sedbergh and later a wing or centre three-quarter of considerable ability for England and the Lions, was chosen, quite understandably, ahead of me. His future successes on the rugby field have been well documented.

On the Saturday of my last 1st XV match for the Dulwich College team, I was scheduled to have two scholarship examinations. After discussions with Bryan Richards, the former Wales fly-half and current 1st XV coach at the College, it was agreed that I would sit the first exam at 6.30am until 9.30am, have half an hour's break before sitting the second exam from

10.00am until 1.00pm. Mr Richards would invigilate and then drive me to St Paul's, where the match was due to kick off at 2.30pm. It is perhaps unsurprising that I failed to win a scholarship, which had always struck me as unlikely anyway, and that I played poorly as Dulwich lost to St Paul's.

At Christmas I decided that another two terms at school were a better option than a gap year. I had been offered a place at St Catharine's College, Cambridge and, as a nineteen-year-old in the summer of 1966, I averaged 74.20 as a batsman in the 1st XI, including four centuries, a school record, with a highest innings of 163* and another of 159. I continued to take wickets as an off-spinner, including a hat-trick against Tonbridge School, the third wicket through a catch by Jon Destefano, another of the highly talented sportsmen in my year group at Dulwich. The batsman played a perfectly respectable forward defensive stroke and dropped the ball just in front of him, but Jon dived forward and caught the ball inches from the pitch.

I took German A level for a second time that summer and turned a mediocre pass into an A grade, but most of the term was spent on the cricket field. I even managed to teach a couple of younger classes, when their teachers were absent for a day or two, so there were already signs that a teaching career beckoned. As the son of a member of staff, I knew several of the other schoolmasters well and that also influenced my thinking.

Cambridge University

Four years at Cambridge University were a real privilege. I arrived at St Catharine's at the end of September 1966 and enjoyed studying French and German, although I spent rather less time on the academic work than I should have. I had initially decided that I would work hard for the first two terms and then concentrate on trying to gain a cricket Blue in the summer term. However, I was invited to freshmen's rugby trials and found that I thoroughly enjoyed the training and the matches for the LX Club in the Michaelmas term and then the chance to represent the University XV in the Lent term.

We played two matches each week and trained on every other day, with an occasional day off. This was where I teamed up again with Nick Cosh, and we played together at half-back. Those were the days when the university could hold its own against the first-class teams, mainly because of superior fitness and immensely talented individuals, but also because of the inventive coaching of Gerwyn Williams, who was well ahead of his time with his ideas. It did help that in the next couple of years the back division contained Jacko Page, an England scrum-half, Gerald Davies, already a British Lion, John Spencer, by now playing on the wing, Ian Robertson, the future Scottish fly-half who was playing alongside Gerald in the centre, and Tony Jorden, the England full-back. My task was made easy, because apart from passing to the outside-backs and running support lines, I had learned to kick the ball quite a distance accurately with either foot, having practised endlessly with left and right foot while playing 'gaining ground' in the Bell House garden. The other advantage was that, because of the obvious threat of the pace of the other three-quarters to our opponents, there were often gaps for me to exploit closer to the scrum.

The Laws at that time allowed the ball to be kicked directly into touch, though I do remember vividly a difficult match against London Scottish, at that time a top London club side containing many Scottish internationals. Cambridge were leading by ten points to nil at half-time, but the second half was to be played straight into a howling gale at Grange Road. Any kick was likely to end up behind our kickers, as became apparent when either our scrum-half or I attempted to clear our lines and move play away from our goal line. Fortunately Gerald Davies was playing in the centre for us, and he told me to pass the ball to him from a line-out, whereupon he sidestepped his opposite number and raced away, supported by speedy backs on his outside and me, at some distance, trying to be prepared for an inside pass. The score that ensued provided the respite we needed, and we held on manfully, never more than about twenty yards from our own line after that.

I established my position in the team in the Lent term of my first year, and it was disappointing in the following season when I broke a scaphoid bone, which kept me off the pitch for three months. I hoped and believed that I might have been awarded a Blue, though the team did look exceptionally strong with Ian Robertson moving from centre to fly-half. Although I did play quite a few more games for the university team, it was not to be and I was not selected for the match at Twickenham.

In my four years the fly-half position against Oxford was filled by three internationals: Billy Raybould of Wales, Ian Robertson of Scotland and then, for two years, Roger Shackleton, the future England fly-half. It was fun playing in such exalted company and it far exceeded my original expectations. The physical side of the game made me a tougher competitor on the cricket field and also provided opportunities to play a fuller role in the extra-curricular activities as a schoolmaster in the winter terms when I was present at the schools. I always thought that dancing, either at a disco or in a ballroom, made me lighter on my feet for squash. Squash made me quicker in reactions and fitter for rugby. Rugby made me tougher and more aware of the team ethos as a cricketer.

More importantly to me at that time, though, was the worry that the broken scaphoid might prevent my playing for the university cricket team in my second year. I had gained a Blue in my first year and was looking forward to more challenges against the county teams who visited Fenner's. My wrist was in plaster for more than two months, but the bone did not reunite.

The specialist explained that there was still a blood supply to both halves of the scaphoid bone and suggested that I could either consider a bone graft or else discard the plaster and see whether I could strengthen the wrist by constantly squeezing a squash ball. This latter suggestion seemed a far better option to me. I had kept relatively fit by playing squash left-handed. I could keep the rallies going, but I could only win points by slotting the racquet into my plastered right hand to play drop shots. By the time of the cricket season I was nearly back to normal fitness, though my top-hand grip on the cricket bat was slightly different. I have had little trouble from the injury since, so his advice was absolutely sound.

In the summer term it became very important to manage my time carefully. I tended to start work early in the morning and put in three hours before breakfast at 8.30am. After that the days were spent at Fenner's, and any supervisions or essays were completed in the evenings. My supervisor for 17th century French literature was a keen cricketer and was quite prepared to fit me into his schedule at nine o'clock in the evening. That was a huge benefit for me and possibly led me to study that period rather more enthusiastically.

After the first part of the tripos I discarded German and concentrated on French, both modern and medieval, which necessitated a 'Long Vac Term' and six weeks more at Cambridge. When in the south of France I went into a bookshop to ask who might be the best authors and experts on the medieval period, I was not really surprised to learn that Dr Stanley Aston, my Director of Studies in St Catharine's, and Dr Leslie Topsfield, my tutor, were considered the leading authorities. Cambridge University had some outstanding academics, as one might expect in a top educational establishment.

Reading languages, where most Fellows had written books on their chosen lecture course, meant that I could miss lectures and read the critical works in my own time. That made the life of a sporting arts undergraduate much more possible. There was no need for time in laboratories. Despite all these advantages, it was still necessary for time management to play a large part.

I never really enjoyed the tutorials with Leslie Topsfield, who seemed to have no sense of humour, and our relationship never became close. Stanley Aston, on the other hand, was supportive of sport and was always ready to discuss cricket. In the very first French translation class, in which he insisted we all wore gowns and was held in a room under the porters' lodge in the college, he informed all of us St Catharine's first-year modern linguists, that there were six ways into college after 11pm, when we all had to be in and the gates were locked, but seven if we had a 27 inch waist or less. He understood the undergraduate mentality of the time, despite a fierce exterior.

In my first year I arrived at the freshmen's nets and was extremely impressed by the players, who all seemed technically better and more confident than I was. Philip Carling had toured India with London Schools, a tour that I was invited to join but declined because I was playing rugby in England Schools' trials. He seemed unperturbable as an opening batsman, had an excellent defensive technique and had good timing. We shared accommodation in bedsits in Chesterton Road. Mano Ponniah, who had already played cricket for Ceylon, was a marvellous stroke player and never seemed to be rushed as he played his shots. Both of these were in their first year, too. The old Blues struck the ball well. I wondered whether I would be picked and whether I would cope when we played against the first-class counties.

As it happened, I was selected for the first match against Essex in 1967, and I opened with Vijaya Malalasekera, another Sri Lankan and terrific striker of the ball, against John Lever, playing in his debut match for his county. John went on to play regularly for Essex and took 73 wickets in 21 Tests and another 24 in 22 ODIs for England, before, like so many Essex players, turning his hand to coaching in one of the county's independent schools.

My first ball in county cricket as a batsman was also John Lever's as a bowler. I played forward, and the ball rocketed off my bat past cover for four. It was a relief to get off the mark so quickly and positively. John got his revenge a few overs later by bowling me for 15.

However, in the second innings, I played confidently and was well into my stride on 86 when I punched a lifting delivery from Keith Boyce, a West Indian fast bowler, over the head of Keith Fletcher at forward short-leg and called immediately for a single that was easily there, as corroborated by Charles Bray in *The Times* the following day. Tony Cross, a third-year batsman who had not been awarded a Blue in his first two years, was watching the ball and sent me back when I was already halfway down the pitch. I had no chance and was run out. On arriving back in the pavilion, I was greeted by several team-mates who expressed their views about the incident, very sorry that I had not scored a century on debut. Later Tony, who did not apologise, said that it was unfortunate, but that we were all playing for our places at that stage in the season. I remember the incident, but I do not remember the weather on the day. Brian Taylor, the Essex captain, was quoted as saying: "I have never played in conditions as bad as today."

Later in the term, on 18 May, I was delighted to record my first first-class century against Middlesex. The match was delayed until 3pm, and I batted at number three, joining Mano Ponniah at 18 for one, when Chris Hirst was caught at mid-on. I was 92 not out and Mano was in the 80s overnight, when the score was 181 for one. The following morning I went on to score 140. Sadly, Mano, with whom I shared a stand of 194, fell for 98. He thoroughly deserved a century in a rain-affected match. It was one of many partnerships which we enjoyed in the three years we played together. He was always a calm and steady influence at the other end, and his experience of having played for Ceylon was a great help.

Cricket at Cambridge provided the perfect opportunity to see whether the professional game was within my reach; whether I could succeed against the best. Over the four years there were some very good cricketers who went on to play for counties in the first-class game. David Acfield bowled off-spin for Essex for many years, Steve Russell, Nick Cosh and Dudley Owen-Thomas, who won the Young Cricketer of the Year Award in 1972, played in games for Surrey, Peter Johnson played for Nottinghamshire, John Spencer played for Sussex, but the best of them all was Majid Khan, who arrived in my last year and brought the university crowds back to Fenner's.

Majid became a very good friend and I have stayed with him and Seema, his wife, in Lahore and Islamabad and they with us in England. He was a magnificent batsman, who captained Pakistan and would have scored more runs than any other of his country's batsmen at the time, if his cousin, Imran Khan, who had taken over as captain, had not left him out of the team. He had so much time to play the ball, and once, in the nets, he showed us that it was perfectly possible to remain balanced and lean into the ball by facing several deliveries without moving his feet. We were a group of players keen to learn and, although our team was often beaten, we were seldom outclassed. We also won a few matches in those years.

The old pavilion at Fenner's was at the opposite end of the ground from the current one. It had showers in the basement, down some narrow, winding, stone steps and a very good roof, which served as a viewing area for the batting team. The first thing that everyone learned about the history of the pavilion was that Jahangir Khan, Majid's father and a former captain of All India, had once thrown a cricket ball from the last step of the pavilion, which landed alongside the wicket at the opposite end. Apparently he had done this without removing his jacket, although he did button it up.

The pitch was not too bouncy or fast and did not take seam or spin much, which protected our relatively inexperienced batsmen but made it difficult for our bowlers to take the professionals' wickets. The outfield was perfect and made fielding a joy. As Cyril Coote, our groundsman and coach, always insisted, even if batting and bowling were not easy, every Cambridge team should be able to become an excellent fielding unit. It was a wonderful facility for the university cricketers, with adjacent tennis courts for CULTC and hockey on the outfield in the days when all CUHC matches were played on grass.

Another strong memory that I have of that first match took place off the field after the first day's play. Leaving the pavilion with a couple of others and some Essex players, I was asked for an autograph by a small boy. I signed RDV Knight and he returned to his group of friends, who asked who I was. When he replied that I must be Barry Knight, who had been an Essex player up till the previous season, I decided that I would always sign in future as Roger Knight!

All our net practice and most of the cricket matches were played at Fenner's, but we also played counties away from Cambridge. We arrived one year at Scarborough to play Yorkshire and found Fred Trueman sitting in our dressing room. As we went in, he looked us up and down and muttered, "There's another wicket for me." When Vijaya Malalasekera came into the room, Fred asked whether he was the opening batsman, which VJ said he was. When Fred asked whether he hooked, VJ changed colour as the blood drained from his face!

Scarborough was always a favourite place to play with its beach and amusements. Fred suggested that we might like to explore the nightclub scene and told us to go to the 2Bs and mention that we were friends of his, which gained entry free of charge for us. It did not help our cricket, but it made for an excellent evening.

The summer term was a busy time with supervisions, examinations, cricket practice and matches and the years merge. It is strange how some memories are stronger than others. Stephen Chalke, who knows his way round the Wisden Almanack as well as anyone, asked me whether I had any thoughts on a match between Cambridge University and Essex in 1970, my last year at Cambridge. As I could not immediately call it to mind, he read out to me that I had taken six for 65 in 30 overs in Essex's first innings and had then scored an undefeated 164 out of 256 when we batted for a second time. I had started that innings on a pair! How could I have forgotten that sort of performance?

When there was no need to rush back to College to complete an essay, I enjoyed a drink in a pub with the county teams, who also found the relaxed atmosphere of matches against the university very appealing. They were a good source of tips about the game and always fun to be with. It also meant that, when I started as a professional, I already knew some of the opposition players, how the batsmen played and what the bowlers looked to do with the ball.

Both Oxford and Cambridge University Cricket Clubs have a proud history of producing international and county cricketers. The scorecards of first-class fixtures, including the Varsity Matches, are full of names of amateurs and professionals who have made their mark on cricket.

CUCC has produced 22 Test captains, from Ivo Bligh, who regained the Ashes in Australia in 1882/83, to Mike Atherton who captained England for five years from 1993. Since the Second World War 13 Cambridge men have captained their countries: Gubby Allen, Norman Yardley, George Mann, Freddie Brown, David Sheppard, Peter May, Ted Dexter, Tony Lewis, Mike Brearley and Mike Atherton (England), Gerry Alexander and Deryck Murray (West Indies) and Majid Khan (Pakistan).

Cambridge has also produced 62 other Test cricketers. The most recent have included: Richard Hutton, Ian Greig, Steve James, Tim Curtis, Phil Edmonds, Mike Selvey, Paul Parker, Derek Pringle, John Crawley, Ed Smith and Zafar Ansari (England), Greg Loveridge (New Zealand) and Andy Whittall (Zimbabwe).

Oxford can boast, among others, CB Fry, Douglas Jardine, Colin Cowdrey and MJK Smith (England), the Nawab of Pataudi senior and junior (India), Clive van Ryneveld (South Africa) and Imran Khan and Abdul Kardar (Pakistan) as international captains. In addition Claire Taylor, who played for the Women's Blues, represented England more than 150 times between 1998 and 2011, was the first woman to be named a Wisden Cricketer of the Year and still holds the record ODI score at Lord's, ahead of all the men.

When I return now to Cambridge, in my position as President of Cambridge University Cricket Club, I enjoy nostalgic walks that bring back the very happy memories of my four years; three years of a degree in modern and medieval languages and then a diploma of education. The walk from Churchill College, where I often stay, takes me past Grace Road (rugby), Sidgwick Avenue (the modern languages department), King's Parade (St Catharine's College) and as far as Fenner's (cricket), where I support the current players, both men and women, who represent the cricket club.

University was a time for growing up and exploring the many opportunities available to develop further skills, experiences, friendships and pastimes. Phil Carling and I shared a double room in College in our second year. I lived for the third year in a double room above the College chaplain, David Sparrow, who often came out of his room when my new room-mate, John Tredwell, or I were passing. John was a rugby Blue. David's view was that his role in College was to get alongside those whom he called the 'hearties', often sportsmen who were the group leaders, rather than be with the already converted, whom he called the 'God squad'. John and I enjoyed many glasses of port and discussed faith, which was preferable to writing essays. It also helped to focus my thoughts on religious and ethical topics, which has served me in good stead as a schoolmaster, a cricket captain, a father and a person.

2

My Cricketing Life – as an Amateur

Between 1967 and 1970 my cricket was split between Cambridge University and the Surrey 2nd and 1st XIs. I remember a game for the Surrey 2nd XI against Kent, when Ken Barrington was coming back from his first heart attack. We arrived at the Metrogas Ground in Greenwich, where there were bars separating the changing rooms. Ken stood behind one set of bars and pretended to be in prison, saying, "This just about sums it up!" What a contrast for him after playing Test cricket.

A game of cricket on a club ground was not so foreign for me, but playing alongside an international cricketer was a new experience. Ken, as every cricket lover and certainly the Surrey members will remember, was a fine England number three. He adapted his game from being a free-flowing stroke maker to batting with bulldog determination and awesome concentration. He was well-known for his sense of humour in the dressing room and became a much-liked England selector and tour manager before he suffered another heart attack and died in 1981 during the Third Test against the West Indies at Kensington Oval in Barbados, where he had made his maiden Test century 21 years before.

In 1967, my first season of first-class cricket, I managed in 14 matches for Cambridge to score 691 runs at an average of 27.64 and, as an off-spinner, to take my first wickets: four at 56 runs per wicket.

The following year there was an increase in the number of my wickets to 14 at 40.92, but the runs decreased for Cambridge to 493 from 13 matches averaging 22.4. The second year syndrome, perhaps! After the term ended I went to play for Surrey 2nd XI, where in seven matches I scored 523 runs at an average of 74.71, with two centuries and two fifties, and then was selected for four matches in the 1st XI, scoring 205 runs and taking seven wickets. By this time I was bowling medium-paced seamers and topped the county's bowling averages at 17.71.

1969 was even better. After a successful season at Cambridge, scoring 641 runs in 10 matches and taking 13 wickets, I was selected by Surrey for eight matches in the championship and seven matches in the John Player

League, which had started as a competition that year. It was in the JPL, the 40-over matches on Sundays, where I started to develop my bowling. Tom Cartwright, one of England's best medium-paced bowlers, topped the bowling averages in the competition that year, but I took 16 wickets in seven matches and was second in the national JPL averages, as Surrey finished in fifth position.

My last year at Cambridge again produced a reasonable number of runs (603 in 11 matches) and 29 wickets at 22.89, so it was disappointing that I only played three matches for Surrey in the championship and three in the JPL, plus three for the 2nd XI.

Cambridge cricket was relaxed but at the same time a challenge, against professional county teams, especially for the players who wanted to take the chance to play professionally after university. After the day's play the county professionals were happy to have a drink and pass on all sorts of hints about batting and bowling, which we undergraduates lapped up.

Surrey 1st XI was different. I was playing as an amateur, collecting travelling expenses and meal allowances from Mrs Poole's office at the Oval, but always seemingly welcomed by the other members of the team, some of whom had started at the same time as I had in the 2nd XI. It was a different atmosphere in the dressing room in a team which had high expectations and was ambitious to live up to the county's very successful record of the 1950s. There seemed less readiness amongst the senior players to help the younger members of the team, though there were exceptions, amongst them Intikhab Alam, who was a wily, experienced Pakistani Test cricketer and a marvellous man to have in the dressing room.

For a student it was exciting to travel away for county matches, stay in hotels and play the game that I loved. It never seemed a chore and, whilst some of the team kept to themselves, some of us went out for a meal together on away trips. As a young bachelor this seemed an ideal existence and pushed me towards a professional cricket career. I always thought that I would teach, but there would be time for that after cricket, though I was not aware of the possibility of combining them at that stage.

At Cambridge the groundsman and coach, Cyril Coote, was a legend. He had seen countless generations of undergraduates and was always available to talk about batting. At Surrey the coach was Arthur McIntyre, a former England wicket-keeper, and, whilst he was always around to help 2nd XI players, I do not remember him doing much coaching with me. He was encouraging and friendly and treated me rather more kindly than the young professionals, on whom he came down hard whenever they did not measure up to his high standards on or off the pitch.

The four years of playing university cricket against county players convinced me that I had enough ability to play professionally. I had scored sufficient runs to gain confidence and had turned myself into an accurate medium-paced bowler, despite bowling off-breaks at school, with the ability to swing the ball either way and extract bounce from most surfaces. I always preferred to bowl with the keeper standing up to the stumps, so that I could 'hit the deck' without worrying about reaching his gloves if he was back.

In the summer vacations I had returned to Surrey, where I opened the batting in the 1st XI when John Edrich was selected for the England team. Having been promoted I remained in the team, both in 1968 and 1969, and opened with John when he returned for the county matches. It was slightly frustrating to have to start each year in the 2nd XI, especially as I had by then scored centuries in first-class cricket for Cambridge, but Surrey had a strong batting line-up: John Edrich, Mike Edwards, Micky Stewart, Younis Ahmed, Graham Roope, Stewart Storey, all first-team capped players who scored over 1,000 runs in 1970.

They were a good batting combination. John Edrich, a top England left-handed batsman, opened with Mike Edwards, a Cambridge University graduate who had not gained a Blue but who scored 12 centuries and 57 fifties for Surrey in first-class matches as a dogged right-handed batsman. Micky Stewart had opened with John for several years and so was the perfect number three, if needed to go in to bat early in the innings. He was an outstanding close catcher and might have played more than the eight Test matches for England, had he not contracted dysentery after only one innings on his first overseas tour to India in 1963/64, when selected as vice-captain. Younis Ahmed was a left-hander, born in Pakistan and younger brother of Saeed Ahmed. He played four Tests for Pakistan and was a highly talented batsman who averaged over 40 in first-class cricket. Graham Roope was an outstanding slip fielder, a free-flowing batsman and a medium-paced bowler who could swing the ball either way. Although he was selected for England in 21 Tests and eight ODIs, he never quite fulfilled his potential because of a lack of self-confidence. He had wonderful eyesight and could identify every plane and the airline that flew over the Oval on its way to Heathrow Airport. He would regularly forecast rain when there was not a cloud in the sky, and he never seemed happier than when we were off the field and he could not be tested as a cricketer. He was superstitious and one Sunday, when we were playing a John Player League match at Trent Bridge, he turned down the lunch because there was duck on the menu. He asked just for a dessert but, when he learned it was a pear, he turned that down as well despite the match only being one innings. Stewart Storey was the team's all-rounder. He finished his first-class career with over 10,000 runs, almost 500 wickets and more than 300 catches. He did the double for Surrey in 1966, the only occasion since the Second World War when a Surrey player achieved the feat.

To support that first six and playing in the 2nd XI were a young Geoff Howarth, the future captain of New Zealand, and Roy Lewis, who batted 68 times in the 1st XI from 1968 to 1973 and scored 13 fifties averaging 29.59 in first-class cricket. There were also Mike Hooper, who scored 805 runs at an average of 53.66 in 1968, when Surrey won the 2nd XI championship, but could not convert his fierce hitting of a bad ball into runs in the 1st XI, and Dudley Owen-Thomas, who was named the Cricket Writers' Club Young Cricketer of the Year for 1972 but, although he had a reasonable season with Surrey in 1973, lost his form and retired from first-class cricket in 1975.

Playing under Micky Stewart as captain, and with such good players in a competitive team, was a wonderful learning experience. Micky never allowed a game to drift and was forever encouraging his bowlers and fielders. He was always positive, and players responded well to his confident approach. He welcomed me into the side as an amateur during the university holidays and made me feel comfortable in a team that challenged strongly in the championship.

In 1968 I had made my debut in the county championship against Northamptonshire, scoring 62 in the second innings, after having scored two centuries for the 2nd XI. It is staggering to remember that in that year, in my second match for Surrey 1st XI, I opened the batting at Hull against Fred Trueman. I was brought up on the exploits of England bowlers such as Trueman and Statham. 1968 was Fiery Fred's last year for Yorkshire, and he was not the express fast bowler he once had been, but he was still an intimidating sight as he ran in and swung the new ball.

The dark background of a low stand at Hull did not help a batsman to pick up the ball. His second delivery swung perfectly into the middle of my front pad, missed my tentative forward defensive shot and the great England opening bowler roared an appeal, which, for some unaccountable reason, the umpire turned down. I was relieved, but Fred questioned my parentage and sexual activities at length before turning away to bowl again.

I remember the match well because I scored 64 in that first innings and 36 in the second, which made a satisfying total in the match. My other strong memory from that match, though, was when Younis Ahmed swept a ball from Don Wilson, Yorkshire's slow left-arm spinner, straight on to the shin of Brian Close, the Yorkshire captain, who was fielding in that ridiculously close position of forward short-leg, which he made his own and where he never flinched. The ball must have hit him full on the shin because it bounced back exactly to where it had been hit. Astonishingly he did not rub it; just looked daggers at his bowler and walked down to the other end for the next over. Forty minutes later Yorkshire bowled us out to win the 1968 county championship and, as Close came off the pitch, his trouser leg was red from the shin down. He later went to hospital for several stitches. This made a huge impact on our team and typified Close's approach to pain, which cricketers of that time respected and, in some cases, tried to emulate.

3

My Cricketing Life – County Cricket and Captaincy

The 1970s and early 1980s were arguably a golden age of domestic cricket. In the decades before, the championship was dominated by a few counties, particularly Surrey and Yorkshire. In the years since, there have been few opportunities for the overseas stars to commit to a full season in England, because of the constant demands of the international fixture programme, which has expanded into our summer months. The championship then was a shop window and testing ground for the England team, and the England players all participated because there were no central contracts. There was little international cricket except for the home Test matches, so other countries' players wanted to gain experience in English conditions and keep involved during their off season.

In 2019 there was an Ashes series taking place and, while England players were predominantly involved in the successful World Cup competition, some of the Australian batsmen and bowlers were practising for the longer game, while joining a county team on short-term contracts. In the 1970s the best of the world's cricketers regularly played for the counties, and English cricketers benefitted from playing with and against these overseas stars. Most counties seemed to have two bowlers from overseas although, as limited-over cricket grew, there was more demand for batsmen.

There was a plethora of quick, some very quick, overseas bowlers: Andy Roberts, Michael Holding, Malcolm Marshall, Joel Garner, Colin Croft, Wayne Daniel, Sylvester Clarke, Keith Boyce, Vanburn Holder, Gregory Armstrong all came from the West Indies; Garth le Roux and Vintcent van der Bijl came from South Africa.

There were also so-called 'second division quicks' like Ezra Moseley, George Ferris and Winston Benjamin, also from the West Indies. The Australian fast bowler Graham McKenzie was one of the first to come to England and play for Leicestershire. England had its own group of quick bowlers in John Snow, Bob Willis, Alan Ward and Harold (Dusty) Rhodes.

The world's best all-rounders also found their way into county cricket and played throughout the summer. Garry Sobers, the best of them all,

Mike Procter, Richard Hadlee, Imran Khan and Clive Rice were all capable of bowling fast as well as dominating with the bat. Ian Botham was the Englishman in the same league, with Tony Greig not only a batsman and fast-medium bowler but also an off-spinner. There was no place for a shrinking violet in the county batting order, especially as helmets did not make their appearance until the late '70s. Having seen off the fast bowlers, there were then several overseas spin bowlers to face: Intikhab Alam, Srinivasaraghavan Venkataraghavan, Lance Gibbs, Dilip Doshi, Bishan Bedi and Mushtaq Mohammad amongst them.

As a top-order batsman it is too easy to concentrate on the overseas bowlers, but we should not forget the batsmen, such as Barry Richards, Zaheer Abbas, Javed Miandad, Kepler Wessels, Geoff Howarth, Glenn Turner, Clive Lloyd, Alvin Kallicharan, Rohan Kanhai, Gordon Greenidge, Viv Richards, Ken McEwan, John Wright, Peter Kirsten, Ron Headley and Eddie Barlow, who was also an all-rounder.

My education came through the county system. The world's best cricketers were playing in the county championship and became true members of their county, returning for several seasons. It helped them all to learn how to play on English pitches, providing testing conditions and allowing them to tighten up their defence, seemingly without losing their attacking instincts honed on the harder pitches in their own countries. Pitches that had been uncovered when it rained helped the spinners, taught batsmen that it was not always possible to hit through the line as was the case in indoor nets and on true pitches abroad and encouraged medium-paced bowlers to bowl a length to avoid the ball sitting up to be pulled when they pitched short. Line and length was the mantra for bowlers, and protecting the wicket was considered as important as scoring runs for batsmen.

Most county cricketers represented the county of their birth or where they had learnt their cricket, but only Yorkshire insisted on a player being born within the county boundary. I came through the Surrey system and always thought that, if I was to progress in cricket, it would be along the pathway from the Surrey Young Cricketers, to the county 2nd XI to the Surrey 1st XI. There was little movement between counties at that time, though it was not unknown. In fact it was only in 1968 that it became possible for a cricketer to change counties without missing a year to qualify, which was helpful for me in 1971 and again in 1978.

Although I saw Surrey as my county, circumstances brought huge changes into my career path. The reasons for moving on were never for an increased salary or because I was disgruntled with an employer. I could easily have been seen as a mercenary, moving through two counties and finally back to Surrey, but there were practical rather than financial reasons to move, and I was able to transfer my loyalty to the team in which I was playing. I still enjoy the company of team-mates from all three counties.

There was a sort of macho approach to the game then – no helmets, thin thigh pads on the front leg and perhaps a towel to protect the back thigh. Arm guards and chest protectors were few and far between. It did encourage batsmen to watch the ball and stay sideways on, and those who did not get in line were quickly spotted and subjected to the faster bowlers at every opportunity!

The generation of cricketers in my era used to say that a batsman in first-class cricket is only likely to be hit by a fast delivery for one of three reasons: losing sight of the ball, trying to play a shot beyond his capability or playing on an uneven surface. Batsmen who turn their heads away and stop watching the ball when they duck are in danger of being hit on the side or back of the head. Batsmen who try to hook a short delivery can be early or late on the shot and again in danger. An uneven pitch is the most problematic of the three reasons for a batsman being hit.

The top batsmen of any era always seem to have time to see the ball early and play it or avoid it late. A batsman playing in line can usually sway out of the line if the ball is at head height. It is more difficult if the ball is aimed more at the chest or neck. If a batsman tries to stay outside the line and the ball moves in towards him, there is nowhere to go without falling backwards. That is one reason why so many batsmen seem to be hit nowadays. In limited-over cricket batsmen like to give themselves more chance of hitting the ball by staying on the leg-side of the line of the ball, but the natural line of a right-handed bowler, bowling over the wicket to right-handed batsmen, will angle the ball in towards them.

When playing against Middlesex at the Oval in 1978 and facing Wayne Daniel, I saw him approach the crease from wide, so that he was just in line with the edge of the screen. Normally that meant that he was going to bowl a bouncer and I had taken those deliveries on the soft part of the leading shoulder several times in the past, which was painful but unlikely to lead to anything more than a bruise. However, on this occasion it did not bounce as much as I thought it would and so it hit me full on the forearm, as happened to Steve Smith the Australian batsman, who was hit on the arm by Jofra Archer at Lord's in 2019.

Determined to emulate Brian Close at Hull and his refusal to show pain, I stood there and looked down the pitch at Wayne, who looked back at me in slight surprise and disappointment. However, slowly my arm went dead and I suddenly realised that the bat had slipped out of my hand and landed on the floor, which brought the most enormous smile to Wayne's face. I was taken for an x-ray where, fortunately, it turned out to be nothing more than another bruise. So much for showing no pain!

I was much more conscious of self-protection when playing against Hampshire in 1982 on a pitch that had recently been re-laid and ideally needed another six months to settle down. Harry Brind, the excellent head groundsman at the Oval, had taken the grass off the pitch, and there was a lot of concern about the cracks, which resembled soup plates. They had Malcolm Marshall; we had Sylvester Clarke. The medium-paced bowlers on both sides were just about playable but, when the two fast, hostile West Indian bowlers were running in, it was an entirely different game. The ball bounced completely inconsistently. When it hit the far side of a crack it took off, when it landed in the middle of the plate it bounced normally and when it hit the nearside of the crack it shot along the ground.

Sylvester and Robin Jackman bowled Hampshire out for 148. The atmosphere in the dressing room before our innings was tense. We had all seen the variations in bounce, and now it was our turn. The pitch was not likely to get easier. When Hampshire bowled, Alan Butcher was soon forced to retire hurt after a nasty blow to his face. He had been wearing a helmet, but he had no face guard and the ball cut him on the forehead.

As I went out to bat I made the decision, for the first time in my career, that I should wear a helmet. I had never even tried one in the nets (probably still labouring under the prevalent macho approach to the game), and so I borrowed a 'lid' and, with no grill or visor and no chin strap, I prepared to bat three and face Marshall, some way back and holding a lethal weapon. Predominantly a front-foot player, I was keen to try to play as normally as possible.

The third ball he bowled me was a good-length delivery so I was moving forward, when the ball hit a crack and reared straight at my throat. I jerked my head back, my helmet fell off behind me and I managed to protect my head only by parrying the ball with the glove on my top hand. I had no time to duck, no chance of playing or leaving the ball, which flew to third slip. Caught Nigel Cowley bowled Marshall nought. I picked my helmet up and walked back, rather ingloriously, to the pavilion to watch others do what they could. David Thomas and Robin Jackman bravely attacked and somehow managed to provide us with a lead of 66. Clarke, Thomas and Jackman then bowled Hampshire out for a second time for 170, with only Gordon Greenidge, at his belligerent best, somehow scoring 84, so we fancied our chances in a low-scoring match of scoring just over 100 to win, despite the state of the pitch and the fact that the bounce of the ball had become even more unpredictable.

At number three again, I put on the helmet and, after what was another very short wait, went out at eight for one wicket to face Marshall for the second time. This time my plan was to move back in front of my wicket to give me as much time as possible and wait for anything overpitched that I might score off. This time it was the fourth ball when Marshall bowled an attempted bouncer. I was already back, but the ball hit another crack and shot straight along the ground, hitting me on the ankle. I tried desperately to drop my bat on it and in the process my helmet fell off my head again, this time forwards. Lbw Marshall nought. A dreaded 'pair'.

Malcolm bowled magnificently and took seven wickets for 38 in 20 overs. Nick Pocock, the Hampshire captain, could not take the ball off him, although he did not try very hard. He won the match for Hampshire by three runs. He was a real handful on any surface. On that pitch he was unplayable.

Although I was not superstitious as a batsman, unlike many county professionals, perhaps unsurprisingly I was never keen to wear a helmet after recording a 'pair' and did so again on only one occasion later in the same season. I remember that Gordon Greenidge and Viv Richards often took their helmets off in those early days, so that they were forced to concentrate on watching the ball. It certainly concentrated the mind when there was a five-and-a-half-ounce piece of hard, round, solid leather flying at you above waist high. Those were the days, though, when batsmen could afford to avoid bouncers and not worry about scoring off every delivery, as is now almost de rigueur in a limited-over match.

There was also some sort of code amongst fast bowlers that the ball would be generally pitched up to numbers nine to eleven, who, in most cases, had the sole objective at the crease of swinging the bat and hoping. They had few pretensions about being batsmen and had limited opportunities to bat in the nets. I remember Pat Pocock, who batted number eleven for the Surrey team, complaining that, in limited-over matches, the early batsmen scored at three an over and then left the tail-enders to win the match by scoring at seven runs an over. Not only that, the tail had not had the chance to practise their batting because, when it was their turn in the practice nets, nobody wanted to bowl at them.

It was a time of many changes. The championship consisted of three-day matches, but the 40-over JPL started in 1969 on Sunday afternoons, following the success of the 60-over Gillette Cup knock-out competition, which began in 1963. Three years later, the Benson & Hedges tournament began; another limited-over competition, this time of 55 overs and played in area groups until the semi-finals and final. Pitches were initially uncovered except for the bowler's run-up.

One-day matches suited me as an all-rounder, and I enjoyed the longer two competitions particularly. The JPL was more akin to today's T20, and players began by seeing it as rather a joke and purely for the spectators. It soon established itself, as has the T20, and became a popular way to spend a Sunday afternoon for players and crowd alike. For the players it was a question of scoring more quickly, without adapting a technique too much. Although some batsmen did clear the front leg to allow a bigger swing, there were no reverse sweeps and no ramp shots. Without a helmet the risk would not have been worth taking, even if the shots had been invented. There were no bats that could hit the ball twenty rows back in the stand, even off a thick edge.

Basically batsmen played as they did in the longer game and the scores reflected that: 160 was considered a good score. Fields were set with a couple of slips in place in the first year of the JPL, and I remember catching Fred Goldstein, the Oxford University and Northamptonshire batsman, at second slip in Geoff Arnold's first over in a JPL match at St John's School, Leatherhead. There were no fielding restrictions and no circles, so it was possible to place all the fielders on the boundary, which happened on more than one occasion. Even the wicket-keeper went back to the boundary in one game, which led to new regulations being introduced.

It was also a game of many grounds. I always loved playing at Lord's, the Oval, Edgbaston, Headingley, Trent Bridge and Old Trafford, but counties used so many grounds, all of which had a charm or distinctive feel of their own. Gloucestershire played at Cheltenham, the Wagon Works ground in Gloucester, Tewkesbury and Moreton-in-Marsh besides the County Ground in Bristol. Surrey took matches to Guildford. Kent played on some beautiful grounds: Tunbridge Wells when the rhododendrons were out in May, Dover, with its pavilion high up a grassy bank, Maidstone and Folkestone. In Yorkshire we enjoyed Bradford Park Avenue, with its football stands distorting the shape of the cricket oval, Hull, Sheffield, bleak Middlesbrough, Harrogate and Scarborough, my favourite, with its sea frets and festival atmosphere, the band starting to play just before the lunch interval. Running up to bowl was not easy as the rhythm of the brass band did not always match the stride pattern of the faster or medium-paced bowlers.

There were too many grounds to list, but I always seemed to do well, in particular, at Hove, the United Services Ground, Portsmouth, Chesterfield and Worcester, as well as the international grounds. The pitches suited my game as an all-rounder and the ball came on to the bat well. Each ground round the country welcomed the county teams and provided a different pitch and conditions to challenge the players' adaptability and technique.

Above all, there was a camaraderie within the county game at that time. We all met, played and socialised on a regular basis through the season. With the increasing number of T20 competitions around the world, where international cricketers play with and against players from other countries, I hope that they, too, are able to experience the joy of meeting and making friends of opponents and team-mates. It used to be the case for touring parties, but the shorter tours with fewer matches have made it more difficult to mix with opponents. Added to that, some captains, coaches and managers have encouraged their players to keep to themselves after the game, and the increasing number of one-day matches has meant less time in one venue.

Gloucestershire CCC 1971-1975 – The Glorious Glosters

When it became apparent that it was more likely that the six capped batsmen at Surrey would start the season in the first team, particularly as they had all scored over 1,000 runs in the championship in 1970, I was concerned. Eastbourne College had agreed that I could teach modern languages for two terms a year and have the summer term free to play professional cricket. I had been excited at the thought that I could combine my two careers from the start, but beginning the season in the 2nd XI was not part of my plan and I am sure that the College's Headmaster did not envisage releasing me to play second-team cricket.

Clearly there were advantages for me in the combination of playing first-class cricket and teaching at the College. The pupils responded readily to a sportsman who appeared from time to time in the papers. I know that it also helped the College when I was mentioned in the press as the Eastbourne College schoolmaster who had made runs or taken wickets. Arrangements were made for other people to take my lessons during the summer term.

Despite lengthy discussions with Surrey's Chairman of Cricket, Stuart Surridge, who assured me that it would not take me long to push my way into the team, I remained less certain. Younger players in county cricket have always felt that age and experience will be preferred until the older player shows that he is not scoring heavily enough. That was certainly the way then at the Oval. It was not a risk that I wanted to take, although, by then, I did have a few centuries to my name.

My father knew Grahame Parker, the Secretary of Gloucestershire CCC, and he arranged for me to meet him. The outcome of that meeting was that I went to play professional cricket for Gloucestershire, with the opportunity to start the season batting at three, but with no guarantee that I would stay in the team unless my results were good enough. That was a risk that I was more prepared to take, as the matter lay in my own hands and not in the failure of someone else.

Eastbourne in the winters and Bristol in the summer months was not an ideal lifestyle, though I enjoyed the challenge of packing and driving a three-ton box lorry full of our furniture back and forth in late March and early September. East Sussex and the Oval would not have been much easier, except that my parents still lived near Dulwich, so I could have lived back at home for the summer. As it turned out, the College in Eastbourne and the County Ground in Nevil Road provided a home for the next five years.

At the end of the Lent term in 1971 I married Chris (Christine Ann McNab Miln), a Bart's nurse who was working as a BOAC stewardess. Flying mostly long-haul meant she was somewhere else in the world for days and weeks but was free to come to stay with me wherever I happened to be playing when she returned. It worked well for us but was not universally popular with other team members, some of whom would have preferred to keep their post-match activities less known outside the dressing room. We were able to see each other more than most county cricketers saw their wives during the summer months of travel to the other sixteen counties.

We started married life in rented accommodation close to railway arches in Bristol, later sharing accommodation with Roy Swetman, the former England, Surrey and Nottinghamshire wicket-keeper, when he arrived to play for Gloucestershire. In September we moved back to my bachelor quarters above a boys' changing room in Eastbourne College. There was no more privacy there, as there was a four-desk study used by dayboys along the corridor between our bedroom and sitting room.

In the second season we decided to buy our first house in Bristol, which we would rent out while we lived in College accommodation in Eastbourne for the winter months. It was a stretch at £7,500, but we have never regretted getting on to the housing market at an early stage.

In 1971 Gloucestershire was just the right team for me to learn about the professional game. They were a really friendly group of cricketers who welcomed me into the fold. Tony Brown was a captain who believed in discipline and expected everyone to contribute to the team effort. He batted in the lower middle order and took 1,223 wickets with his medium pace, often having opened the bowling before Mike Procter and Jack Davey and occasionally John Dixon took over.

There were several senior players: Arthur Milton, David Allen, John Mortimore, Ron Nicholls, Barrie Meyer, David Shepherd, David Smith and Roy Swetman, all of whom had a wealth of experience, some of them at international level. They approached the game in their different ways. Shep was grateful to be selected and aimed to score around 600 runs in a season, as he told me as we lay in adjacent baths after a net session. I was surprised, because it always seemed to me that 1,000 runs was the starting point for a batsman. Shep, though, was content to bat at number six and play as the situation in the game dictated. He was nervous as a cricketer but outstanding later as an international umpire.

When I arrived, Ron Nicholls always seemed to bat with the worry of not being awarded another contract in the following season although, in a game in 1962 against Oxford University, he and Martin Young had put on 395 runs for the first wicket. Their partnership remains the highest for any wicket by Gloucestershire, and Ron made his career best score of 217. He helped the team in some John Player League games by keeping wicket and also took 11 wickets with his occasional leg-spin. He, like several of the team, was a professional footballer. He played for Bristol Rovers, Cardiff City, Bristol City and Cheltenham Town.

Barrie Meyer was in his last year before retiring and becoming one of the world's best umpires. He too had played football for both Bristol teams and scored 100 league goals in his career. In most other eras he would have kept wicket for England, even though Gloucestershire was not a fashionable county as far as the selectors were concerned. He stood up to the medium-pacers and held 707 catches and made 119 stumpings, keeping to three top spinners in John Mortimore, David Allen and, at the start of his career, 'Sam' Cook.

David Smith played for 16 years as a medium-fast opening bowler and was selected five times for England on tour in India in 1961/62, when Trueman and Statham opted not to tour. He took 1,250 first-class wickets and was another of the footballers, playing for Bristol City and Millwall.

The two England off-spinners, David Allen, who spun the ball prodigiously, and John Mortimore, who preferred to beat the batsman through the air, were a terrific combination, especially at Bristol and Cheltenham, where there was often turn for the spinners. I shall never forget a nightmare of a session at Cheltenham, when we had lost, having been bowled out too easily on a sharply turning pitch. After the match, Tony Brown ordered a practice in the middle facing these two. Off-spinners, with the ball turning away from a left-hander's bat, were always my most feared opponents and, on a third-day pitch which had considerable wear and tear, I'm not sure I middled many deliveries in my innings.

I played what I still call the left-hander's 'play and leave', where I played up the line of the ball and tried desperately not to follow it if it turned. I did not look to score unless it was full enough to drive safely or short enough to pull. The only other shot that I attempted when well set was a good old-fashioned heave over mid-wicket, which was always in danger of going straight up in the air off a top edge but brought me many boundaries.

Mike Procter was the star player and an inspiration to the team and to some Gloucestershire members from Birdlip, who had come together as a supporters' group, followed us around and shouted 'Proctershire' at every wicket he took or run he scored. He was probably the world's second best all-rounder after Garry Sobers at the time, a batsman whose off-drive was likened to Wally Hammond's and a bowler who swung the ball into the right-handers at extreme pace off his long and impressive run.

I took the place of Mike Bissex at number three. He played 212 first-class matches, scored 6,492 runs with only two centuries, held 132 catches and took 237 wickets with his slow left-arm spinners. He was one of those strange cricketers who bowled with his left arm and threw with his right, which often confused batsmen looking to steal a run.

I benefitted enormously from listening to the advice of these senior players, though I always thought it was important to work out my own technique and method of playing, guided by Graham Wiltshire, the coach. I had very few extended lean spells with the bat but, on one occasion when I had three or four innings without a reasonable score, the conflicting advice from John Mortimore, Tony Brown, Barrie Meyer and Ron Nicholls was to stand up taller at the wicket, to crouch a little in my stance, to keep my back-lift short to avoid being yorked and to raise my bat higher for more rhythm. Graham Wiltshire, a moderate former player but the straightforward and genuinely supportive county coach, told me to ignore all those comments and took me into an indoor net where he threw a tennis ball underarm and told me to hit it as hard as I could. Whether this approach would work in this day of unending analysis I rather doubt, but it relaxed me and made me realise that watching the ball was the key factor so that my head and eyes led my feet, hands and bat into the right positions. In the next match I scored a century and was back on track again.

I agree with the current Surrey captain, Rory Burns, when he said: "Growing up in county cricket, a lot of the time you have to try and work it out for yourself, though you obviously talk to the coaches around. If you can establish yourself every time you take a step up, you take confidence from that. No one can bat for you. It's about having a clear game plan in your head." That was how I approached cricket.

Pre-season training consisted of a few runs, a few nets and some fielding practices. On one run, where we set off from the County Ground, did a few exercises at Ashton Gate Country Club and then prepared to run back to the ground, David Shepherd was left a long way behind. We waited while he completed his exercises and then Tony Brown led us on the way back. It was unfortunate for Shep that Tony checked that we were all following and saw him hitching a lift in a milk float.

Most of the coaching seemed to be done during the matches by the senior players, perhaps because Graham Wiltshire was not confident enough surrounded by players with better cricket credentials than his. He concentrated on the 2nd XI. That said, I did chat a lot with him and found his advice simple but helpful.

One example of Arthur Milton's coaching support during a match was against Warwickshire when I had played forward to Bob Willis and missed the ball outside off stump and then, next ball, had tried to move back and across and play off the back foot and also missed that. Arthur sauntered down the pitch (he rarely moved faster than necessary, particularly when stealing a run, where he would arrive at the crease without apparent haste just as the ball arrived) and asked what I was going to do next as playing first forward and then back seemed to have exhausted my options. He said that I should remember that Bob was not as fast as one might think and did not do as much with the ball as one might expect. I knew very well that he was not right on either count, having played alongside Bob at Surrey, but it did reassure me and help me to locate the ball more readily.

Arthur was a talented sportsman, who played both football and cricket for England. He was a real team man who enjoyed the success of others as much as he did his own considerable achievements. We used to call him 'Clothbat', as he appeared to move around behind the ball and, with the softest of touches, ease it into gaps. Mike Procter, on the other hand, we called 'Thunderbat', because he never went in for half measures and played his off-drives in a way which reminded some of our older supporters of Wally Hammond. Their batting styles could hardly have been further apart.

In the next few years there were inevitable changes to the team as senior players retired. David Graveney, who had been a leading figure as a schoolboy at Millfield, was the son of Ken, a former Gloucestershire fast bowler and captain, and nephew of Tom. He played for the county from 1972 to 1990. He was a right-hand batsman and a tall, orthodox left-arm spinner who took over as captain from 1982 to 1988. He moved for a year to Somerset and then had three years at Durham, the first two years as captain as the county moved from minor county to first-class county status. He later became chairman of the England selectors, chairman of the Professional Cricketers' Association and subsequently the ECB national performance manager.

Andrew Stovold, who scored 17,705 runs from 1973 to 1990 and kept wicket regularly, opened the batting with Sadiq Mohammad, an experienced opening batsman, brother of Hanif and Mushtaq, who played 41 Tests for Pakistan and brought his experience to the county. Alastair Hignell was not only an immensely talented batsman but also the England rugby full-back. As a player he infuriated bowlers with his ability to hit seemingly straight deliveries square on either side of the wicket. He was an outstanding fielder and a great man to have in the dressing room. Julian Shackleton, son of the metronomic Derek, who took 100 or more wickets in 20 consecutive seasons for Hampshire, was similar in mentality to his father in trying to bowl maiden overs but not as consistently successful as a medium-pace bowler.

Our other star player was Zaheer Abbas, who arrived in 1972. He was an outstanding overseas player, widely called 'the Asian Bradman'. He is still regarded as one of the finest batsmen to have played international cricket. He scored 108 first-class centuries, 12 of them in Tests of which four were double-centuries. He averaged 44.79 in Tests and 51.54 in all first-class matches. He is the only batsman to have scored a century and a double-century in a first-class match four times, finishing each of the eight innings not out. I was relieved to bat ahead of him and Mike Procter because, if they had been at three and four instead of four and five, I might never have got in.

Cricket in Gloucestershire was fun and seemingly less pressurised than at the Oval. At Surrey there was greater expectation that the team would do well and would be challenging to win one of the competitions: the championship, the John Player League, the Gillette Cup or the Benson & Hedges Cup. That did not mean that the Gloucestershire team was unambitious, and Tony Brown and Mike Procter ensured that we competed whole-heartedly in every match, which suited my competitive nature. In 1972 the county finished third in the championship and in 1973 fifth. Best of all, Gloucestershire won the Gillette Cup in 1973.

In the five years that I played for Gloucestershire there are several matches that remain firmly entrenched in my memory. In 1971 we played in the Gillette Cup semi-final at Old Trafford, one of the most famous games of all time, which ended in near darkness just as the BBC News was starting at 8.50pm. For us, as the beaten team, it was a heart-breaking moment of abject dejection. For Lancashire it was a moment of absolute elation as David Hughes took the game by the scruff of the neck. For the cricket supporters at the ground it was an astonishing end to the game.

The final five overs, after delays for rain, started as the evening gloom descended. There had been an announcement at 7.30pm that the train for Bristol was leaving, but no Gloucestershire supporter moved. Another announcement at 8.30pm received the same response. Lancashire needed 25 for victory off the last five overs; Mike Procter had two to bowl, Jack Davey, our more than useful left-arm seamer, also had two and John Mortimore, our England off-spinner and a canny bowler, who had already taken three wickets, had one.

The decision to get Morty's overs out of the way and then leave the two quicker bowlers to finish the game seemed a reasonable option. In hindsight perhaps we should have used the quicker bowlers first and then left the off-spinner to bowl the last, if necessary, in the almost complete darkness that would have fallen by then. Tony Brown talked about this option for the rest of his life. Hindsight is a wonderful thing!

David Hughes, who had only just come to the crease, smashed a six, and the wily off-spinner, as was his usual response to being hit, bowled the ball a little higher, a little more slowly and a fraction shorter. This ball went a little further into the crowd at long-on. There is, on film, one delivery of that over where the ball was hit through extra-cover and I ran round the boundary from long-off to stop the four, only to be thwarted by some young boys who gleefully rushed to pick it up just inside the boundary rope, which had become closer to the action as the crowd became more and more excited. Rory Bremner, one of our best impressionists and comedians, uses the film, which shows me shouldering one boy out of the way and kneeing another to try to get at the ball and prevent a boundary. It goes for four and Rory's comment is: "Here we see the future Secretary of MCC fielding on the boundary." Suffice to say the 24 runs off that over made the 25 to win off five overs a foregone conclusion, and Lancashire won and went on to win the final at Lord's.

A personal highlight was a match in an earlier round of the Gillette Cup between Gloucestershire and Surrey in the same year. Gloucestershire were bowled out in 56 overs for 214 and Surrey were coasting to victory at 193 for five with plenty of overs left. Tony Brown recalled me to bowl, and one by one the remaining Surrey batsmen surrendered to my bowling. It seemed unaccountable at the time, and Micky Stewart, the then Surrey captain, has never quite come to terms with the final result, which was a victory by 15 runs for Gloucestershire at Bristol, where the Man-of-the-Match was a very recent recruit from Surrey who had taken five for 39. Perhaps I had more to prove, but I often had a good match against former team-mates. Alan Gibson described the spell by writing that 'Stewart edged a harmless looking ball from Knight. Knight, by keeping his head and bowling a length, took four wickets in two overs. There were scenes of jubilation on a scale not known at Bristol for many a long year'.

There were other limited-over matches where we did not have the same successful ending and, after the disappointment of losing some key one-day matches, everyone at Gloucestershire was delighted to beat Sussex in the final of the Gillette Cup in 1973, the county's first major success since 1877, when they last won the county championship.

I was due to open the batting with Sadiq Mohammad. A friend's grandfather, who had never seen me bat but was always a great supporter, switched on his television at 11am to see the start. However, the game started earlier than some matches, at 10.45, in order to accommodate the 60 overs for each side, and he missed my dismissal, bowled by John Snow for two runs. As he was housebound he never saw me bat, but we continued to chat about cricket whenever I called.

Gloucestershire were in trouble at 27 for three, but the captain Tony Brown (77*) and vice-captain Mike Procter (94) took us to 248 for eight, which, in those days, was described by Wisden as a formidable total. Sussex started well, but from 155 for two they collapsed, losing the match by 40 runs. One of the turning points was Jim Foat swooping from cover point to run out Tony Greig, the England captain, before he had scored. In the end Mike Procter's pace and my medium-paced seamers were, in Wisden's words, 'too much for the tail'. It is always a bonus as a medium-pacer to have a genuinely quick bowler at the other end, because batsmen are keener to weigh in and score runs before the ordeal of facing the fast bowler, particularly as Mike was sprinting in with his legs pumping, his hair billowing behind him and the Birdlip Boys chanting "Proctershire" around Lord's.

Celebrations that night went on well into the early hours in the Clarendon Court Hotel, near to Lord's. It was a wonderful feeling for the team to have won a tournament at the Home of Cricket and to have brought Gloucestershire back as a force to be reckoned with. However, there was a John Player League match to be played on the following day in Chesterfield and, although that did not cut short the celebratory drinks, it did necessitate a drive in the morning up to Derbyshire for the 2pm start. Our two successful batsmen of the final were due to be opening the bowling on the Sunday. However, John Mortimore won the toss, standing in for Tony Brown who, with Mike in his car, had not arrived in time, and elected to bowl on the usual green pitch that was prepared at Chesterfield. He opened at one end and I bowled at the other, which, on a green top, was not a fearsome duo. We lost that match, perhaps unsurprisingly, but nothing could detract from our victory of the day before.

Travelling, often long distances at the end of a day's play, was a large feature of county cricket in the '70s and '80s. Rest was not scheduled into the summer programme, and most top-order batsmen had the chance of five innings in a week. The bowlers also had to perform and bowl many overs on most days, which was accepted if not popular amongst the fast bowlers. Perhaps the workload suited some of them, because they did not break down as often as present-day bowlers. On the other hand they did not dive or throw themselves around in the field as today's bowlers are required to do. Nor did they bat other than to slog a few runs without getting in line to the quicker bowlers.

There are different thoughts about the amount of cricket we played and the distances we travelled. When in nick, batsmen were happy to bat as often as possible. When it was more of a struggle, batsmen split into those who wanted to practise constantly in the nets and those who wanted to get away from the game. It was the classic battle between the batsmen who agreed with David Gower, that too much practice would bore them and take an edge off their appetite for runs, and those who followed Graham Gooch's approach whereby the more practising he found time for the better he became. I was a strong believer in the former method. If I was out of touch, I wanted to hit a tennis or squash ball and forget about cricket for a day or two.

Bowlers, especially the quick bowlers, understandably wanted to rest and did not want to run up in nets where the footholds were loose and often underprepared. Fast bowling has always been hard work and, in the days when there were many more three-day matches, which involved twenty or more overs a day four times a week, it is astonishing how fit most of the top bowlers remained. The bowlers did their fitness training on the pitch and most did not consider going running during the season. A warm-down was more likely to be a few pints of beer than a stretching session in front of the pavilion.

Travelling long distances in a car seat straight after the exertions of a match, as a batsman, bowler or wicket-keeper was also just about the worst way to look after your body. However, those were the days before the breathalyser and most journeys were broken by a stop for a drink and a meal, which meant arriving quite late at the hotel.

One weekend in 1972 exasperated the Gloucestershire team. We left Bristol on a Friday evening, after a match that ended in the last over of the day, to drive to Westcliff-on-Sea to play Essex on the Saturday, a trip that took us right across the country through London with no M25 motorway in place. The only saving grace was that we were travelling east and not straight towards the setting sun, as was often the case when driving back to Bristol in the evening. For the Sunday league match, then played in the middle of the three-day championship match, we had to drive on Saturday evening after the day's play to Derby. Once that game was finished, the cavalcade of five cars set off once again for Westcliff to resume against Essex on the Monday and Tuesday. It did not seem to affect Mike Procter, who scored a century and then followed that up with a hat-trick on the Tuesday! For the start of the next match, a 60-over Gillette Cup match on the following day, we drove on Tuesday evening to Canterbury to play Kent. Those of us at breakfast on Wednesday were slightly bemused to see Roy Swetman coming down the stairs with his leather gloves on. He announced that he was going to drive round the ring road to keep in practice.

I enjoyed one-day cricket and, as an all-rounder, there was always a chance that I could play a meaningful part in the match. Whether it was a Gillette Cup of 60 overs (reduced from 65 after the first year in 1963), a Benson & Hedges Cup of 55 overs or a John Player League match of 40 overs, as a top-order batsman and a first or second-change bowler, there was always an opportunity to contribute to the team's success. On ten occasions during my career, I was either Man-of-the-Match or the Gold Award winner in limited-over matches.

We did not have to learn to adapt to the T20 or even the T10 format, both of which have encouraged imaginative and innovative batting and athletic fielding. However, on Sundays, faster bowlers had their run-up restricted, which most managed without any problems, though John Price of Middlesex found a way to run the full distance by incorporating a long curving run in his approach, so that he did not cut the white line drawn 15 yards behind the stumps. Our generation of cricketers still regards the longer format of the game as the best test of an individual's skills and techniques, but the range of shots has increased enormously in the last fifteen years.

Occupying the crease with a sound defensive technique was then a key objective, though there was also a desire to dominate the bowlers whenever possible, encouraged by the overseas batsmen playing for counties. Time was on the batsman's side and more deliveries were allowed to go through to the wicket-keeper than in a limited-over match. As the bowlers were not restricted in the number of overs they could bowl in championship cricket, one of the aims was to tire out and frustrate the quicker bowlers and make them think that they were wasting their time by bowling bouncers. The batsmen who hooked and those who flinched always encouraged more bouncers to be bowled, so swaying out of the way or ducking were useful ways of using up a bowler's energy.

There have always been demands on professional sportsmen. In the '70s and '80s the county cricketers played much more cricket, had far less time for fitness training or practice, had long car journeys from place to place and played every other county once or twice in the championship each season, once in the Sunday League, as well as meeting most counties in the other one-day competitions. It could become a grind, but success always made it worthwhile.

There was a good deal of after-match socialising with the opposition and conversation about cricket and the merits of other players around the counties. Without the analysis of videos, the knowledge of how batsmen played, who was afraid of quick bowling, who favoured the leg-side, what bowlers did with the ball was learnt and passed on by word of mouth to be stored away for the next encounter with those players. Umpires shared the bar and on occasions travelled with players.

After one match at Lancashire, Gloucestershire were travelling home to Bristol and the umpire Tommy Spencer had to travel to Worcester to officiate there the following day. He had no car so we offered him a lift in our car and agreed to drop him at his hotel. On the way I asked how he normally travelled, and the two other Gloucestershire players in the car and I were amused and more than surprised by his answer that he preferred to travel by train as he did not trust his eyes for driving! I don't think that any of us have repeated that story since. The relationship between umpires and players was generally respectful and friendly. I had known Tommy since I was aged eleven when he had coached me in the MCC Easter Coaching classes at Lord's and encouraged me to keep playing my off-drives, which he assured me were a great strength and would bring me lots of runs, as indeed they did.

The vast majority of umpires were former first-class players, and there was an easy rapport between players and officials. The umpires knew the batsmen who walked when they had nicked the ball and the small minority who did not at that time and, with that knowledge stored away, they shot the latter out the moment the ball hit the pad, almost pleading to bowlers to appeal. It was a case of natural justice, which, along with the benefit of the doubt going quite often to captains, who had to mark the umpires after each match, was broadly accepted by the players. There was no recourse to a third umpire or slow-motion replays and players knew who might give them out if hit on the pads when sweeping and adjusted their game accordingly. For the most part decisions were remarkably accurate within these parameters, and the batsmen and bowlers accepted their lot without acrimony. I remember 'Sam' Cook, formerly a Gloucestershire slow left-arm bowler, giving a batsman out on the sweep when David Graveney was bowling. He put his finger up with huge pleasure and said: "They didn't give them out when I was bowling, but that's out today!"

With sometimes lengthy stints in the bar in the pavilion after the day's play, much was passed on and discussed. Very early in my career, sitting on a barstool in a group at Trent Bridge, Garry Sobers explained how he swung the ball either way and how it was all to do with the position of the thumb either on its edge for his left-arm in-swinging deliveries or flat for the ball that left the right-handed batsman. That was often how we learnt the skills, and it allowed me to develop the ability to swing the ball either way, which was vital at my fairly gentle medium pace. No coach had ever mentioned the thumb. It had always been the position of the feet and the left shoulder to stay sideways on, and the follow-through across the body to bowl an out-swinger and being more front-on to bowl an in-swinger.

I did try to run up faster and jump higher in the delivery stride at one stage in my Gloucestershire career, but I was never cut out to be a fast bowler and wanted to concentrate on batting in the top three or four whilst contributing as a third or fourth seamer. The result of the experiment was that I lost 'the gather', as John Snow, one of England's greatest fast bowlers with whom I later played at Sussex, used to call the position before releasing, and I lost any semblance of length, as the ball came out very gently and floated rather than hit the pitch hard. The advantage that I had was the ability to swing and seam the ball either way with the keeper standing up to the stumps and to use my height to get bounce. That was a short-lived and not very committed attempt to speed up as a bowler. At the start of my career at Surrey, the county probably saw me as a successor to Stewart Storey, batting at number six and bowling as a third seamer and thus a genuine all-rounder. I was more certain that I was primarily a batsman who bowled and, indeed, I am confident that, if I had batted against my own bowling, I would have scored a stack of runs!

Gloucestershire provided me with five formative years as a professional cricketer, and I shall forever be grateful to the county for giving me my chance to play the game.

Sussex CCC 1976-1977

After five years with Bristol as the home ground, Chris and I spoke at length about our plans. We now had a daughter, Catharine Elisabeth (Katie), who needed to settle into a school. There was now a third aspect to my twin careers – the family needs. The options seemed either to look for a school in Gloucestershire, if I could find a similarly generous headmaster who would release me for the summers, or to see whether Sussex would be prepared to take me on so that I could remain at Eastbourne College, which was an excellent base for us and had been extremely accommodating for the past

53

five years. The third option was to stop playing cricket and concentrate on teaching, which I always saw as my long-term profession but, ideally, not yet. We decided that Sussex was where we wanted to be.

During these deliberations I was chatting to a local reporter in Bristol and discussing the possibility of not continuing with Gloucestershire. He asked me whether I would definitely consider retiring or leaving if I was offered the captaincy of Gloucestershire or if I was selected to play for England, which had been suggested as a possibility in some newspaper articles. I explained that, although it was likely that I would leave Gloucestershire at the end of 1975, I would obviously have to rethink if either of his hypothetical situations arose. Unfortunately, although he wrote a reasonable article, the headline writer put a banner at the top, saying that 'Knight will only remain at Gloucestershire if he is offered the captaincy or selected to play for England'.

Tony Brown was not at all impressed and, the following morning, I was called into the office by the captain where I had to explain how this complete misunderstanding had occurred. It did bring home how careful one needs to be in expressing any opinions to the media. However, this is also a moment to say that, over my thirty years of involvement in cricket as a player or as an administrator, the media have been, for the most part, accurate and supportive. I have enjoyed an excellent relationship with the cricket writers and have avoided the few gossip columnists who have, from time to time, made unworthy or unnecessarily provocative or negative comments.

I had a meeting with the Sussex coach, Tony Buss, and the chairman, Tony Crole-Rees, sitting in the back of the chairman's Jaguar, and the end result was that Sussex offered me an opportunity to move on and play for the county, which allowed me to remain in my teaching post at Eastbourne College and enjoy two summers at Hove.

Tony Greig was captain, John Snow, with whom I shared a car on many trips to away matches, and Mike Buss were the senior players, but Tony's intention was to bring on and encourage younger players. Javed Miandad and Kepler Wessels were an exciting couple of overseas players, John Barclay, Paul Phillipson, Paul Parker, Jerry Groome, Roger Marshall, John Spencer and Giles Cheatle were forcing their way into the team, and there were two former Surrey players in Arnold Long and Chris Waller. Peter Graves captained the side when Tony Greig was involved in England matches, and we were a happy team playing at Hove where the pitch had pace and favoured my batting and seam bowling. Peter and I always joked that, together, he and I would make the perfect left-handed batsman. He was much stronger on the leg-side, and I always favoured the off-side.

It was in my first season in 1976 that I scored my highest first-class score of 165* against Middlesex and ended the season with the highest aggregate of runs in the championship for the county. I was also ninth in the national limited-over averages with 848 runs at an average of 44.63, sharing the prize, with John Shepherd of Kent and the West Indies, for the leading six-hitters (13) in the John Player League for the season. So much for playing the ball straight and along the ground, as I had learnt in the Streatham garden. So much, too, for Peter Graves' analysis of me as an offside player, although he was predominantly correct.

The change of county had worked, and our home lifestyle was more settled, living in Sussex for the whole year. Katie attended her first school, Chelmsford Lodge, and Graeme Edward Verdon, our son, who had been born in the August of my last season with Gloucestershire, completed our family as we settled into Granville Court, a block of flats owned by the College, five minutes' walk from the school and even closer to the boarding house, Gonville, where I was a house tutor. Life seemed very good.

Perhaps serendipity should be accepted more readily. Chris's birthday is 27 June. I scored my first-ever century as a batsman for Dulwich College on that date in 1964, although I had not yet met her. On that same date in 1976 in a John Player League match, Stonegate Farmers, the county sponsors, offered an egg to any batsman on either side for each run scored, half a dozen for a four and a dozen for a six. Bowlers were offered a dozen eggs for each wicket. Barry Richards made our bowling look relatively easy as he stroked the ball majestically around for 97, supported by David Turner with a much more workmanlike method.

It was a swelteringly hot day, but their total of 220 for six did not seem out of reach. I had taken three wickets in the Hampshire innings, so we would be ready for omelettes over the next week or so. At the end of the match, which Sussex did not win, I had scored 127, with four sixes and 15 fours. It did not help when John Spencer came out to join me at the crease towards the end of the innings and, in his dry way, joked that we could win by 'getting them in threes'. After the match, when I had recovered from heat exhaustion, helped by our physiotherapist rushing to my aid with a couple of glasses of sherry sweetened with sugar, I was able to meet the sponsor, receive my prize and agree that we would not take the 25 dozen eggs with us but would collect them on a fortnightly basis from a local store.

It was another day to remember and an unusual way to celebrate my wife's birthday.

1977 was the first season for six years when I did not score over 1,000 runs in the championship, which was a disappointment to me and Sussex. For the first and only time in my career I had to face being dropped for the match being played in Eastbourne, my home town and ground, which was a difficult decision to accept. There was no argument to be made about weight of runs, so I could have no complaints, but I hated missing out, especially at the Saffrons in front of a home crowd. Perhaps the main redeeming feature of my season was a century against Surrey at the Oval in the last championship match of the summer in September, which may have heralded the next opportunity in cricket.

It was not an easy season in the Sussex dressing room, with rumours and then confirmation that Tony Greig, John Snow and Imran Khan, who had recently arrived, had signed up to Kerry Packer's World Series Cricket in Australia. Uncertainty did not help us as a county, nor did Kepler Wessels' departure to military service in South Africa halfway through the summer. Sussex finished 8th in the championship, were well beaten by Derbyshire in the first round of the Gillette Cup, lost to Kent in the quarter finals of the Benson and Hedges Cup, but were joint fourth in the John Player League.

My two years at Hove were another opportunity to develop as a professional cricketer. They were contrasting seasons of success in the long, hot summer of 1976, where in one match we all arrived at the ground to see the outfield completely bare of grass because of the hosepipe ban and the square red because of a plague of ladybirds, and disappointment in 1977, the only year in which I was ever dropped from a team.

It was easier for us as a family to live in one place throughout the year and life at Eastbourne College was very fulfilling, now that I had taken on running the rugby and coaching the 1st XV. That ran alongside teaching both French and German and coaching squash to boys and the VIth form girls. I was also around to help John Lush, my housemaster in Gonville, who ran the cricket for 25 years, to coach his team when Sussex did not have a match. The 23-mile drive along the coast from Eastbourne to Hove for the cricket was straightforward and was the longest commute that I had in my whole working life. Coombe Dingle, where we had our first home, to the County Ground in Bristol had taken 15 minutes, although Cheltenham, Gloucester and the other Gloucestershire home out-grounds were further away.

56

There were different characters in the Sussex team, and we were led by a less measured captain. Tony Greig was more demonstrative than Tony Brown, less able to contemplate any defensive cricket, even when circumstances demanded it, and more inclined to aggravate a situation within his own team or with the opposition. Having won the toss on a green Hove pitch, he came back into the dressing room rubbing his hands in glee and said to John Snow: "Snowball, this is your pitch! We're bowling." John Snow reacted by saying that the captain never looked at a good batting track and said it was an opening batsman's pitch, so why did he assume that this was his? He followed this up by running in and bowling medium-paced leg breaks, until Greig took him off and resorted to lesser bowlers. Later in the day, when the green tinge had disappeared from the pitch, John Snow ran in hard and took five wickets. He had made his point and then wanted to perform for the team, as he always did.

John was a very fine fast bowler, but he started life as a number four batsman at Christ's Hospital School. He volunteered to be Sussex's first pinch-hitter in the Sunday League and went out, threw his bat and scored 50 in next to no time. He then opened again in the next game but, unfortunately, under the illusion that he had proved himself as an opening batsman, he played much more conventionally with much less success.

He was an enigma to many but a great travelling companion for me. I drove and he did the *Daily Telegraph* crossword, occasionally asking me for assistance as we travelled from match to match. We also discussed cricket, and I continued to learn about the game. On another occasion in a Sussex match he infuriated Tony Greig again. John had just finished his over and was sauntering down to field at square-leg near the pavilion, his sweater over his shoulder, when the captain bowled his first ball. He was bowling off-breaks and pulled it down short, so that the left-handed batsman hit it in the direction of the still-retreating John Snow. Tony Greig's anguished cry was ignored, and the ball went past him while he was still facing the other way. The captain's volley of abuse was greeted with a quiet comment that "Bowlers should wait until their fielders are in position before bowling."

Arnold Long was a wicket-keeper with a sardonic wit. In a match at Hove in 1976 against Somerset he asked Ian Botham, who was just starting in the first-class game and was on 97 not out, whether he had ever scored a century. When the answer came back that he had not, 'Ob', as he was known, suggested that Ian might celebrate by reaching the landmark with a six. In attempting to do so, Ian missed his hundred and had to wait a little longer.

On another occasion he asked Barry Richards whether he could hit any ball wherever he wanted. Barry was well into his innings and proceeded to prove that he could. 'Ob' nominated that the ball should go through extra cover, and Barry moved slightly back and gave himself room to hit the next delivery through extra cover on the up for four. The following delivery 'Ob' said that fine leg would be a good place to hit it, so Barry moved across his wicket and glanced the ball for four in that direction. We always thought that Barry had three ways of playing a delivery. The orthodox stroke in the coaching book, a slight movement to hit the ball to an unexpected place and, only very occasionally, a defensive shot. He was the best batsman against whom I played, which is saying something when I played against other great batsmen such as Colin Cowdrey, Tom Graveney, Rohan Kanhai, Zaheer Abbas, Clive Lloyd and Viv Richards.

Kepler Wessels and Javed Miandad were both exemplary overseas players. Kepler never stopped practising, and when he was out he would often retire to sit in his car at Hove with his pads still on until he could persuade someone to bowl at him in the net. As the nets were worn and often made batting difficult, if not almost impossible, most of us had a reluctance to use them later in the season. Kepler's view was that, no matter the surface, he was always prepared to try to play and improve his batting. Javed instilled a greater sense of fun amongst other members of the team. He was always mischievous and loved upsetting opposition bowlers by stealing a run or challenging them to throw the ball at his wicket when he pretended to do so. He made us all run harder and was good as a batting partner with his unbounded confidence, although he did seem to invite more bouncers from the quick bowlers, which had an impact for his batting partners. Both players were beginning their careers, and there was little doubt, even in the early stages, that they were destined to be top performers. Both loved scoring runs in their own way and contributed hugely to the team.

It was during my time at Sussex that I took the NCA Advanced Coaching Certificate, a course led by Les Lenham, probably the best demonstrator of batting that I have ever met. I remember him batting against Intikhab Alam in a net and calling out each delivery, whether a leg-spin, a googly or a top-spinner, as the ball was coming down the pitch. He not only called each delivery correctly, he played the most immaculate stroke to each ball.

On the course were several established cricketers, Clive Lloyd and Robin Hobbs amongst them. In one session, when Les was teaching group coaching skills, we all stood and picked up our bats as he called out that the bowler had reached the wicket and we should play a stroke to the ball, which was short of a length on off-stump. We were expected to move into a backward defensive stroke, which we dutifully did, with the exception of Clive Lloyd, who played an attacking shot on the back foot, ending with his bat over his shoulder. Les's cry of "It's a good length, Clive! It should be a backward defensive" was met with the comment: "I never play the shot!" There was no answer to that from a competent county player to a great Test batsman. I also remember playing squash against Clive on one of our evenings when we were free. I kept hitting the ball to the corners and stood on the T in the court, but I was never able to get the ball past his extendable arms, which seemed to reach the side wall on either side with ease. No wonder he was an outstanding cover fielder as well as a top batsman.

There is no reason why very good cricketers should be good coaches, because often they do things naturally, without having to work out why. Robin Hobbs was an example of this. A top-class leg-spinner, he was asked by Les Lenham to explain which finger he used predominantly to spin the ball. He was initially flummoxed, looked at his right hand and then asked if he could be given a ball. It was only then that he realised that he used the finger, next to the smallest finger, to put purchase on the ball. It was a fascinating course that taught me more about my own game. As most schoolteachers will tell you, teaching is an excellent way of learning for yourself, as it demands real knowledge of a subject in order to put it across to pupils.

I rather thought that Sussex would be my last chance to enjoy cricket at first-class county level and combine it with teaching. After seven years at Eastbourne College, teaching for the two winter terms, it was clear that I had to consider the future more seriously. Cricket and the school holidays had given me the chance to go on tour to East and West Africa with MCC and to South Africa with a Derrick Robins XI. It had brought in twice as much salary in the five months of the summer as in the seven months in the classroom. It had also been an ideal break from the routines of teaching as well as providing a huge amount of pleasure and a sense of achievement. I had proved to myself that I was able to play at this level and that I could score runs and take wickets against the best. I had been playing against some of the greatest players in the world, had bowled out Tom Graveney and had Garry Sobers caught. I had scored a century against Andy Roberts and runs against other great fast bowlers and managed to keep involved in the teaching profession at the same time.

Surrey CCC 1978 – 1984 ... Leadership in the Oval Office

At the end of the 1977 season it was clear that I had some serious decisions to make. Simon Langdale, the Headmaster of Eastbourne College, had suggested that it was time for me to retire from cricket and concentrate on teaching, with a view to becoming a boarding housemaster in the next couple of years. At Sussex, despite my poor season, there would be a search for a new captain as Tony Greig would not return. One or two local committee members mentioned that I could well be under consideration, which was an appealing thought.

What changed everything, though, was a telephone call, very much out of the blue, from Alf Gover at the Oval. He asked whether I would be interested in returning to Surrey as captain for the following season. This came as a complete surprise, because there had been no other conversation or inkling of a change. He said that he could not promise anything, but he wished to put it to the Surrey Committee and thought that they would be pleased to have me back as captain, as John Edrich was to retire.

I was now in a turmoil and totally uncertain what the right way forward was. Should I start my full-time teaching career? Could I remain, with the same arrangements, at Eastbourne College if I decided to wait for the outcome of the Sussex Committee's deliberations over a captain? Should I hope that Surrey wanted me back and, if so, could I find a school where I could teach for two terms each year? I had discussions with my father who was still teaching at Dulwich College and decided that I could delay a decision for a few weeks, while the two counties went through their committee meetings. I also had an exploratory conversation with David Emms, the Master of Dulwich College. I approached him, asking that, based on the hypothetical situation that I would be offered the captaincy at Surrey, would he consider my teaching modern languages for the two winter terms. In the meantime I continued to teach that winter at Eastbourne College, having explained my dilemma to Simon Langdale. He had always been most supportive of my twin careers and I was very grateful to him for his understanding and his balanced advice.

The two likelier options were full-time teaching or a change of home to the Dulwich area and the chance to captain a county cricket team, which definitely appealed to me. Surrey was my original county and a return to the Oval was a challenging prospect, were it to materialise. I was always going to be a schoolmaster, but I hoped that added responsibility in cricket could keep me a little longer in a career which I still enjoyed. There would be plenty of years ahead to teach, but high-level sport, with the additional dimension of captaincy and leadership, still attracted me. It would not be easy to leave Eastbourne College, where we had been extremely happy, having made friends with others on the common room staff and locally in the town, but both Chris and I were prepared to look at opportunities and take them if we felt them to be right, despite a feeling of loyalty to Simon Langdale, his two predecessors, Michael Birley and John Kendall-Carpenter, and the school governors, who had provided me with the opportunity to continue with my two careers.

When Surrey formally approached me and invited me to captain them in 1978 and Dulwich College agreed that I could teach during the winter terms, all we needed to do was explain to Eastbourne College and Sussex CCC what we had decided, find a house that we could afford near enough to the Oval and Dulwich College and get the children into schools in the new area. Looking back it sounds a lot to achieve in a short space of time, but it all went amazingly smoothly. We sold a house in Eastbourne, which we had let while we continued to live in College accommodation, and bought a home in a quiet road in which to live in Herne Hill. It was ten minutes from the College and fifteen minutes from the Oval when there was no traffic. Another couple of easy commutes. Simon Langdale could not have been more supportive of our decision, though I did feel that I had taken advantage of his kindness since he had become headmaster of Eastbourne College and then deserted him. Sussex appointed Arnold Long as captain, which was the right decision and brought experience to a young side. Katie went to Dulwich Hamlet, the local state primary school, and Graeme started his early schooldays at Dulwich College Preparatory School, thanks to a generous remission of fees allowed for the staff at the College. We moved on and it was a start of another chapter for us all from which we never looked back with any regret.

As had been the case at Eastbourne, Dulwich College needed to find someone to take my lessons while I was at the Oval and elsewhere on the cricket circuit. In London it was easier, and for several years Mademoiselle Béatrice Delaunay stood in for me. She was a qualified teacher and, one year when I returned to the College after the summer, I asked one of the VIth form boys how the class had got on with their teacher and what she had covered. Boys being straightforward and honest, he replied that Mademoiselle Delaunay spoke better French than I did and was much better looking! Both were undoubtedly true.

One of the perks of a school such as Dulwich College was that there were endless contacts and, when I returned to the area, I met a former school friend who was now running SG Smith, a local chain of car dealers. He was happy to let me use a Peugeot 505 and later a Volvo Estate with my name and signature emblazoned on the sides with some advertising for his garages. It was not always ideal to be recognised when driving, but there were advantages. First I had a large reliable car, and secondly cricket supporters were generally pleased to acknowledge me, especially if I had done well on the cricket field. On one occasion Chris and I, plus my parents, were going to the theatre in London and running a little late. Parking was a nightmare, but there was a space coned off in front of another theatre. I drew up and asked the member of staff outside if he could recommend where I might park.

He looked at the name on the car and said: "Hello, Roger. Just go left, left and left again and come back here and you can leave the car in this space. I'll move the cones." When we parked, it was a little embarrassing and my father insisted on going into this theatre and out of another door to reach the theatre which was our destination. The other helpful moment was when I was finding it difficult to break into a line of traffic on the South Circular road near Dulwich. Nobody was prepared to let me in, so I edged out slowly. One of the drivers, who was determined to stay close to the car in front, suddenly saw the writing on my car and, as he read the wording, the line of traffic stopped and he drove gently into the car in front. I waved to thank him and joined the queue as the two drivers got out to swap details.

1978

Six years of captaincy at Surrey were very much a highlight of my cricket career. Although I had not captained Cambridge University in the four years at Fenner's, I had captained school teams and had played under the two Tonys, Brown and Greig, as well as Micky Stewart.

In the first year, with Fred Titmus as coach, after his very long playing career at Middlesex, I steered the county to 16th out of 17 in the county championship, so the less said about this year the better. It was the lowest position that the county had ever occupied. John Edrich had relinquished the captaincy but continued to play and open the batting. Geoff Arnold had departed for Sussex, almost in exchange for my arrival. Robin Jackman led the bowling attack manfully but without a pace bowler at the other end.

It should be added that Robin was understandably very disappointed, having been told that he would be the preferred captain, to learn, fortunately in a letter from me and not through a press release, that I had been invited back to Surrey and had accepted the captaincy. My first thought on being appointed was how the senior players at Surrey would receive me. Robin was an obvious choice as a captain and would have relished the task. I was keen to make contact with him, although he was overseas for the winter, and I believe my letter broke the news in a more sensitive way, asking for his support as vice-captain. It did not make for an easy relationship initially, though we knew each other from the matches in the 1960s, and I am grateful for the way he received the news and reacted to it. He remained a whole-hearted cricketer.

Younis Ahmed, a most talented batsman, who had not contributed as many runs in the first team in the latter years as his ability should have produced, was dropped and from then on was constantly telephoning me to ask why he was not selected in the first team. He was also upsetting other players in the 2nd XI with his carping. Surrey had a reputation of being moaners, and there was little success in bringing about a change in that attitude in the first year, though some of the leading contributors to this reputation had moved on.

There were one or two encouraging signs when David Smith, who returned to the staff after an unhappy end to the season in 1977, recorded his maiden century in first-class cricket and Monte Lynch scored a century against Pakistan. Jack Richards began to show his strengths as a wicket-keeper who could bat. David Thomas and Hugh Wilson, both teenagers, showed fleeting signs of becoming the faster bowlers that we needed to support Robin Jackman. But the most reassuring part of that year of poor results was knowing that Surrey possessed two of the best spinners in the game in Intikhab Alam and Pat Pocock, both of whom were incredibly supportive and helpful through the difficult year. The other relief was that I did get back to scoring runs and continued to bowl economically, which at least proved to any doubters, if they were around, that I could justify my position in the team. Captaincy is almost impossible if the rest of the team begin to doubt the worth of the captain's contribution. It was a frustrating year, but it led into several much improved seasons in the years to come.

The John Player League, which began in 1969, the fast-moving game of 40 overs, made it vital that the captain knew how many overs each bowler had delivered. In one JPL match I was bowling Inti and Percy Pocock in

63

tandem, relying on the scoreboard to remind me of the overs they had each bowled. When the board showed that Inti had bowled his eight overs and Percy had bowled six, I took off our leg-spinner and went back to the seamers. To my utter horror, when I next looked at the board, Inti's overs had gone back to seven and Percy's had moved on to seven. The scoreboard was momentarily, and very unusually, incorrect. It soon became apparent to me that I had miscalculated, and Inti would have to bowl one of the last overs of the innings. Inti was always most reliable and economical, so we ultimately won the match, after Robin Jackman had kept his final over to very few runs, but it was a salutary lesson for me to keep a closer check on overs bowled by each bowler. When I asked Inti afterwards whether he had realised that he still had one over left to bowl when I took him off, he replied: "Yes, but I thought it was a tactical plan."

Inti was always a great support to me, with his experience of captaining Pakistan, and a very good friend. On another occasion I asked him whether he could open the bowling for us in the fourth innings of a match when the ball was turning. Pat Pocock was concerned that the new ball would be difficult to grip, but Inti's answer was straightforward: "I shall hold it tighter." It was an education standing at slip when he bamboozled many batsmen with his googlies, one shown and one concealed, his top-spinners, his leg-breaks and the magic ball bowled from twenty-four yards. His forceful batting was also a great asset to the team in the lower order. Few batsmen hit the ball harder at that time.

It was a hard first year as captain. We tried younger players, and there were definite signs that some of them might make the grade at county level. Geoff Howarth was required by New Zealand later in the season, but Alan Butcher, who had started the summer with little success, came back strongly with two centuries. Graham Roope was on England duty for Test matches, so we were an inexperienced batting side and that showed in the number of times we were dismissed for low scores.

Some of our batting was embarrassing in 1978, no more so than when we went to play Ireland in Dublin. After being generously hosted and plied with wine and other alcoholic drinks on the day we arrived at the airport, in the hotel, at the restaurant and again at the hotel where there was a discotheque which seemed to go on for most of the night, we even found a crate of Guinness in the dressing room. In a two-day match Ireland declared at 211 for five and bowled us out for 111. We had a serious discussion that evening about professionalism and the need for personal pride in our own performance. We followed on. The second day was very much better. We declared on 254 for six, and Ireland ended the match on 64 for nine. Honours even, but reputations not fully restored!

Our bowling was equally inconsistent. At Tunbridge Wells, where we were caught on a wet pitch and had a terrible time against Derek Underwood and Graham Johnson, we even played Fred Titmus as our second spinner in the absence of Pat Pocock.

Fred Titmus, after a very brief time as Surrey coach following his many playing seasons across the Thames at Lord's, resigned at the end of the season, although he did find and offer a contract to Sylvester Clarke before he left. That was the best legacy of his time at the Oval.

Sylvester arrived one cold day in 1979 when we were practising in the middle. Hugh Wilson was bowling and Jack Richards was taking the ball knee high behind Alan Butcher, who was standing at the batsman's wicket playing or leaving the ball. Sylvester had managed to find the Oval after getting lost on the underground. He had a cold and came on to the field wearing several sweaters and a pair of trainers below his track-suit trousers. He jogged in off a short run, and the first ball pitched and arrived at Jack Richards head high. When he repeated this a couple of times, we all knew that we had found what we desperately needed: a genuine fast bowler to share the new ball with Robin Jackman, break up partnerships and roll over the tail. We signed him up with great anticipation.

1979

1979 saw key changes. Micky Stewart, who, as he told me on his appointment, was one of only two Surrey Cricket Committee members who had spoken and voted against my returning as captain, became the Cricket Manager and transformed the whole cricket set-up. He did explain that he would have chosen me to captain a team of younger players, but he had concerns about throwing me into the cauldron of the Surrey team of 1978. Looking back on the first year, I can see why he had reservations, but I think that, over the next few years, he saw my resilience in many different situations. He and I worked extremely well together. In the 1960s we were captain and player, for the next five years we were to be manager and captain, and our relationship was excellent.

Younis was not retained on the staff and left to play for Worcestershire. He was particularly unhappy, but both Micky and I believed it was right for Surrey. As he scored over 1,500 runs and Worcestershire finished second in the championship, after being 15th the year before, the move was clearly a good one for him and them. Surrey ended in third position and reached a one-day final, so the move of a rejuvenated player to another county, as often happens, led to improvements all round.

However, perhaps the most influential change for us was the arrival of Sylvester Clarke to be our spearhead and provide the pace and fire that not only brought him his wickets but also helped Robin Jackman to take 93 first-class wickets as his opening partner. They were a marvellous pair who took early wickets, broke partnerships and blew away the tail of our opponents. Pat Pocock also took 70 wickets. It suddenly made me a much better captain, as is always the case when there is a match-winning fast bowler around to intimidate the opposition! Joe Root must have felt the same with the arrival of Jofra Archer. The first question our opponents always had on their minds was whether Sylvester was playing. Surrey players had a spring in their step again, although we did miss Sylvester during his period of injury.

In March 1979 we arranged a pre-season trip to Singapore, Hong Kong and Bangkok, which was an excellent way to bond the whole playing squad, although Micky did have reservations. Singapore allowed us the freedom to stretch, train, field and play in the sunshine and warmth of the Padang. Hong Kong was better practice for the English summer, because it rained. However, we played football and shared a curry with the Gurkha regiment, of which Robin Jackman's brother was a senior officer. Bangkok was an interesting experience. We played at the Royal Bangkok Sports Club against a hastily selected team, including some of our own squad. The pitch was uneven and the huge crowd, which from time to time spontaneously burst into applause, was encouraging and motivating for us, even though they were in the grandstand watching and reacting to the horseracing, which was taking place around the cricket ground and several football pitches, which surrounded our ground. The club is an amazing place where there are facilities for a great number of different sports with a clubhouse in the centre.

We were very well hosted by an MCC member living and working in Bangkok who opened the batting for the opposing team, asking that we gave him one to get off the mark. We agreed, and Graham Roope opened the bowling. Even his medium-paced away swing was testing on the uneven pitch, and the first ball reared off a length. It was fortunate that the batsman managed to get his glove in front of his face to avoid possibly a serious injury. He ran a single and Graham, who always hated batsmen scoring off his bowling, told him that we had delivered our side of the bargain and now he should find a way to get out, which he managed without too much difficulty.

We returned from our Far East tour fitter, more united and ready for the new season with a reshaped team and a different manager, who had Surrey cricket running through his veins. The final position of third in the championship showed what we, as a team, were capable of doing and the AGM that year was much easier for captain and manager than in 1978. At the end of the first year one of the members had stood up and asked me a question. "Captain, the year after you left Gloucestershire they won the Benson & Hedges Cup, the year after you left Sussex they won the Gillette Cup. Is there any chance that you might be leaving us soon?"

The 1979 championship brought out the best in Robin Jackman and Pat Pocock. Sylvester Clarke was injured for a part of the summer, but Hugh Wilson and I took our fair share of wickets to lessen the impact of his loss. Our batting was helped by Grahame Clinton, who joined us from Kent and scored over 1,000 runs in the season as an opening batsman. Geoff Howarth and Alan Butcher had much better seasons, and Graham Roope contributed as well. It was, though, our 70 bowling bonus points, the most of any county, which took us up the championship table.

Our improvement was noticeable not only in the first-class matches but also in the Benson & Hedges Cup, where we lost the final to Essex, having beaten them in the qualifying rounds. Geoff Howarth and I scored well in both matches, combining in the first match in a partnership of 105 and in the final putting on 89. In those days the Essex total of 290 for six was an enormous target, built around a magnificent 120 by Graham Gooch, but we only fell 35 short.

In the earlier rounds we beat Northamptonshire by five runs, after rain had interfered and led to my bowling Sylvester out much earlier in the innings in order to keep Northants behind the run rate in case of no further play. Oxford and Cambridge were beaten easily. Essex lost to us for the sixth time out of six matches in the B&H tournament, this time by seven runs. Although we lost to Sussex, we qualified for the quarter-finals. Younis inevitably made a century for his new county, Worcestershire, against us, but we won by seven wickets as Monte Lynch scored 67 and Geoff Howarth 51. In the semi-final we were restricted to 166 by Derbyshire, but, by staying in attacking mode with close catchers, Sylvester, Robin, Hugh

Wilson and I bowled them out for 160. Pat Pocock bowled his eleven overs for 22 runs, which kept the pressure on the home side on a slow pitch. We arrived at Lord's with high hopes. However, without Sylvester and with Robin only just fit enough to play, it was always going to be a struggle to keep the Essex batsmen to a manageable total, despite our success against them in past B&H matches.

Despite this disappointment, it was a very encouraging season and, as the new system developed and players grew closer, there were more opportunities for a smile on the pitch, which had not been a noticeable part of the Surrey team over the few years before.

1980

This was a year when Surrey players carried nearly all before them. We finished second in the county championship, a long way ahead of third-placed Nottinghamshire, but we just could not beat Mike Brearley's Middlesex. They won the championship, beat us in the Benson & Hedges competition and the John Player League and, as a final blow, they won the last Gillette Cup Final against us by seven wickets, thanks to Mike Brearley himself scoring 96 not out and Roland Butcher a quick-fire 50. We were close in the championship and only 13 points separated us from Midlesex at the end, but it meant that, although we had improved by one place from 1979, a title still eluded us.

As so many sportsmen say, we 'should look at the positives'. We had played competitive cricket throughout the summer. Sylvester Clarke stayed fit for the season and took 79 first-class wickets at an average of 21.51, including a hat-trick against Nottinghamshire. Robin Jackman took 121 wickets and was selected for England in both Prudential Trophy matches against Australia. He was also close to playing in the Centenary Test. He was chosen as one of Wisden's five cricketers of the year. Of the batsmen Alan Butcher had a tremendous year and was selected for one of the Prudential Trophy matches. Seven of our batsmen averaged over 30. Perhaps more significantly, four bowlers averaged under 25.

One of the highlights of the year was a victory over the Australian touring team. After three declarations in a rain-affected match, the Australians were asked to make 300 in five hours but were bowled out for 240 with Pat Pocock taking five for 61. Jeff Thomson, Dennis Lillee, Geoff Dymock and Ashley Mallett had been well played by Alan Butcher, Geoff Howarth, Graham Roope and Monte Lynch, all of whom scored over 50. I had succumbed, as so many others before and after, for nought, caught Marsh, bowled Lillee. There had been criticism by the Australian team of the negative approach of most counties so, to declare twice and beat the tourists for the first time since 1956, was a great feather in our cap.

Giles Cheatle joined us from Sussex. The thought was that he, as a left-arm spinner turning the ball away from the bat, would be a successor to Intikhab. Towards the end of the season, though, Intikhab returned to the team and again proved his value in helping us to win six out of the last eight matches. Duncan Pauline forced his way into the side for a few matches from weight of runs in the 2nd XI, but Hugh Wilson faded as a fast-bowling prospect and bowled only 63 overs in the championship.

Our success was well received by the Surrey membership. The opening batsmen, Alan Butcher and Grahame Clinton, provided us with good starts to support Sylvester Clarke and Robin Jackman who were often devastating with the new ball. One of the difficulties that was beginning to emerge was that the TCCB only permitted two overseas cricketers to play at any one time, so Geoff Howarth, by then captain of New Zealand and a fine player, had to battle it out with Intikhab Alam for the second overseas player position. Sylvester Clarke was always going to be the first choice. Geoff had a poor start to the season and never really had a chance to rediscover his batting form in the 1st XI, which was sad for him and a loss for us.

One of the personal memories of 1980 was being invited to Calcutta to play in the Bengal Golden Jubilee cricket match. Geoffrey Howard, a former Surrey Secretary, had taken a team, 25 years earlier, to celebrate the Silver Jubilee and now selected a team, captained by Mike Brearley, to take on Bengal, captained by Venkat, in a five-day match at Eden Gardens. It was my first experience of India, the country of such incredible contrasts. We stayed in the Oberoi Grand Hotel and walked to the ground past slum dwellings.

The ground, with a capacity of over 100,000, looked positively deserted with the 18,000 who had turned up to watch from behind the metal fences. Small boys thrust books, caps and paper through the fences asking the boundary fielders for autographs. I was happy to oblige until the police and stewards arrived and used their sticks and batons to keep the youngsters' hands on the spectators' side of the fence. The enthusiasm of those in the stands was obvious, and there was a buzz whenever the Bengal team was playing well, which was almost throughout the match. We had five Test players, but Bengal had a formidable line-up with Amarnath, Gaekwad,

Madan Lal, Arun Lal, who became head coach of Bengal, and Sunil Valson, the only man in the winning Indian World Cup squad of 1983 who did not play a match.

We were due to be introduced to Mrs Gandhi at lunchtime on the fifth day, but there was a grave danger of us being beaten earlier in the morning. With no chance of reaching the 474 we had been set in the fourth innings, Mike Brearley suggested to Venkat that it might be sensible to prolong the match, so the Prime Minister would have something to watch, but Venkat explained that it was a competitive match. As it happened, John Lever batted brilliantly for 73 and defied the Bengal bowlers so we survived until lunch and duly met Mrs Gandhi, who flew in by helicopter and was charming as she sat for photographs amongst the teams. It was a very sad shock when we learned that she had been assassinated a few months later.

India was a wonderful experience, and I still feel a great affinity with that part of the world.

1981

Another final, another loss. Yet again we came second in a one-day final at Lord's, losing this time to Somerset in the Benson & Hedges tournament. We slipped from second to sixth in the championship, missing Sylvester Clarke for half the season and Robin Jackman taking only half the number of wickets as in the previous season. Sylvester averaged 15.43 when he was available and Robin still averaged 24.16, but their combined tally of 104 wickets paled into insignificance compared to the 200 they had taken in 1980.

David Thomas took on some of the fast bowling duties, but he and Hugh Wilson, who had not developed in the last season, both ended 1981 with back problems, the scourge of several young England fast bowlers. Intikhab had another excellent season, his last before returning to Pakistan, and was our leading wicket-taker. Only two batsmen averaged above 30, compared with the seven in the year before. It was a disappointing year for us all. Through all this, Jack Richards, our wicket-keeper, was improving with the gloves and the bat and was rewarded by selection for the England tour to India.

In Jack's absence Alec Stewart made his first-class debut against Gloucestershire at Cheltenham, scoring 2 and 8 batting at number nine, but keeping well, taking three catches and conceding only seven byes in the two innings. As Intikhab bowled 42 overs and Pat Pocock 47, that was quite a baptism of fire for a young keeper.

Micky, his father, had asked me whether Alec should start with another county, as there might be resistance from players in having a father as manager and a son as player on the staff. Micky was not usually uncertain about decisions, but it was an understandable concern. I explained that I had more than survived at Dulwich College with my father teaching there. Alec was clearly a talented batsman and wicket-keeper, and I was not at all keen to lose him from Surrey. I am sure that Micky also wanted him to stay but just needed reassurance. Although a county staff is very much smaller than a school of over 1,600 boys, it was definitely manageable.

Throughout the time that I was captain and Micky was manager, Alec always referred to his father as 'Manager' or 'Ger' and Micky usually called his son 'Stewie'. Occasionally he did call him 'son', but that was also Micky's regular approach to any young player in the team. There were absolutely no problems within the staff and Alec's ability became increasingly apparent over the years, so there was never any accusation of nepotism. His Surrey and England records stand for themselves, and his devotion to the county of his birth has extended to his becoming Director of Cricket, thus continuing a Stewart dynasty at the Oval, where a gate is named after Alec and the pavilion after Micky. They are both Surrey men through and through.

There did not seem to be many highlights in 1981, but one was Sylvester's attack on the Glamorgan bowlers at Swansea, where he recorded the season's fastest century in 62 minutes. For a couple of seasons he had intimidated batsmen by his fast bowling, now it was the turn of the bowlers to fear the wrath of the man from Barbados. His score provided us with the chance to declare after the two first innings had ended with scores only one run apart. On the third day Pat Pocock and Monte Lynch bowled Glamorgan out with four and three wickets respectively. Much as we enjoyed Sylvester's merciless attack as a batsman, it was the six wickets he took in the first innings that we were to miss later in the season. Despite his unavailability, we were clear that one man does not make a team, and the rest of us did not stand up as well as we should have done.

June started as a good month. We beat Glamorgan away, Worcestershire in a run chase led by four left-handers, Grahame Clinton, David Smith, David Thomas and me, and Lancashire by four wickets at home. It then tailed off with a draw against Northamptonshire, where Sylvester broke down with a leg injury. It was not until mid-July that we won again.

I remember our victory against Sussex at Guildford, not for the result, though it was welcome, but because of two deliveries when I was batting. Imran Khan was quick in that match, and he always bowled two lengths to me – short and shorter. In the second innings, when we were chasing 119 to win, I decided that it was time for me to take Imran on when he bowled a bouncer. It was not one of my usual shots, as I preferred to watch the ball go past and the bowler to waste his energy. Perhaps, if helmets were more the order of the day, as they are now, I would have tried to hook more often but, as predominantly a front-foot batsman, I did not play that shot much. On this occasion I set myself to move back and pull him, and the first attempt sent the ball like a tracer bullet towards the scoreboard at square-leg. Probably too carried away with my success, I tried the same shot to the next ball, which was also predictably short but rather more on the off side. It was my last shot in that innings as the ball spooned up to mid-on off the top half of my bat. Not a great example to the younger members of the Surrey team, who were always much keener than I to take on the fast short-pitched deliveries. In the end the reliable Intikhab saw us home by five wickets.

I remember the match against Leicestershire, when I was caught by Mike Garnham bowled by Andy Roberts for two ducks, another dreaded pair. I also remember the next match when we at last beat Middlesex in the championship for the first time since 1973, and we did this soundly in two days and by ten wickets at the Oval. Intikhab (eight wickets), Pat Pocock (four) and Alan Butcher (four), bowling slow left-arm as opposed to his normal medium-pace, bundled out our north London opponents twice. It did help that Mike Brearley, Mike Gatting and John Emburey were all playing for England, but we too were still missing Sylvester Clarke.

It is strange that certain memories come back for no apparent reason. I remember the second innings against Lancashire, a game which we drew at Old Trafford. Michael Holding was, as always, exceedingly quick and, when he started off against me with one lone fielder in front of square at bat-pad or forward short-leg and the rest placed as four slips, a gully and a backward point on the off side and leg-slip and a fine-leg on my leg side, I knew that I was in for a barrage. As it happened, I can tell my grandchildren that I smashed him for ten in the over. Well, perhaps 'smashed' is not quite accurate! I nicked the first ball through the gap between fourth slip and gully, not entirely safely, but on the ground. The third ball was a yorker which I jabbed down on, and an inside edge took it too fine and too quickly for the boundary fielder to stop. So eight off three balls, which brought

72

about a bouncer, which I avoided. On the last delivery of the over I played an ordinary forward defensive shot to a straight ball, which went towards the vacant mid-off position and, as there was nobody closer to the ball, Michael had to fetch it himself, while we scored two more runs. It was probably my only real victory over a great fast bowler, who was and remains one of the nicest men in cricket, as well as a tremendous commentator. He never needed to 'sledge', he let the ball do the talking and it always did its job.

The final time that I played against Michael Holding was in a charity day at Victor Blank's ground. We were both rather older and had retired from the serious game, but we still turned out occasionally in these charity matches. Earlier in the match I had bowled to Richard Branson, who had paid a substantial sum to the charity to take part. I bowled a couple down the leg side so that he could score without any danger of being bowled, but he failed to connect with either. I tried outside the off stump and he nearly decapitated himself off a top edge, but he did score a couple. I was unsure whether to repeat the 'dangerous' delivery outside the off stump or return to the less dangerous, but for him less easily hittable, leg side. In the end I decided on the latter but, very unfortunately, the ball hit the seam and turned into a leg break, which he missed and which just nudged the leg stump, disturbing the bail as it passed. I was embarrassed, he was not best pleased and, as he passed me on his way back to the pavilion, he suggested, I think jokingly, that I should not consider flying on Virgin planes.

The line-up between Michael and me came at the end of our innings, when he was bowling and we needed ten to win with a couple of overs left. He was bowling at medium pace and, as the ball arrived on a perfect length, I hit through the line and must have timed it perfectly, because it disappeared over the sightscreen for a straight six, something unthinkable when he was in his prime and something that I would not have even considered as possible. We were both extremely surprised. He summoned up his strength for the next ball and attempted a bouncer, but not at any pace, which I pulled for four. I was quite glad that there were no more balls to be bowled, but it had been the second time that I had hit ten runs off a Holding over!

And so, on 25 July, to our second B&H Final in three years. The preliminary rounds were ruined by the weather, which definitely favoured us. We lost to Sussex, had no result against Hampshire and Middlesex and won against the Minor Counties. Middlesex, who lost their first match to

Hampshire, then had three no result matches. Hampshire were surprisingly beaten by three runs by the Minor Counties, which was a bonus for us and only the second time the Minor Counties team had won a match in this competition. Sussex and Surrey progressed to the quarter-finals, where we beat Nottinghamshire and Sussex lost to Leicestershire. In the semi-final against Leicestershire we ended victorious after a very tense finish. Ken Higgs, not the swiftest of number eleven batsmen, was run out on the penultimate ball attempting a single to Pat Pocock, not the fastest of fielders to the ball. It was an interesting contest won decisively by Pat, so we were through to our third consecutive final at Lord's.

It was a particular relief to get through to this final. In the preceding week we had endured a ridiculous amount of travelling. On Friday 3 July, after 64 overs fielding in the last innings, we completed the three-day match in Taunton and drove, as leaders in the championship table, the 270 miles to Harrogate. After the first day of the match against Yorkshire, we drove to Scarborough for the JPL Sunday League match and then back to Harrogate, a round trip of 125 miles. Two more days and then, on Tuesday evening, after another 76 overs in the field, we drove back home, a distance of 220 miles to London and considerably more for most of the team who lived further south in Surrey. 615 miles, two three-day matches, a 40-over game and then on the next day, Wednesday 8 July, we arrived at the Oval to play a very important semi-final.

In our third consecutive final, our total of 194 for eight was never going to be high enough to worry Somerset, with Viv Richards, fresh from 196 in his last innings, in dominant form again once he had played and missed several times at the start of his innings. It gave us hope initially, as we had already taken the wickets of Brian Rose and Peter Denning. Once Viv had his eye in and his timing right it became a foregone conclusion, especially as Ian Botham was smacking the ball around at the other end. It was, though, Somerset's other overseas player, Joel Garner, who did the real damage. He took five for 14 in his 11 overs and was quite a handful with his steep bounce from well-pitched-up deliveries. He always hit the top of the bat, so middling the ball was extremely difficult. Somerset won with more than ten overs and seven wickets to spare. I was personally pleased with my own score of 92, but we did not make enough runs on the day.

The second half of the season was very mixed for us and we departed for the winter, with the expectation that we would be touring Hong Kong and Australia at the end of September. This was obviously problematic for me as a schoolmaster already absent from the summer term and David Emms, the Master of Dulwich College, suggested that I should take the whole winter away from the College and return the following year.

Surrey agreed that I could work as part of the administrative staff for that winter and report on the situation regarding cricket in schools and in junior club sides. That was a very worthwhile exercise, which I enjoyed, but what was galling was that ultimately it was an unnecessary break from teaching because the tour was cancelled as a result of our fast bowlers' injuries. I missed running the 1st XV rugby team and teaching French, but administrative tasks and setting up a database of facilities around the county kept me busy and were interesting work.

1982

This was, at last, our year for a trophy. The fourth consecutive final, in the NatWest Trophy, which had replaced the Gillette Cup, gave us all a taste of success after so many near misses. To finish fifth in the championship was acceptable, though a little disappointing as we had challenged strongly and been in second place for some of the season. Sylvester was fit throughout and he and Robin Jackman took 110 and 87 wickets in all matches for Surrey. Pat Pocock had an ongoing back problem and missed several matches. This provided an opportunity for Andrew Needham, who was developing well as an off-spinner. The retirement of Intikhab gave more chances to Giles Cheatle, but our spin attack was considerably weakened and, although the faster bowlers, David Thomas and Kevin Mackintosh, showed promise, taking 32 and 28 championship wickets respectively, we needed our spin bowlers to take more wickets than the 24 from Andrew and Giles.

Now that Sylvester was back to his hostile best there were some comments about his action. My honest appraisal was, and is still whenever I see films of him bowling, that the arm was ramrod straight, but that there was a moment when his shoulder jerked through and then the arm followed, giving him extra leverage and an action that was more difficult to pick up. I, along with others, scrutinised his action on film taken from all angles, and I was convinced that it was fair according to the laws. I suppose I am bound to say that, as his captain, but he was cleared by the 'throwing' panel and continued to bowl in the same way throughout his career.

Although there were 17 centuries scored in the championship by Surrey batsmen (it would have been 18 if I had not hit a slow non-spinning long hop from Alvin Kallicharan, playing for Warwickshire, straight to deep mid wicket's safe hands on 99), our batting was still rather inconsistent. With Intikhab no longer taking an overseas player's place, Geoff Howarth came back into the side and averaged 40, which was good news for him and excellent for us. He was a steadying influence near the top of the order and, on occasions, he opened when Grahame Clinton's back problems prevented his playing.

There were two maiden centuries. Jack Richards confirmed his batting ability against Nottinghamshire at the Oval, and Andrew Needham scored his first century against Lancashire at Old Trafford, rescuing us from a precarious 74 for seven, and then followed it up with five for 91 in their first innings. Very sadly, it was all too much for him and, despite several warnings not to continue celebrating, he was found by the manager sitting on the floor of his hotel bedroom at midnight with the fridge door open and a number of empty bottles strewn around. Apart from being dropped for the next match for disciplinary reasons, he was in no fit state to bowl Lancashire out in the second innings and went for 113 runs off 15 overs while managing to take only two wickets. There was no doubting his talent, but he never really capitalised on it for Surrey and a few years later moved across the Thames to Middlesex.

Graham Roope could not find his form despite one century, and he was not retained at the end of the season. David Smith topped our batting averages, Monte Lynch scored over 1,000 runs, but I had a disappointing championship season as did Grahame Clinton.

At the start of the year we had sat down to discuss how we would approach the new season. We had done much better since Micky came back to the Oval, but we were not fully satisfied. As a schoolmaster, I always liked acronyms and so I suggested that we should bear in mind the word 'CHEERS'. To win we needed Character, which we had been showing but inconsistently. The cricket season is a long period and we all agreed that Humour had a part to play in keeping up the team spirit. It was essential that we did not treat the game as a daily drudge, so we accepted that Enjoyment was part of why we played. As professional cricketers we were conscious that we were employed by the club, so Entertainment was needed to keep the membership and other spectators on board. We all accepted that every individual in the team had to take Responsibility at all times, aware of the situation in each match, which had not always been the case. We all hoped that following the mantra of C-H-E-E-R would lead to the final 'S', which was Success.

The pre-season encouragement was received by individual members of the team in their own way but, to me, it provided a reminder that we had not yet reached where we wanted to be. I was conscious that I was often seen as the schoolmaster by some of the players. In fact, in my first season, I had sat the team down during one lunch interval and, in my own way, had read the riot act. Robin Jackman, my vice-captain, came up to me quietly afterwards and said that, whilst he agreed with everything that I had said, the players would respond much better if I were to 'f-- and blind' much more. That did not come naturally to me and for the most part I did not resort to that approach, but he made a relevant point, which has always stuck with me. I was aware of the danger of my pre-season chat being seen cynically in the same way as a schoolmaster's words to his pupils. Nevertheless, whether it had any effect or not, we did win a trophy at the end of the season.

It is always easier to play enough good cricket to win a knock-out tournament, without the consistency needed for a league or a longer one-day competition. So it proved in 1982. Apart from finishing fifth in the championship, we were twelfth equal with Derbyshire in the John Player League. In the Benson & Hedges competition we beat Essex comfortably, lost by three wickets to Sussex, lost by one wicket to Kent and ended by beating Hampshire by 13 runs. We failed to qualify for the quarter-finals.

However, it was in the knock-out competition of the NatWest Trophy that we came good. Monte Lynch's 129 and Graham Roope's 77 were too much for Durham, still at that time a Minor County. In the second round Northamptonshire were swept aside by six wickets as David Smith scored an excellent 103. In the quarter-final against Hampshire Robin Jackman took six for 22 and was deservedly winner of the man-of-the-match award in a game we won by eight wickets. In the semi-final at the Oval against our nemesis, Middlesex, Sylvester was pumped up and won the man-of-the-match award for his four for 10 in seven overs, well supported by Robin Jackman and Graham Monkhouse with three wickets apiece. Our 205 for nine was 125 runs too many for Middlesex and was a welcome victory for us.

That took us to Lord's for the fourth year in a row to compete in a final, this time against Warwickshire, captained by Bob Willis. Bob and I started our cricket careers in the Surrey 2nd XI. He was selected by England before he received his first-team cap and subsequently left to play for Warwickshire, seeing little future for himself at the Oval. I left for Gloucestershire and then Sussex, but the return to the Surrey family for me had brought great pleasure, if quite a lot of heartache initially.

We went out to toss in the middle on an overcast morning in a game scheduled to start at 10am in order to beat the onset of dusk in a match of 60 overs each. I was invited to toss the coin while Bob called, fortunately, wrongly. When Peter West of the BBC asked me why I had chosen to bowl first, I explained that any early morning dampness would be welcome to our bowlers and, at Lord's, an overcast sky was usually just what the seam bowlers wanted. The pitch would not break up or deteriorate at all, and I was hopeful that we could turn our three-year wait into a victory in a final. Bob stood next to me with his arms folded and a rather hangdog expression. Peter West asked whether he also would have opted to bowl first. Bob, at that time captain of England, kept his arms folded and answered: "Yes, probably, but no sweat." He finished with an audible sniff, which ended the interview, and we returned to our respective dressing rooms.

I suspect the mood in the Surrey room was better and more positive than in Warwickshire's, but that was their problem, not ours. The ball undoubtedly did a little more in the first innings than it did later in the day as the sun came out, but it was by no means impossible to play properly. There was some movement for the seamers, but the pitch did not bring about the downfall of the first few batsmen. One opener missed a straight ball from Robin Jackman early in the innings. Then David (Teddy) Thomas took over. He persuaded the other opener to tread on his wicket. Dennis Amiss was bowled by a good swinging delivery, and Geoff Humpage chased a wide ball and nicked it to the keeper. David had made real inroads into the Warwickshire batting.

I was allowed to bowl twelve overs, taking two for 14, with the help of two brilliant catches at slip by Geoff Howarth. As the innings developed, Asif Din showed that the pitch did not hold any real terrors and put on 62 with Gladstone Small, taking Warwickshire from 74 for eight to a total of 158 all out, but the damage had been done in the minds of the batsmen once the toss was lost. Surely this was going to be our match?

The most important thing was not to lose early wickets to Bob Willis and Gladstone Small, both England fast bowlers. Once Alan Butcher and Geoff Howarth had seen them off and put on 80 for the first wicket, David Smith joined Alan and we coasted to victory in 34 overs. I was sitting in the dressing room padded up through their partnership, trying to concentrate in case I was needed to bat, but I was constantly interrupted by various committee men wanting to say congratulations before we had reached the total.

We were all pleased when the winning run was scored. It was a huge relief to win a competition and, although it was not much of a spectacle for the crowd and, therefore, did not totally fulfil our objective of ENTERTAINMENT, we were delighted to have achieved SUCCESS. Whether our pre-season reference to CHEERS worked or not is irrelevant, but certainly the team's minds were fully focussed on that day, and I was able to celebrate my birthday two days later, saying 'cheers' to the family and friends. David Thomas won the man-of-the-match award for his three for 26, including a spell of three wickets for one run at the beginning that set the tone. He bowled quickly and accurately and was the perfect complement for Sylvester Clarke's two for 17 in 11.2 overs and Robin Jackman's two for 27 in 12. Our two children were thrilled to have their photographs taken at home where we kept the NatWest Trophy overnight.

So the season ended with some silverware at the Oval at last; the first success since 1974 when John Edrich's team won the Benson & Hedges competition by beating Leicestershire.

This was also the year when I was called into the England one-day international squad for the match versus India at Headingley in June. Barry Wood had injured his wrist and, when I arrived, was in the hotel with a machine stimulating muscle movement on his wrist. It looked as though I would open the batting on the next day. In the morning, though, he felt better. He asked me to throw a few balls to him to see whether his wrist would cope. Luckily for him and for England it seemed fine and he won the Man-of-the-Match award with a well-judged 78 not out as England won by nine wickets.

Sadly for me it was the nearest I came to being an England player, although I stayed with the squad for the second ODI at the Oval. I was given all the kit, sweaters, shirts and tie, but I have never felt justified in wearing any of it.

1983

This was my sixth and last year as captain of Surrey. Robin Jackman had retired after his many successful years with the county. Geoff Howarth was wanted by New Zealand. Although Sylvester continued to take wickets and ended the championship season with 79, he was not operating with his opening partner at the other end. David Thomas took 57 wickets, Graham

Monkhouse took 45 and Pat Pocock, now fully restored to fitness, took 68, but we finished 8th in the championship, lost in the early rounds of the NatWest Trophy, ended 11th in the JPL and failed to qualify for the Benson & Hedges quarter-finals. Three of us scored over 1,000 runs and eight averaged over 30, but we could not finish the opposition off. We drew 13 matches in the championship, won seven and lost four. Bowlers are such a key element in a successful team.

There were good moments. David Thomas came on as a batsman and scored two centuries, his first in first-class cricket being against Nottinghamshire. It did not help us when he broke his finger later in the season and missed several matches, joining Kevin Mackintosh, who had a chronic back problem, on the side lines. Duncan Pauline, against Sussex, and Alec Stewart, against Oxford University, made their maiden first-class centuries. Graham Monkhouse took seven for 51 against Nottinghamshire, his best figures.

There was also one bad moment, when the decision was taken to release David Smith from the staff. It had happened in 1977, but he was reprieved when I took over the captaincy. He was extremely talented, fearless as a batsman, but not an easy man to motivate if he was not in the mood. It was a sad moment when Micky and I accepted that the time had come to part company with him. There had been a few moments over the years when others had complained about his behaviour towards them in the dressing room. I had had a couple of unpleasant incidents to deal with on the pitch, but I always hoped that he would learn to control his temper, which was never far from boiling over.

He had one stand-up row with Micky Stewart after a match at Edgbaston, where Micky, despite my suggestion that it was the wrong moment to criticise the batsmen, weighed in and called our batsmen cowards for not taking responsibility and winning the match. It was aimed at all the players, but David took it personally and, after almost threatening the manager, he stormed out of the dressing room and ground, but not before thumping the wall outside and badly cutting and bruising his hand. I had thought, at one stage, that I might have had to pull them apart as David towered menacingly over Micky, who seldom took a backward step. We were all concerned, and Micky drove home via David's house to find him entirely calm, now that he was in his own environment.

On another occasion he had a bad toe and tried to insist that he was fit and that he would cut a hole in the end of his boot to take the pressure off his toe. We accepted his opinion that he was fit to play, very naïvely as it happens, because he left the field a few overs after the start and came back on without a shoe on that foot. I sent him off to get a boot, and there was a glowering presence behind me as we walked to the other end of the pitch for a new over.

It was not always his own team-mates or captain who stirred him up. There was an incident at the end of a match against Leicestershire. Ken Higgs, as he often did, had several times rubbed out David's block-hole mark and dropped mud on a length. When Ken was run out, David taunted him but then decided he should shake hands and thank him for the game. As Ken pushed his hand away with his bat, it all exploded and David had to be ushered away, when the two of them were eyeball to eyeball with each other, threatening all sorts of repercussions.

These were not regular occurrences, but they did occur too often. After the moments of blind rage David was often calm and occasionally even gentle, but his volatile nature was a liability when he erupted. Nevertheless, I was sad to see him go because I liked his competitive spirit and his fearless approach, especially to fast bowling, which saw him represent England in two Test matches and two ODIs. He was a fine player and, although he did suffer a number of injuries, he could have played more international cricket.

Probably the main memory that I have of 1983 was the extraordinary match at Chelmsford. Cricket has a strange way of raising and lowering the spirits. We were on a high after winning the NatWest Trophy the year before, but at the end of May we plummeted to the depths. The story has been told from various perspectives but, as captain, I cannot understand how conditions could change so dramatically in the course of a day. We had lost the whole of the first day because of rain so, in winning the toss and asking Essex to bat first, we all thought that we would be in the prime position towards the end of the game to chase a target, either by bowling Essex out or their declaring to set us a target. The pitch played well and Keith Fletcher led the way in scoring a century, but we were not unduly concerned when we bowled them out for 287, leaving an hour for us to bat. Our plan to declare and then expect Essex to do the same and set us something to chase seemed on course. Keith Fletcher obviously thought differently.

As many spectators will know, the pavilion at Chelmsford is situated at mid-wicket and not behind the bowler's arm, so batsmen waiting to bat have little idea what the ball is doing. Alan Butcher and Grahame Clinton started by leaving quite a lot of deliveries. Then Alan Butcher was caught behind for 2, and Andrew Needham, who went in three, looked to be in difficulty immediately, as the bowlers found their range. Grahame Clinton added six runs, but by then we were 8 for five, with Andrew Needham, me, Monte Lynch and Jack Richards back in the pavilion, all for ducks. At 8 for eight, with David Thomas and Ian Payne both departing for ducks, it was an unbelievable scorecard. At this stage Graham Monkhouse was dropped at slip, the ball running away for two runs. If he had been caught, we would almost certainly have registered the lowest-ever score in a first-class match, beating Oxford University and Northamptonshire who shared the undesirable record with 12.

In the dressing room there had been an enormous scramble for the bowlers to drag themselves out of the bath or the shower, to put back on their cricket clothes and get into some sort of mental state to bat. There was a sense of complete shock in our room. Most of the lower order were preparing for their evening in Chelmsford and resented having to go out again to bat after a day in the field. We all know that it only takes ten good balls to bowl out a team, but there is always the feeling that something will change and someone will come to the rescue. But not on this occasion. At this point, with the score on 10 for eight, Sylvester played a horrific slog shot and connected with the ball, which just trickled over the mid-wicket boundary. At least we had passed 12.

Norbert Phillip, immediately after that, had Graham lbw, and that left Sylvester Clarke and Pat Pocock together. We watched as Pat, who was never short of advice on what to do in any situation, went down the pitch and spoke to Sylvester, presumably telling him that in this dire situation he needed to play sensibly. He duly did and played an immaculate forward defensive stroke, covering the middle and leg stumps. Unfortunately Neil Foster bowled it on off stump, which disappeared out of the ground. All out for 14 in 14.3 overs, with six batsmen registering a duck and Pat Pocock nought not out.

It was by now twenty past six, so the ten-minute break between innings spared us any further embarrassment as play finished at 6.30pm. Keith Fletcher did ruefully say afterwards that he considered claiming the extra half hour believing that he might bowl us out again and win the match, but we returned to the dressing room shell-shocked to say the least. Micky had left earlier to watch some of the 2nd XI match, so he was spared the debacle.

Norbert Phillip (7.3 overs, 4 maidens, 4 runs, 6 wickets) and Neil Foster (7 overs, 3 maidens, 10 runs, 4 wickets) bowled unchanged, and every time they bowled it straight we seemed to miss the ball. Every time they bowled it off the stumps we appeared to nick it and, barring one chance, they caught it. There was no reason why it had all changed from when we were bowling at them. Perhaps it was a better ball; maybe it was slightly more overcast; perhaps some sort of mini-tide had come into the stream alongside the ground. In the end there was nothing we could really say to exonerate the worst innings that Surrey had ever had. In almost complete silence we dressed and returned to the County Hotel for the night and prepared for the third day, which had taken on an entirely different perspective, with our original plans in tatters.

Slowly, while sitting around in the hotel and thinking back to the innings, reality set in. There were several attempts at humour, but it was not an obvious time for uproarious jokes. In the Essex first innings there had been 20 extras (4 byes, 10 leg byes and 6 no balls), and Alan Butcher put everything into perspective when he said that we should realise that we needed another six runs to avoid an innings defeat by the extras.

There was not much that I or anyone else could say. The batsmen said that they had never seen so much swing and seam in their lives. Certainly, I faced three balls, which all swung prodigiously and, when I padded up to a ball some way outside the off stump and was given out lbw, I was fairly convinced that it was going to miss the leg stump. Seven wickets were either bowled or lbw, so we were not given much width at all. It was one of cricket's freak scores.

Henry Blofeld, who was reporting on the match, tells a lovely story against himself. He was due to go to the theatre and had left early. He telephoned his report into his editor after the end of the Essex innings and left the last sentence as: 'At close of play Surrey were ---- for ----.' When he later called the editor to check that he had inserted the score, as requested, he was mortified to learn of what had happened and that his last sentence would read: 'At close of play Surrey were 14 for 10.'

The following day we batted through the rest of the match and ended up at 185 for two, leaving the result as seven bonus points for Essex and four points for Surrey. At least I could look Micky Stewart in the eye after joining Grahame Clinton at 18 for two. His determined 61 not out from 78 overs and my undefeated 101 drew the match. In the second innings the ball was doing much less than it had in the hour before close of play, and we survived.

There was little point in ordering 'naughty boy nets', as sometimes happened after a poor batting display, but we did have a few nets before the next match a week later in Worcester. As we came to terms with what had happened, we began to see the funnier side of it. We struck a tie consisting of a figure seven made up of ducks with Chelmsford 1983 underneath. Pat Pocock was allowed to have an honorary duck despite remaining not out on nought. Micky showed much less of a sense of humour and banned it from the Oval. He never liked to admit failure or mistakes and once told me never to refer to anything which might be construed as such either by the media or people listening. Perhaps he was right but, although we were not at all proud of our performance on 30 May 1983, it was a memorable occasion that we did not want to forget.

A couple of days later I received a letter from a prep-school headmaster, saying that his side had been bowled out for 19, 24 and 23 in the last few weeks. He wondered whether we would like a fixture.

1984

Being awarded a benefit season in 1984 and having taken on a boarding house at Cranleigh in September 1983 meant that captaincy was not possible. I had enjoyed my six years at the helm, and I retired from the position so that Geoff Howarth could take over and bring his experience of Test captaincy of New Zealand and victory over England to the team.

There are many happy memories of my time as captain, and it was a marvellous opportunity to work closely with other cricketers, some with great experience, some starting out in the game, and attempt to merge them all into a successful team. On the whole, looking back, I felt that it worked well. There are areas of captaincy, in hindsight, where I would probably have done something different. For example, in my first year in a match against Sussex, we needed to take two wickets in the last over to win, but Sussex were also in a position where a good over would lead them to victory. I should have bowled Intikhab but opted for safety first and bowled Robin Jackman, who kept the last over under the required nine runs so the game ended in a draw. I should have been more confident and would have been in later years.

The relationship with Micky Stewart was crucial, and his guidance helped enormously, particularly in his early years as manager. We had some good players and I think that most, if not all, enjoyed those years, even though there were so many occasions where we just missed out on a trophy or the top spot in the championship, which we all dearly wanted. Players developed, and some went on to represent their country as a result of the atmosphere at the Oval.

1984 was a most disappointing year, as we finished 8th in the championship and in the JPL. Geoff Howarth was not suited to the day-to-day routine of county cricket after experiencing success in the Test series against England and could not find the form or patience to make as many runs as he should have done, averaging 23.37. He was a fine batsman for the big stage and loathed playing in front of a small crowd on a dismal day in some of the less inspiring county grounds.

There were positive notes in the season, though. Jack Richards came of age as a batsman with two centuries, and Monte Lynch continued to play freely and scored the most runs in the championship (1,511). Alan Butcher and Grahame Clinton were still too inconsistent, but Alan made big scores when he was in form and ended with over 1,300 runs. Wickets were spread between seven bowlers, with Sylvester taking 78, the off-spinners Pat Pocock 56 and Andrew Needham 28, and the other seamers Graham Monkhouse 45, David Thomas 56, Mark Feltham 28, another talented all-rounder from the Surrey conveyor belt, and me 27. We found another left-arm spinner in Keith Medlycott, who was to become a more regular player in the years ahead and, in later years, the coach. However, we only won six matches in the championship, which was not enough to finish higher up the table.

I continued to bat at number three or four and, as my benefit season wore on, I was told by one of the Surrey supporters that very few cricketers had scored centuries against every county. As someone who had played for three, it was pointed out to me that the only county against whom I had not scored a century was Yorkshire. I had scored centuries in first-class or one-day matches against Gloucestershire, Sussex and Surrey, plus all the others, Oxford and Cambridge and Pakistan as well for good measure. It provided added incentive as my cricket career approached its end.

Our only championship match against Yorkshire was at the Oval, starting on Saturday 18 August. On the first day of the three-day match we bowled out Yorkshire, and Alan Butcher and Grahame Clinton started the Surrey reply. They were both unbeaten overnight when we all went home and prepared for a Sunday League match against the same opposition on a different pitch, but still at the Oval, which we won by 12 runs. On Monday they continued their record-breaking partnership and put on 277, the highest first-wicket partnership for Surrey against Yorkshire at the

Oval and only 13 short of Surrey's record against Yorkshire, established in 1914 by Hobbs and Hayward at Lord's in a match that had been moved because the Oval had been requisitioned for military purposes. Was this my opportunity to score a century against Yorkshire on a good Oval batting track and complete the full house? At that time only Glenn Turner and Viv Richards had achieved this.

Grahame Clinton and I put on 100 before he fell for 192, and Monte Lynch and I had a partnership of 91. Then it happened. I was on 77 when Phil Carrick bowled me a full toss on leg stump, which I hit rather tamely to Kevin Sharp at mid-on. So it was not to be, and I felt the usual disappointment of any batsman when his innings is over.

After an opening stand of 277, I had my chance. But for mis-hitting the full toss, I might have completed the full house of 17 counties. From a team's perspective Surrey declared on 518 for five off 139 overs and gained a victory by an innings and 195 runs, which was the most important aspect of the match. Looking at Phil Carrick's figures of 36 overs, 6 maidens, 102 runs and one wicket, I clearly missed out.

I was pleased personally to finish on a real high before retiring from the game to concentrate on teaching. My last five first-class innings in that year were 142 against Gloucestershire at Cheltenham, 77 against Yorkshire, 114 against Somerset, 109 and 16 against Essex, all at the Oval. My cricket career nearly went full circle. My first innings was against Essex at Fenner's, where I scored 15 and my last against the same opposition at the Oval, where I made one run more. John Lever, who took his first wicket in 1967 by dismissing me, could have repeated the dose, because he was playing for Essex, but Neil Foster got there first.

Teaching duties meant that I missed the last match against Worcestershire, but I did have one last chance to captain the team against Glamorgan at the end of August, when both the captain, Geoff Howarth, and his vice-captain, Alan Butcher, were unfit. Swansea was always a favourite ground for me. It was generally a flat batting pitch, and the Welsh crowd was always good humoured. Rodney Ontong was captaining Glamorgan, but the weather forecast for the three days was not promising. The match was severely disrupted by bad weather, with only ten overs on the second day and none on the third, after the first day had seen attrition by Glamorgan batting on a slow turning pitch. Before the start I said to Sylvester that the pitch was obviously low and slow and I thought that he would be best bowling at full pace, but in short spells. There would be low bounce but possibly some slow turn for the spinners, Pat Pocock, Andrew Needham and Keith Medlycott.

Sylvester, who was never a man of many words, looked at me and said: "I'll bowl, captain!" After an early wicket, he was finding little bounce, but he kept running in and whenever I said that I thought it was time for him to take a break he repeated his three words: "I'll bowl, captain." After 12 overs on the trot, he agreed that he would take a break, by which time he had taken two wickets for 17 runs in conditions totally unsuitable for a fast bowler. I never had cause to doubt that he tried wholeheartedly whenever I captained him, but this was a phenomenal feat of endurance and determination. He just wanted to continue. He eventually ended the day having bowled 21.1 overs and taking three for 28. It was a mammoth effort, and I was very grateful to him for trying everything he could to break through. David Thomas had also tried hard to extract bounce and pace from the pitch for 20 overs without any success. The three spinners between them had bowled 60 overs with figures of two wickets for 167 runs. It was not an inspiring pitch, and the cricket had been extremely dull. At the close of play Glamorgan had reached 266 for five.

On the second day the Welsh rain took us all off the ground and ruined any real chance of a competitive match. Before the heavy rain came, our openers, Duncan Pauline and Grahame Clinton, had put on 17 without loss. On the third morning it was still raining hard and there looked to be no prospect of any play, let alone a situation whereby a result could be achieved by either side. The rain persisted through the morning, and the delightful woman who ran the catering at Swansea told us that she had prepared an end-of-season lunch for us. There was turkey, roast potatoes and vegetables, followed by delicious puddings and several bottles of wine. She had even bought some balloons.

We tucked in, as none of us thought we had any chance of play. However, after lunch at about 2.30pm, the umpires interrupted our party to say that the rain had stopped, the sun was shining and the tide had gone out, leaving the outfield and square wet but drying quite quickly. Spectators and members were coming into the ground, so Rodney Ontong and I had to go out with the umpires to inspect the pitch and surrounding areas. The two umpires, David Constant and Bob White, both seasoned former cricketers and sensible officials, said that there was potentially a chance of some cricket later in the afternoon. They also pointed out that the ground had been opened, and spectators were coming in.

Neither Rodney Ontong, captaining Glamorgan, nor I saw any point in going through the motions with no result at all likely, especially if we were unlikely to start for another hour or so. We agreed that we should at least show willing and inspect the square, which had not yet fully dried, and the outfield, which was not yet playable. We went out, prodded the square with the umpires, who were also loathe to play but conscious of the need to appear keen for the match to restart. As we walked around the outfield, water came up at every step. Back together on the pitch, we all agreed that it would be pointless cricket. There was little chance of Glamorgan taking ten wickets on the flat pitch, so Rodney was not keen. The likelihood of a start no sooner than 3.30pm made the run chase impossible, and most of the players had been drinking wine at the lunch. Bowlers would bring dampness up to the bowling creases, making them slippery, batsmen would slip and slide if they ran off the main pitch and fielders would be soaked if they dived. There was going to be a delay of at least another hour or so before we could start, which would make it all meaningless.

We all preferred an early departure to get to London on a Friday night, particularly as rain was forecast to interrupt the match again later in the afternoon. The umpires had also enjoyed the lunch, and they too wanted to get home. The problem was that the sun was now out, and everything looked fine from the boundary edge. Finally we all agreed and it was announced over the ground's public address system that the game had been abandoned "because the conditions were still wet and slippery and it was felt that the players would not be able to stand up", both of which were factually correct – but not necessarily linked! The match was declared a draw, and the Surrey team returned home up the M4. It was not the best way to end my stint of captaincy at Surrey, but it was a common-sense decision.

At Surrey there was the most professional approach of all three of my counties. Micky Stewart, as manager, was insistent on fitness and high standards. He took an active part in the coaching and constantly reminded me in pre-season nets at the Bank of England ground in Roehampton that I must keep my hands high when batting. He loved the game, talked endlessly about it and cared deeply for us as a county staff. We set targets for the players and agreed on maintaining a strong disciplinary regime.

Our relationship could not have been better. We both understood and kept to our roles, although, on one occasion, when Micky was very disappointed by our performance and came into the dressing room to criticise the way we had capitulated, I did joke to him afterwards that perhaps we should swap roles as I could, at times, be more objective and less caught up in the emotion of the match. Surrey enjoyed some good years in my time there, though not as successful as those between 1952 and 1958 under Stuart Surridge and Peter May or between 1997 and 2003 under Adam Hollioake.

To Summarise

As captain of a county cricket club I was, perhaps, fortunate to have taken over at a low point in the county's history, though improvement was not evident until the second year. Success was founded on the relationship that was created between me, as captain, and Micky Stewart, as cricket manager. This was a key part of the transformation at the Oval. Between us we rebuilt the confidence and spirit of the players and found ways to help them combine and develop their skills so that better results followed on the field.

Leadership is often more about bringing out the skills of others as a collective unit rather than demonstrating great personal skills, though a cricket captain's confidence and decision-making ability is always bolstered by personal success. The outstanding cricket captains basically fall into one of two categories: very good players or very good managers of people. The rest of us do our best. Throughout a cricket team there needs to be a healthy balance between the individual's personal ambitions and the needs of the team. There cannot be more than one ego in a team or the team ethos is likely to be destroyed. The improved team results in 1979 led to a much happier and more contented environment, with growing competition for selection, which brought with it the need for sensitive managing.

Micky handled most of the off-field issues, such as fitness and net practice, and I took responsibility once we had crossed the boundary rope. We both handled individuals with their concerns, complaints and questions. Cricket is a game where decisions often have to be made in an instant on the field, and there is usually insufficient time for any advice from the boundary. There will have been discussion before the game with senior players and manager about selection, about the pitch, about the strategy for dealing with opponents, both batsmen and bowlers. We considered the balance of the team for each particular match, whether to play the extra batsman, play two spinners or four seamers, dependent on the pitch, the weather forecast and individual preferences. Ultimately Micky and I always agreed that the captain should have the final say about the ten other players to take the field with him.

In the six years that we worked extremely harmoniously and productively together I can only remember two occasions when we really disagreed on the final selection of the team. We had three cricketers registered as overseas players and only two were allowed to play at any one time according to the governing body's rules. Sylvester Clarke was a potent weapon as one of the most feared quick bowlers in the world and was, if fit, the first choice for one of those two positions. Geoff Howarth, a fine batsman from New Zealand and later the country's very tactically astute captain, was an important part of our batting line-up. Intikhab Alam, one of the best leg-spinners in the world, added variety to our attack and was also capable of scoring rapidly lower down the batting order. He had also been captain of his country, so there was no shortage of sensible advice, whenever I asked. But we could only play two of them in any one match.

We arrived to play Hampshire away on one occasion to find a green pitch and this brought about one of the very few disagreements between Micky and me. He said that runs would be at a premium and therefore we should play our strongest batting unit, which would include Geoff Howarth. I felt that Intikhab's ability to take wickets on any pitch and also to contribute middle-order runs swayed my decision in his favour. Added to that, David Smith was developing into a more than useful batsman and was in form after runs in the matches before. I did not want to leave him out. There was no doubt that Sylvester would play.

After a lengthy discussion Micky accepted, reluctantly, that I should have my way. I told Geoff and Inti of the decision, and they accepted it. However, several senior players then rushed up to me, saying that the decision was madness. That was when I started to have doubts and, the more I listened, the more I realised that I did not have the full support of either the manager or the senior members of the team. It was clear that we should have discussed this more widely at an earlier stage. However, I was now faced with another decision just before I was due to meet the Hampshire captain to hand over details of our team and toss for innings.

I decided that the weight of opinion was against me and therefore I should change my mind. I went to Geoff and said that I had reconsidered, after conversations with the other senior players, and I now wanted him to play instead of Intikhab. Understandably, because of the botched way I had approached the situation, he told me forcibly what he thought of me and my decision-making and said that he would prefer to play in the second team.

The outcome was that we went with my original preferred team and we won the match. That did not make the decision right, but it was a relief. It made me understand that changing a team at the last minute is not an example of strong leadership. I had managed that situation poorly and had allowed others to change my mind at the wrong time. I should have had the courage of my convictions. Perhaps the main lesson to be learnt from this episode was to discuss decisions fully with key advisors early and to take on board their opinions before reaching a final decision.

On the other occasion of disagreement between Micky and me, I went with his suggested selection, and we won that match too. No one person has a monopoly of correct decisions.

The years as a cricketer in the first-class game provided many happy memories. There were moments of disappointment but many more times when the team or I can look back on successful highlights. The Gillette Cup victory with Gloucestershire, the NatWest Trophy victory with Surrey, leading Surrey to second and third place in the championship and beating the Australians were all memorable occasions.

Personally I was delighted to score 35 centuries in first-class and one-day cricket, only missing Yorkshire from the full set, to win the man-of-the-match or gold award ten times, to contribute runs, wickets and catches for three counties in first-class and limited-over matches and to have led the county of my birth for six years. It was particularly pleasing to end my professional cricket career on a batting high. Statistics are in Wisden for everyone to see, and others will interpret them more objectively than I can.

Ultimately, though, what brought the most pleasure to me was playing against and meeting the best cricketers in the world, proving to myself that I could compete with confidence and success in their company and making so many long-lasting friendships. It was a wonderful experience from 1967 at Fenner's to 1984 at the Oval, and I loved it all.

4

My Cricketing Life
Balancing Cricket with Teaching and Family

The fourteen years of professional cricket during the summer months and teaching during the winter were always going to come to an end at some time. Few people were as fortunate as I was. I remember hearing that Nigel Popplewell, the Somerset cricketer, and Eddie Butler, the Welsh rugby player, worked in a job share at Cheltenham College. Nigel taught in the winter months, while playing cricket in the summer. Eddie taught in the summer and played rugby in the winter. The main difference was that I always intended to become a schoolmaster, while Nigel later qualified as a solicitor and Eddie became a journalist, novelist and broadcaster. Those split years would not be possible today with full-year contracts for cricketers and the demand for schoolteachers to be ever-present with the increased emphasis on examination results.

Dulwich College is a marvellous London day school, but I had always seen myself emulating my father and becoming a boarding house master. At Eastbourne College I had thoroughly enjoyed the pastoral and extra-curricular aspects of the school environment. At Dulwich there were only four boarding houses in 1983, meaning there would be fewer opportunities to pursue that area of education. As my cricket career was coming to an end, with Surrey granting me a benefit season in 1984, my teaching career became the priority.

I was running the 1st XV rugby team at Dulwich, and one of the opponents was Cranleigh School. Over the years I had come to know Lyn Adam, a New Zealander who coached their team. He and I had discussed schools on a couple of occasions. It was, nevertheless, a great surprise, as we were walking up and down the touchline watching our respective teams, when he said that he was returning to New Zealand and leaving his Cranleigh boarding house. He asked whether I would be interested in moving schools. I was quite distracted as my team was playing well and leading as we approached the end of the game, but I had to concentrate rather more when the Cranleigh Headmaster, Marc van Hasselt, came to stand next to me and asked the same question. I explained that I would have to speak first to David Emms, the Master of Dulwich College, but it sounded just what I was hoping to do.

With one last season ahead of me and the benefit commitments, it would not be easy but, after discussions with David Emms and further conversations with Marc van Hasselt, I was appointed housemaster of Loveday House in September 1983. It was a purpose-built house with double studies for most of the boarders after their first year. Only three years old and built around a quadrangle, it was a marvellous new home. I always thought that it was important to retire from cricket before being retired by the county, and this was the right time to move on again.

Now was the time when I started to think far more seriously about educational methods. I thrived on the pastoral side of teaching, probably because I was confident about dealing with youngsters. The classroom lessons, particularly at VIth form level, needed greater research into the grammar and the literature that I was teaching. My one concern was the oral side of language teaching. I should have spent more time in France and Germany, but the summer holidays had been reserved for cricket, so I always felt a little under pressure, particularly when pen friends were in the lessons. As it happens, I learnt a lot and improved my oral French the longer I taught.

The pupils were a delight for the most part, and I often related as well if not better with the rebels. They were the ones with character and, provided they could be kept onside enough to survive at the school, it was a joy to see how successful most became once released from the strictures of school routines and boundaries. One of my hookers in the 1st XV at Eastbourne College, Michael Prince, used to steal away from the school on some evenings and go into town. I intercepted him once on his return, just before lights out, and we had a long conversation about playing to the rules enough to stay at the school and his responsibilities to the rest of the rugby team. He has become Michael Praed, a successful TV and film actor, so it was definitely worthwhile taking the time to keep him on some sort of straight and narrow. Several years later, he made contact and offered us two tickets to his performance as Frederic in 'The Pirates of Penzance' at the Theatre Royal, Drury Lane, and it was good to go backstage afterwards to catch up.

Sport was often a huge help to the less academically-minded people. That, music, art and other extra-curricular activities were a welcome break from the rigours of the classroom for them, and I always thought that a sporting background gave me an advantage in maintaining discipline and good order in my lessons.

It is interesting, looking back, to realise how much one changes from the first days of teaching through the years as a person in more responsible positions. In some ways I felt closer to the pupils than the common room when I started. They were nearer my age. At Eastbourne College, when joining in the 1st XV rugby practices to help Robin Harrison, the Head of Geography, who had represented Cambridge University at Twickenham some time before and remained an excellent coach, the captain Mike Pyrgos asked whether he could call me Roger in training and practice games, as they all saw the newspaper articles referring to 'Roger Knight, the Gloucestershire cricketer'. I said that, so long as it remained on the pitch and was not audible off the field, I would accept that. That worked well for a couple of days but, after one training session, I was walking along the cloisters going home to change when he shouted loudly from the other end of the cloisters – 'HANG ON, ROGER'. The agreement ended! When he became a Harlequins player and subsequently a successful coach of Bryanston School 1st XV, he ruled with a rod of iron and I suspect no boys called him Mike. I have always felt relaxed in sporting situations, whether cricket, rugby, tennis or squash with pupils and encouraged them to be confident in their approach themselves but, as a schoolmaster, I have always believed in a need for a certain formality. Back to the understanding of boundaries!

Those fourteen years of teaching and cricket, with the increasing responsibilities of a family, left little time for holidays. We escaped at Christmas, on several occasions, to Crieff Hydro near Perth in Scotland. The hydro was a 'dry' hotel, which was ideal for families, because parents and children were together a lot with plenty of activities. We went with Chris Rea, the British Lions rugby player, Terri, his wife who was a former colleague of Chris as a BOAC stewardess, and their daughter, Alison. We set off in our car at about 4am and stopped for breakfast north of Birmingham, before arriving just around lunchtime at Crieff. Packing was easy. We started with a box of wine and whisky for the room parties, added a box of Christmas presents and packed a suitcase with track suits for the constant sport during the day and evening dress for the dinner and the Scottish dancing after it. We enjoyed four hearty meals each day from Christmas Eve to 27 December, Chris Rea and I competed with each other at table tennis, snooker, golf, cross country running and swimming as well as joining in the soccer and hockey between the guests and the staff. The children had activities arranged for them and ate in the nursery, minded by delightful staff members.

The Scottish dancing was one of the highlights for us all after dinner. The children joined in the Dashing White Sergeant, the Gay Gordons and other simple reels before the deadline of 9pm, when there was a compulsory half-hour break so that children went to bed and then the more complicated reels continued from 9.30pm. Chris and Terri Rea were excellent dancers, Chris, my wife, and I learnt fast, though dancing the Duke of Perth was a challenge. We were encouraged to join the Reas' eight, but we found they already had enough, so we were moved to the next group, a Yorkshire family, but they too were already in an eight. As we joined the next group down the room, I turned to a rather austere-looking Scottish woman wearing dancing pumps with laces up her leg, who was standing next to me, and said that I hoped she would push me in the right direction. It was slightly unnerving when she replied, in her deeply Scottish accent, "There's no time for that." We managed but, when there was an encore and the dance was twice as fast and half as long, we ended in a mess.

During the cricket season, especially in Bristol, Chris used to join me for a drink in the pavilion after a day's play, with Katie asleep in the back of our estate car. Once Katie was born, Chris retired from being a stewardess and did not travel to away matches for the most part. There were occasions when she came with me to Yorkshire, staying with a nursing friend, and London, staying with my parents. As the children grew older, they spent a lot of time at cricket grounds. Chris was very friendly with Maryna Procter and spent time with her and Greg, their son, when Mike and I were playing matches away from home.

When we were back at Eastbourne College I was busy in the boarding house as a tutor. I coached rugby. I was often involved in mid-week training sessions and with matches on Saturdays, so Chris did most of the child care. She was able to do some part-time theatre nursing when time allowed. Getting to the County Ground in Hove with two small children when we only had one car was challenging, particularly as there were no facilities available. Eventually the wives clubbed together to buy an old caravan, so that they had a base and running hot water.

It is not ideal for a married couple to spend so many days apart, as we did during the cricket seasons, but it showed that our relationship was strong. Chris had given up any thoughts that she might have had of developing a long-term career and was a full-time mother at home bringing up our children. I was fortunate that she was prepared to do that, because without her support, I could not have continued to enjoy the twin careers for as long as I did.

Time management became a necessary skill for me. That was not easy in two roles that dealt with people. Schoolchildren are always demanding and socialising with cricketers was an important part of the job, especially once I was a county captain. The role as a father, arguably the most important of the three, could and should have had more time devoted to it. As a grandfather I understand what is required, how fulfilling it is, and I am loving that relationship with the next generation down.

Cranleigh School

We moved to Cranleigh towards the end of the 1983 cricket season, and I travelled to the Oval each day. The senior housemaster was Andrew Corran, the former Oxford cricket and hockey Blue and Nottinghamshire fast bowler, and he and his family welcomed us all to the school, where he and Gay, his wife, took us under their wing.

We lived in a modern four-bedroomed house for the first time in our lives and we were surrounded by the fields of Surrey. The boarders' accommodation took up three sides of the quad, and our house adjoined the fourth, with a resident married deputy housemaster and another bachelor tutor on the opposite side. We were responsible for sixty resident boys and ten sixth-form boarding girls, who were with us from after breakfast until ten o'clock in the evening, when they went to their sleeping accommodation elsewhere on the campus. It was a large family to take on, but John Thompson, our deputy housemaster, and Christopher Mann, our house tutor, were both experienced, dedicated schoolmasters and helped us through the first couple of terms, aided by an excellent set of house prefects and an outstanding school captain, Andrew Hobbs, who was a member of the house but, in his position, had a study bedroom in the main school. They ran the house during the summer term of 1984, while I completed my last season and tried to be available for my benefit manager, Alan (AC) Shirreff, a great friend and a former county cricketer.

It was a busy term, but I tried to be a cricketer, beneficiary and schoolmaster all at once. There was no teaching programme, but being in the housemaster's house meant that I became very involved in the life of the boarders. What I forgot at times was that I was also a father and I was brought back to reality when Chris said that our daughter, Katie, who was by now eleven, had asked whether she needed to make an appointment or go and knock on my study door to speak to me.

Everyone was very supportive and, when we reached September 1984, I said goodbye to professional cricket and embarked on the career that I had always envisaged as a schoolmaster in a boarding school. I was able to teach examination classes, whereas, when I was teaching for half the year, I was restricted to the younger classes and the Lower VIth. Having started after Cambridge as a schoolmaster who played cricket, changing to a county cricket captain who taught, I was now going to be a schoolmaster who was a former professional cricketer. However, I clung to playing cricket for two years for Bedfordshire, captaining the team in the second year, and represented the Minor Counties in the B&H competition.

Chris was invaluable as the housemaster's wife and later as matron as well. She greeted the parents, entertained other staff, friends and the boarders in our home and listened in the Laundry Room at nine o'clock in the evening to the worries of the junior boarders. Katie changed schools and, after a year at a local preparatory school with a delightful headmistress, Miss Ursula Fairfax-Cholmondley, known by everyone as Chum, she went to Cranleigh's sister school, St Catherine's Bramley. Graeme, who had enjoyed the competitive and hard-working life at Dulwich College Preparatory School, moved to the Cranleigh Preparatory School, which was less disciplined and less competitive. He was already developing as a talented sportsman and, although he was clearly academically able, the staff did not push the pupils as much as at Dulwich Prep.

The SG Smith-sponsored Volvo, with my signature on the front doors, was a hit with the pupils in that first year and when we decided that we should have a dog, a retriever, we thought that we had really joined the M25 commuter belt set. Sydney was in his element with rabbit-filled fields in which to roam, kitchens to explore, biscuits and socks to collect and endless boys and girls who loved to take him for a walk. He was also a comforting presence for some of the homesick youngsters when they started as boarders.

Marc van Hasselt was an excellent headmaster, but sadly he retired after our first year. He was a true schoolmaster and understood the issues which arose. His successor, Tony Hart, came from the Treasury, with little experience of teaching. In the view of most of the boarding community he struggled at first and yet chose not to ask for advice. There were a number of tense moments, and the atmosphere was not as relaxed in the common room. Nevertheless the staff pulled together, and the school continued to run relatively smoothly.

The boarders in Loveday House were a joy, and the vast majority of parents appreciated all that the school did for them. The house competed in every sport and provided quite a few school team players ranging from rugby, cricket and hockey to tennis, clay pigeon shooting and cross country. We had an outstanding polo player who went off to matches outside the school and a variety of musicians, actors and artists. One of the musical highlights was a wonderful evening when Oliver Strauss, a good cellist, played cello duets with Caroline Dale at a dinner party, which we gave for a few parents and sixth formers. Caroline was the Young Musician of the Year and came to teach at the school. The academic standards were strong, and the girls played a full part in the life of the house, especially in one year when I appointed one of the sixth form girls, Shani Peters, as house captain.

I have heard it said that teachers do not see real life, but we encountered so many of life's difficulties from death to divorce from serious illness to drunkenness, the blight of cigarettes and the ups and downs of adolescent relationships. We were perhaps fortunate to have no contact with drugs and, of course, there was no internet with social media and the readily-available distractions and dangers, which are around today.

I shall never forget our having to contact a parent in Kenya to say that his son had suffered an aneurism and was in the Atkinson Morley Hospital. Hasit Dodhia was a charming boy whose family had had several early deaths and he was seriously ill in the hospital. Mother and father arrived within twenty-four hours and, miraculously, Hasit recovered though remained hemiplegic. He returned to the school about eight months later after his recovery and the other pupils were brilliant with him, carrying his tray in the dining room, making sure that he could cope with whatever he was doing. In his final year he and several other sixth formers, led by Shani Peters, our inspiring house captain (not easy for a girl to lead a boys' boarding house after only one year in the school, but she was a natural leader), abseiled down the multi-storey barracks in Kensington and raised a fair amount of money for charity. Hasit was a very game boy who passed his A Levels well enough to gain a place at Bath University. It was an appalling moment when we heard that two years later he suffered another, more serious aneurism and died.

One of the delights of the house was a senior common room which had its own kitchen. Some of the lower sixth form boys chose to have cooking lessons and, on one occasion, three of them asked whether they could cook dinner and invite three girls from other houses to join them. They intended to wear black tie and the girls evening dresses. I was always keen to support initiatives such as this and agreed that they could and accepted that they could have one bottle of wine. I thought there would be little problem with six people sharing only one bottle.

During the evening I went up to see how they were coping and saw that they had only drunk half the bottle. Half an hour later I went up again and there were only five of them at the table. I found the sixth, one of the cooks, lying on the grass outside, considerably under the weather and clearly having drunk too much. As I questioned them, they insisted that they had only had one bottle, but they then admitted that it was topped up regularly from a wine box under the table. Boys will be boys, but school housemasters have to be housemasters and so I punished them by stopping their exeat weekend at home and getting them to do some gardening around the house. It was not a major crime, but they understood that they had let me down and betrayed my trust. I had to smile on the following weekend, though, when we found a washing line stretched across the quad with countless wine boxes hanging from it. There was a sixth form bar in the school at that time and the whole of the upper sixth had access to it, so the empty wine boxes told the story of how the senior pupils spent their Saturday evenings.

Whether we live in a safer environment nowadays when there are many fewer, if any, bars in schools and yet still quite a lot of illicit drinking, I am not sure. There is no doubt that too much alcohol was consumed, but it was accepted that boys and girls over the age of eighteen were entitled to spend time in the sixth-form bar, served by other sixth formers and overseen spasmodically by a member of staff. When we reached the end of term I received a Christmas card in the shape of a wine box from the guilty trio of boarders, which was a good touch.

On another Saturday morning Chris had asked one of the sixth-form girls to show some prospective new parents round the house. When the parents arrived, the girl had not appeared, so Chris went up to her study, which was empty. However there was music coming from the study at the end of the corridor, so she knocked and went in. She was faced with four bare feet poking out from the end of the duvet and one of our sixth form boys and his girlfriend lying in the bed. She called me and I went up to find the culprits hastily trying to pull on more clothes. Sadly the headmaster had little alternative but to ask them to leave the school, particularly as the boy in question had had a slightly chequered disciplinary career at the school. As they were both in their last term and in the middle of A levels they were allowed to return in the following week for their last examination. It was ironic that this examination was a biology practical, for which they had presumably revised thoroughly! The headline which appeared in the Sun newspaper was 'Matron interrupts saucy romp in public school'. We never thought that Chris would appear in the *Sun*, but at least it was on page seven, with all her clothes on, and not on page three.

The position of housemaster was a very fulfilling part of teaching. I still enjoyed teaching French and I was fortunate to have another outstanding head of department in Michel Marty. His approach was to get to the photocopy machine at 6.30am and print out all his paperwork to share with the department. He had no time for other heads of department who moaned about not being able to use the photocopier and suggested that they should get up earlier and beat him to it.

I found immense satisfaction in running first the rugby and later the cricket, coaching squash and even producing a couple of plays, helped by a first-class senior boy, whose father was a film director. He knew far more about the direction of a play than I did, so we agreed that I would book rehearsal times and ensure that the cast appeared at the right time and he would do all the directing.

As a housemaster there is always variety and the chance to deal with young people who have so much energy and enthusiasm. Table tennis after prep was one favourite; making and tossing pancakes on Shrove Tuesday was another. This was the dog's favourite, as he lay drooling near to where any misdirected uncaught pancakes would land. There were some very talented pupils, and the majority of parents were delighted with the end results. It was, though, sad to have one parent who complained that he had wasted his money because his son had not got into Oxbridge, had not played in a school first team and generally had not reached this parent's expectations. I did explain that Jeremy had gained three good A level grades, had a place at Exeter University, had taken the lead in the main school play, had enjoyed his rugby in the 3rd XV and had made many good friends during his five years. The boy was pleased, but little would convince his father. At least his mother had the good grace to say thank you to his teachers.

We had a memorable incident when we were just leaving for a day away over an exeat weekend, when all the boarders had been dispatched to parents or guardians. We had forgotten something and returned to the house, only to find a painter's ladder up against an open upstairs window to a dormitory. I went to investigate and found a parent, a barrister, collecting his son's tennis racquet. As he had found the house locked he had decided to go in through the open window. I just wished that I had removed the ladder and not gone into the house, because there was no way out from the locked door of the dormitory. He might have learnt a lesson and would have had to jump or wait until we or the boarders returned.

After six years under an uninspiring headmaster, I felt unsettled and thought that, if he could do it, perhaps I could be a headmaster. It had never been an ambition, but there was something appealing about being in charge of your own destiny and leading a team rather larger than a team of house tutors, which by now had grown to six, with two living on site. The other four came in as academic tutors to do an evening's duty. I applied to a couple of schools and had interviews at King's College, Taunton and Framlingham. It was no surprise to me when a good friend, with whom I had taught at Eastbourne College and who was more experienced than I, was chosen as headmaster of King's College and did an excellent job for a long time. I was delighted that Simon Funnell invited me, a few years later, to become a school governor.

Framlingham in Suffolk is very isolated and neither Chris nor I really wanted to live in that area, but we went for the interview and met Mark and Jenny Pyper, applying from Sevenoaks School. We were both in the last three, but eventually the job went to James Miller, who was teaching at Winchester College. It was perhaps a relief not to have been selected, but we had become quite attracted to the prospect of a headship through the interview period. Mark became Head of Gordonstoun.

The following year I received a telephone call from Hugh Monro, with whom I had played rugby at Cambridge. He was headmaster of Worksop College and had been headhunted to go to Clifton College. He suggested that I should apply for his old post and said that he had really enjoyed his three years in North Nottinghamshire. After some research into the school and plenty of advice from other headmasters, I arrived with Chris for an interview at the College.

One piece of advice from Tony Evans, a colleague in the same department at Eastbourne, my former head of department at Dulwich and by now head of Portsmouth Grammar School, was that I should avoid talking about cricket and concentrate on school development and academic excellence. It was, therefore, rather disconcerting when the first question from an elderly female governor was whether I knew Derek Randall, who was her personal cricketing hero. The interview lasted three quarters of an hour, and I felt it had gone well. I liked the governing body and, in particular, the chairman, David Moody. At that stage Chris was invited in and was grilled for a further quarter of an hour, not knowing what I had said. She almost certainly got me the job.

I was invited to take up the post in September 1990 and so we moved house once again, this time to Nottinghamshire, close to the borders of Derbyshire, Yorkshire and Lincolnshire. I always said it was as near to Yorkshire as a Surrey man dared to live!

Worksop College

The College, a Woodard school, is situated in 350 acres of Nottinghamshire countryside close to the town of Worksop, which lost some of its soul when the coalmines were closed. It is part of the Dukeries and, by the time we arrived, had been transformed from a tough all-boys' boarding school to a co-educational school of boarders and day pupils. It was totally unpretentious, and the pupils and parents were very different from those in the commuter belt of Surrey. They were happy to hand over their children to be educated, rather than acting as consumers and expecting results, as was becoming more common at Cranleigh. It had a proud history of producing top sportsmen and in the last twenty years has produced, amongst others, Joe Root, the England cricket captain, his brother Billy, a developing county cricketer, and Samit Patel, an England one-day international cricketer, as well as some outstanding hockey players.

There were 350 pupils and, as with most independent schools, the headmaster's main task was to keep the school full. It did not help that I had inherited a difficult 'O' Level year group in the fifth form, with seven on final warnings. Inevitably they were unable to keep to the straight and narrow for the year, and I was faced with deciding whether the latest misdemeanour of 'borrowing' a parent's car and driving, under age, on the M1 to a motorway service station to buy some teddy bears, which they placed on the beds in the girls' boarding house, to which they should not have had access, had any mitigating circumstances. The boarding house staff were united in agreement that it was more than one step too far, but the bursar kept on mentioning the lost fees, which we could not really afford. The decision was made, and then I spent hours trying to find new schools for them to attend so that they could complete their 'O' Level examinations.

However much a schoolmaster tries to keep rebels safe during their school years, there will always be some who refuse to listen and go too far. I have always believed that school children need firm guidelines and must understand where the ultimate boundaries lie. I dislike the analogy of discipline being like a balloon, which can stretch and extend in some directions, often dependent on the mood of the teacher, and then quite suddenly burst because the teacher at the time has not felt at all empathetic. I prefer the analogy of a fort with solid walls, where pupils can climb the wall and look at the world outside, but if they jump down on the other side it is extremely difficult to get back and be accepted by the community. A disciplinary structure needs to be clear. It can take a long time to cultivate links with other schools and to feel able to call the Head to ask him to take on someone who has been expelled, but there was a very good relationship between independent schools and most were very accommodating, provided they knew the full story

Three years in the post of headmaster is too short, but we did manage to make a few essential changes in the staff and in the boarding and day accommodation, as well as persuading the staff and pupils that the academic results needed addressing. The grades improved, without the sporting successes lessening. While we were at Worksop Chris helped the Sister in the sanatorium, entertained staff, pupils, parents and governors and took over running the Centenary Fundraising Appeal when the chemistry teacher, who had recently retired to run it, had health problems. She worked incredibly hard at a role which she had never undertaken before and created databases, contacted alumni and raised considerable funds, helped by the wife of one of the housemasters.

The year after we arrived I needed to advertise for a historian, a housemaster and a rugby coach. I was extremely fortunate that, when I was at Cranleigh, a New Zealander had been attached to my team of tutors, while on a term's sabbatical before taking on a boarding house at King's College, Auckland. He had left us saying that, if I ever became a headmaster, he would love to teach in the UK. He was a historian, had been a housemaster for some years and was a typical New Zealand rugby coach with plenty of experience. Nobody was better suited to the position that was advertised. Warren Lincoln and his wife, Lyn, moved into Pelham House, which was in the same part of the main building above the headmaster's house, and Lyn immediately joined Chris on the appeal.

The main facility that we were able to build with the money raised was an Astroturf hockey pitch, which has had tremendous results for the College hockey players, two of whom, as I write, represent England, one as captain. In addition we had taken the decision to change from renting 150 of our acres to local farmers at a very low rent to allowing a golf professional to design a golf course and make use of it as a public course for 25 years, when it would revert to the College. The pupils and staff were permitted to play a certain number of rounds free of charge each year. It was beneficial to all concerned, especially as the farmers were not making much use of the land.

Warren and I were good friends, and he was immediately well accepted in the staff common room. We went running together to keep fit and I played squash against the first team boys, so I was not stuck behind a desk. There was a lot of travelling to local preparatory schools, and relationships to be formed in the local community. Life was never dull.

The staff were excellent, hard-working, mainly uncomplaining and prepared to run the many extra-curricular activities that took place. My deputy head for the first term was Ricky Winn, the former England rugby player. He had only stayed to see me in, as his health was not good and he had been due to retire at the end of the summer term. The first major decision was to appoint a new deputy head and I chose a member of staff who had been at the College all his teaching life, was sixty-three and would retire after two years. It seemed sensible to go for experience, as opposed to choosing an outstanding young housemaster, who was keen to extend his experience and move towards becoming a headmaster. I felt that he had time on his side. Arthur Caulfield was a creature of habit and self-discipline and the right man to be the link between the new headmaster and the common room. He told me from the start that he would tell me privately what he thought about my decisions but that he would always support me outwardly, which is exactly what I needed and expected. I did, though, clearly upset him on one occasion early on.

In the College dining hall there was a long high table on the platform at one end of the hall. In the middle, facing the pupils, there was what could only be described as a throne. I had decided that I was not going to occupy the throne and chose to sit, along with staff members, on the chairs at the table wherever there was a gap. One day I collected my lunch from the canteen and joined four senior masters. There was a lot of huffing and puffing and, when I asked whether there was a problem, they said that I was sitting on Arthur's seat. He always sat there. Apparently, during the meal, Arthur came into the dining hall, saw the seat was taken and walked out, missing his lunch. When I caught up with him in the common room, where he was having his daily toast and jam, I said that I hoped he had not missed his lunch because of where I sat. His answer was that, when he arrived at the

College as the youngest member of staff, the then headmaster had told him that he should sit at the end of the table, and he had done so ever since. He was not nearly as concerned as the other four members of staff.

There was an issue regarding the cricket that needed to be decided when I arrived. The master in charge, who had retired from all teaching duties to run the appeal, said that there was no other member of staff with sufficient cricketing credentials. I suggested Alan Kettleborough, who had played for Yorkshire and was an excellent cricket coach and first-class groundsman, but apparently he would not be allowed into the Repton common room when he took our team there as he was not a member of the academic staff at Worksop. Alan and I agreed that the answer was for me nominally to be the master in charge, for him to undertake all the coaching of the 1st XI and a young languages teacher, who was a qualified umpire and loved the game, to take on all the administration. I also joined Alan in the nets, whenever other duties did not intervene. On the Saturday when Worksop played away against Repton, I travelled with the team and Alan, dressed in a jacket and tie instead of his usual tracksuit, came with me into the common room for lunch and a drink after the match. Suddenly it did not seem to cause any problems, but perhaps a head's magisterial presence helped!

Chris and I have many happy memories of our short time in Worksop, not least one Michaelmas term when we were almost cut off by snow. We had power cuts and I was writing reports by candlelight, concerned that a draught of wind would blow the flame on to the pile of completed hand-written reports. The pupils went home early, and we had the staff and their families round to the house for party games and Christmas cake in front of the log fire.

I also remember well an inset day, where a friend and former colleague from Eastbourne College, who now ran leadership courses at schools, suggested that his course, which had been successful amongst the prefects at Cranleigh and other schools, would work well with staff as well. He persuaded me to let him use Worksop staff as guinea pigs. On the evening before the course, we invited all the staff for a drinks reception in the garden, and Philip Le Brocq explained the objectives of the following day. He asked everyone to wear loose clothing or a tracksuit, as we would start with exercises in the gym. This caused quite a stir. We had several new members of staff about to begin at the College and they were enthusiastic, whereas the Director of Music and the Head of Classics were less impressed. The next day the former wore a suit and the latter a bow-tie. The sessions went well, and I felt that the staff gelled and enjoyed them once they had overcome a few inhibitions. The new members of staff thought it helped them to integrate. It helped that they saw the Headmaster and his Principal Mistress make an attempt, not always successful, at some of the exercises.

I always embarrassed Mary Simmonds when I introduced her as my Principal Mistress, but she was an invaluable part of the senior management team, along with her husband, Neil, who was Director of Studies. As every leader will know, it is impossible to please all the people all the time. One set of new parents, whom I showed round a dormitory had very opposing views. The father, an Old Worksopian, regretted the changes from his day, thought the school had gone soft and doubted whether it was the right school for his son. The mother said that she would not have let her son come to the school if we had not put carpets on the floors and curtains at the windows in the dormitories.

Meeting parents and showing them different parts of the school was always better if the pupils took them. However, my predecessor told a wonderful story of one such visit, when he and the bursar led prospective parents through the swimming pool. After they had left, the bursar asked why he had spent so much time telling the mother to be careful about the slippery area round the pool, so that she continually looked down. The head pointed out that he had noticed the large amount of rust on the ceiling and did not want the parents to look up!

There were some interesting characters on the staff. Dennis Hackett, the head of PE and a former Loughborough Colleges rugby player, coached the 1st XV very well and could be heard everywhere on campus as he barked out his loud instructions with no need of a megaphone. The Director of Art had a tattoo and an earring, coached the 3rd XV rugby team, which encouraged sportsmen to consider art and vice versa, and was always positive and enthusiastic. The chaplain had been a prop forward for Wasps Rugby Club 1st XV, tended towards the outrageous and was not on very good terms with the Senior Woodard Provost, who visited once a term.

The boarding-house parents were incredibly dedicated and served their pupils really well in their different ways. One was always keen for his boys to achieve the top academic marks and beat other houses; another, who ran the mixed day house with his wife, always had a wry smile and a sardonic comment. Wendy Bain in the girls' boarding house protected her girls and supported them extremely well.

The Head of Physics, who also ran the sailing and the naval section in the CCF, unfortunately had a lisp, which was highlighted by his insistence on referring to physics, sailing and the CCF, in which he was involved, and which the younger boys mimicked. He was an excellent sixth-form physics teacher, knowledgeable and much valued by those who had chosen his subject at A Level, but he struggled with disciplining the junior classes. Nobody was more dedicated to helping the pupils than he was. In a discussion about his future plans he told me that the only other school which he would consider joining apart from Worksop was Strathallan in Perthshire. When the head of science position came up and he applied, he was asked to travel there overnight for an interview. He was excited and it was quite a surprise when he returned and said that, although he had been offered the post, he had declined it. Apparently, his father had advised him that it was not a sensible time to be teaching abroad!

The seven years at Cranleigh and the three years and a term at Worksop were the period when the educational world was the centre of my life. It was where I thought I would always be and I felt thoroughly at home in the school environment whether as a classroom teacher, a sports coach, a boarding house master or a headmaster. There was a formality with which I felt comfortable. In fact it would be fair to say that I was 'suited and tied' to the profession! Chris played a huge part in the last two roles and our children grew up surrounded by marvellous facilities and the children of other staff members, although we had decided that it would be better for our two not to attend the schools where I was teaching.

Katie moved to Eastbourne College in the sixth form, so we kept our links with that school. Graeme went to Tonbridge and did well academically and on the sports fields, where he represented the school at first-team level in all the major team games, captaining the rugby 1st XV. Katie was a good musician, playing in the College orchestra and singing in the choir and in musicals, as well as playing sports at school level. Graeme persevered with the bassoon, because a sporting friend had said that it was an instrument that almost guaranteed you a place in the orchestra as there were so few players from whom to choose. They both went on to study for degrees at Durham University, which was very convenient when we were at Worksop.

With improving examination results, an artificial hockey and tennis surface and an eighteen-hole golf course and, most importantly, some positive new younger members of staff, whom I had appointed, I hope I left the College in a better place than when I arrived, but then all headmasters need to think that. I should have liked to have stayed a little longer to see a whole generation of pupils through the school, but it was not to be.

As Headmaster of Worksop College there were, as with captaincy, moments when important decisions had to be made. The staff, the pupils, the parents, the alumni and the governing body all had views on most aspects of the College's life. Shirley House had been a boys' boarding house since the College began, but boy boarding numbers were down and spaces for day girls were limited at a time when more girls were applying to come into the VIth form. After much thought and consultation with staff and governors, it was decided that Shirley should become a day house for both boys and girls. This would allow different facilities to be made available and would solve the problem of lack of space for day girls. It was a change to the school's ethos of merging boarders with day pupils in the same houses, but logistically it made sense. The housemaster and his wife were supportive and were the right option to run the new house, both of them full-time teachers and keen to take on the pastoral side of education.

The announcement was met with hostility from some alumni, inevitably perhaps after their memories of life as boarders in Shirley House. The current boy boarders were also opposed to the change, and this spread to some parents. Opposition was vocal and extended to anti-headmaster slogans on a wall. Nevertheless, the decision had been argued fully, and I stuck to my guns. The change was welcomed by the new inhabitants of the house. Boarders from the original house were transferred to other boarding houses of their choice and, very quickly, the new situation was accepted. This decision affected more people than the choice between the Surrey overseas players in a county cricket match, but managing the decision was similar in that individuals were bound to be affected and needed to have their concerns eased and the reasons for the change explained. I had learned a lesson, which helped on this occasion.

Teaching in four schools brought so many friends and acquaintances amongst the staff and pupils. I am still in contact with many of them from the different generations. In fact recently I was telephoned by someone, one Friday evening when I was in New Zealand, who wanted to remind me that I had taught him French. He did not give me his name but asked whether I wanted to see him when he was 'on in Auckland'. He said that he enjoyed ad-libbing both in French and German, and he recalled our French lessons.

As I did not recognise his voice and he gave no name, it was difficult to place him. However, Chris and I scoured the local newspaper and the internet to see who was appearing anywhere in Auckland on the following day. It did not take us long to find out that it was Eddie Izzard, whom I had taught French very briefly and who was spending the evening with another former Eastbourne College schoolmaster in Christchurch. A Dulwich boy, whom I had taught French in the VIth form, has a house on Waiheke Island, where Chris and I now spend most winters, but he and his wife live more permanently in the South of France. As he said, I must have taught him something about the language!

The Change from Headmaster to Secretary

At the end of 1992, after a mere two years as Headmaster of Worksop College, I received a telephone call from an MCC member asking me whether I was going to apply. It took me completely by surprise, because I had no idea what he was expecting me to apply for. He explained that Colonel John Stephenson, the Secretary of MCC, was to retire at the end of 1993 and that he thought that I should apply for the position.

My immediate reaction was that I had not been at Worksop anywhere near long enough to consider moving to another post. I was enjoying the challenge of headship. My predecessor, Hugh Monro, had been headhunted to become Headmaster of Clifton College after three years, and my time at the College would be similarly short were I to leave. I had always assumed that five years, the length of a generation of pupils, would be the minimum period for me to be in that post.

However, it did provide food for thought, especially as I received telephone calls from other people at the Club, suggesting that I might have a good chance were I to apply. I had always assumed that I would pursue a career in education, but the lure of perhaps the best job in cricket nagged at me. Chris and I discussed the two roles and, as we had done in the past when new opportunities arose, drew up a list of pros and cons on a sheet of paper. It was not an easy decision to take, especially as there was no guarantee that I would be appointed. We discussed the issue with David Moody, who had been a most supportive Chairman of Governors and who had appointed me in 1990.

David was really helpful and asked the obvious question. Did I want the job? I explained my reluctance to move out of education and take a step into the relative unknown, my concern about seeming disloyal to the College if

I left and, if I were not appointed by MCC, what the reaction might be if it became known in the College that I had applied. It was clear, though, that the chance of taking on a role that has no equal in cricket, was something that appealed to me.

In our list of pros and cons Chris and I decided that there were more positive advantages in moving from North Nottinghamshire, where I was one of about 230 Headmasters' Conference (HMC) independent school headmasters, to being a cricket administrator in North London, running the most prestigious club in the world. London was still a draw, although the Nottinghamshire countryside and the nearby Derbyshire Dales were beautiful areas and were closer to Durham where our children were still at university. The only downside, as we saw it, was that our retriever would have to give up the 350 acres of the College and Clumber Park and make do with Regent's Park. He would miss the constant stream of VIth form girls who came to take him for a walk and then returned him covered in perfume to hide the smell of cigarette smoke!

David's advice was that I should send MCC my curriculum vitae but not apply formally. That was helpful when my Deputy Head spotted a comment in a newspaper in January before the final interview had taken place, saying that I was tipped to be the next Secretary. I was able, quite truthfully, to say to the staff that I had not applied and I had not been offered the job. That offer was formally made a month later after a second interview and so Worksop College advertised for a Head for the third time in six years.

The reaction within the common room and amongst parents was positive, most appreciating that MCC Secretary was a one-off position for anyone, let alone someone who had been so involved in cricket, administration and people management. It was a wonderful opportunity for me, for Chris and for our two children, who relished the chance to have a London base, when they returned home from university. Even Sydney seemed content, particularly after he had escaped from the house in Grove End Road and found his way into the Lord's kitchen for the first time.

At Worksop Chris had played a full part in the College activities, hosting staff, parents, pupils and governors in the Head's house. She had also helped in the sanatorium, when the Sister was indisposed, and had taken major responsibility for the College appeal. She had found time to work occasionally as a nurse in the local hospital theatre, but she spent a large amount of her time as the Head's wife. In fact, when I was interviewed for the headship, Chris was also interviewed and asked what role she saw for herself. That is not acceptable now, but then it was fairly normal practice.

That interview prepared us both perfectly when the full MCC Committee interviewed me for forty-five minutes and then asked Chris to come and answer some questions for ten minutes at the end, not knowing what I had been asked or how I had answered. I felt that my part of the interview went well, but watching the reaction of the committee members to Chris' responses made me much more confident. She took all the questions in her stride, and it was clear that our approach as a team was what MCC wanted. John and Karen Stephenson had entertained in 4 Grove End Road and Chris and I intended to use the house, with a back gate into Lord's, and the Secretary's Hospitality Box in the Grand Stand to invite MCC's guests from all walks of life and administrators from all the visiting touring teams. Chris, as a former air stewardess, was the perfect hostess, and together we built up close friendships with cricketing people at home and abroad. She was able to combine this with working in Harley Street at a medical practice.

We moved from Nottinghamshire to London, from a seven-bedroomed Head's house which we had had to furnish ourselves, to a partly-furnished five-bedroomed house at Lord's backing on to the Home of Cricket, on 4 January 1994. Another episode in our lives was about to start. It was exciting, but we were apprehensive at the change from the world of education, in which we both felt comfortable, to a complex world of cricket, members, committees, governing bodies and much greater exposure to the politics and pressures of running a cricket ground as a club and a business.

My last class at Worksop College was general studies with a group of third-form pupils aged thirteen. One of the girls was anxious to ask a question, so I gave her the chance. "Sir, when you have been a housemaster, a headmaster and a county cricket captain, why do you want to become a secretary?" It was a good opportunity for a diversion from the planned lesson to discuss the structure of cricket and the role of an administrator, and I suspect it was of much more interest, though clearly of less importance, to the class than the original discussion about bullying or supporting and caring for others.

The girl was not alone in being baffled by the terminology. One of the applicants to the MCC advertisement was keen to stress her typing speed, which, if it had been a key qualification, would have put her many words a minute ahead of me. As will be seen in later chapters, the title has changed from Secretary to Secretary & Chief Executive to Chief Executive & Secretary, but, as far as I can see, the actual job description has altered very little despite these cosmetic changes of name.

I had been an MCC Committee member for three years, so I had an understanding of how the Club worked. I had also toured Kenya as captain in the Christmas holidays of 1992/93 with John Stephenson as manager. As I tore a calf muscle early in the tour, there were several opportunities to sit, watch the cricket and learn more about the role from John. He would have liked to have continued for a few years and I would have been happy to delay my departure from Worksop, but the Committee had made the decision to move forward in a different direction and so I became the 13th MCC Secretary in 1994.

Part Two

MCC – A Unique Club

5

The 13th Secretary of MCC

I have a coffee mug that would have been appropriate when I arrived at Lord's as the 13th MCC Secretary. Printed on it is: "Due to the confidentiality of my job I don't know what I'm doing."

Arriving at Lord's brought back a similar feeling to being the headmaster on the first day of term. As a classroom teacher there is a syllabus to follow, eager faces in front of you, the advice from a head of department and the inspiring words of the headmaster, who has appointed you, ringing in your ears. There is also a bell to tell you when to stop at the end of a lesson. As a boarding housemaster, once the parents have left their offspring in your care, there is plenty to do in helping new pupils to settle in and welcoming back the older boarders, whilst providing guidelines for the newly-appointed prefects. As a headmaster, it was the first time that I had begun the term with a blank diary. Lessons were not scheduled, the pupils went off to their house groups and parents left. After the headmaster's welcome, introductory chapel service and assembly, the headmaster leaves everyone in someone else's charge and retires to the study to remind himself about what he plans to do over the next days and weeks.

It was much like this when I arrived at Lord's and went into my office in the pavilion overlooking the ground with the best view in cricket. I had to lay out my own timetable and decide what priorities should be tackled first. I was really fortunate to have Stephanie Lawrence as my personal assistant. She had experience and great knowledge of the Club, of the staff, of English and overseas cricket administrators and had been the PA for Jack Bailey, the 11th MCC Secretary, so little phased her. She was to be in charge of my diary, and we discussed the many areas of work that would be on the agenda over the coming weeks and months. There were people to meet and, as a start, Steph took me round the ground to meet as many of the staff as possible. Without exception they were welcoming and ready to chat. She showed me the dates of the many committee meetings, which quickly filled up a lot of gaps in the diary. She showed me the commitments that were annual events and the papers which had to be produced or read. Although there was no immediate need for confidentiality, I realised that I did not know what I was doing.

The President, Treasurer and Chairman of Finance all briefed me over the coming days, and the three members of the Secretariat also explained what would be required. I did have to learn quickly and, although Lord's was a place that I knew and many of the people I also knew, the systems and routines were all new to me. I need not have worried about having a blank diary. That lasted about half an hour.

Having seen minutes of recent committee meetings before arriving to take up the position, I was aware of the main issues that would take my focus from the start. Administration can always wait, because people are far more important, so I did not touch my in-tray until the evening.

One letter, which Steph had put separately on my desk, stands out in my memory, though, and still creates a warm feeling. I had met Keith Miller very briefly at Wormsley cricket ground, introduced by Denis Compton at the tea interval of a Paul Getty cricket match. He had wished me luck in the role and here, on the blotter, was a letter from Australia, hand-written by the great Australian all-rounder. He wrote to wish me luck at Lord's, which he said was his favourite ground. I carried the letter around in my jacket pocket for a week. Two days later I received a telephone call from him in Australia, repeating his wishes and saying that he was sure that I would enjoy the job and would do it well. He probably had more confidence than I.

Starting in January did mean that there was no cricket for a few months, so I could concentrate on getting my feet under the table and coming to terms with being responsible for a members' club of 18,000, a ground revered as the Home of Cricket and all the ambassadorial roles that the position required. More urgently, it was important to get round the ground to find out what was happening and who needed support.

The new Indoor Cricket School was due to be completed and opened that year by Prince Philip, which was the first meeting that I had with him. As a President of MCC on two separate occasions, he knew his way round Lord's and was pleased to open the new facility, which used natural light but avoided shadow and direct sunlight. It was a fantastic new building and has been extensively used since that day, bringing cricketers of all ages, standards and abilities to practise in the nets or play indoor matches.

What was a real help to me was the excellent report written by Lord Griffiths' working party, which was adopted by the MCC Committee on

19 January 1994. This formed my blueprint as I started in a world that was very different from the educational world of schools.

In 1968 there had been a major reorganisation of cricket in England. MCC took a step back from the front-line administration of cricket in the UK, as the Test and County Cricket Board and the National Cricket Association took on the running of the professional and the recreational game in England and Wales. At the end of 1993, the post of Chief Executive of the International Cricket Council was created, and David Richards, former CEO of the Australian Cricket Board, was appointed. In July Sir Clyde Walcott, from Barbados, was elected as the first non-British Chairman. So, in 1994, MCC was not running either national or international cricket for the first time in its history, and its new role needed to be defined and understood.

The Griffiths Report proposed the way forward and its recommendations were clear. MCC should still primarily be a members' club with a large home cricket fixture list, tours overseas to ICC Associate and Affiliate countries and an active interest in helping European countries. Lord's was to be maintained and developed as the Headquarters of Cricket, a home for Middlesex CCC, with office space for the County, TCCB and ICC, and there should be a greater emphasis on the commercial opportunities for the ground. MCC was to continue to act as Guardian of the Laws of Cricket, which it had done since 1788, and of the Club's artistic and literary treasures. The Club had always seen itself in a missionary role and Lord Griffiths' working party recommended that MCC should continue to speak out publicly as an independent influence in maintaining standards within the game.

As Secretary I saw my role as combining the three aspects of MCC: as Secretary of a members' club, the senior executive of Lord's and ambassador for the missionary role, although it was now less clear what this last role should entail. The membership club and Lord's, the Home of Cricket, were relatively easily defined, as was the guardianship of the Laws of Cricket. An ambassadorial role was more complicated now that TCCB was taking responsibility for English cricket and ICC needed to develop its own identity for the international game.

There were many different ideas amongst the membership and even within the Committee. Some members believed that MCC should concentrate on domestic, recreational cricket, some thought the emphasis should be to help and encourage developing cricket nations and particularly European countries, with which I had already been involved since the first meeting of representatives of the ICC Affiliate countries in Germany in 1987. There was also an ignorance amongst some of the membership and the general public who thought that MCC still did run cricket. All too often any media comments about English cricket started with "a spokesman from Lord's said ...", which merely added to the confusion. Some of those who knew that MCC had ceased to be responsible for cricket in England thought that it still should be taking the lead. On one occasion, even Sir Alec Bedser mentioned this to me.

Final recommendations of the Griffiths Report – January 1994

- To operate the traditional Members' Club to the high standards that Members expect and in a business-like way that never loses sight of the importance of individuals, and continually seeks to improve its facilities
- To maintain and develop Lord's Cricket Ground as the Headquarters of Cricket with accommodation for ICC and TCCB [Board of Control]
- To maintain a strong and independent presence in cricket both at home and abroad and, as the Guardian of the Laws of the Game, to be prepared to speak publicly in order to uphold the standards of the game
- To maintain a large home fixture list thus encouraging and influencing cricket played in schools, clubs, universities, Minor Counties, the Services, Scotland and Wales
- To maintain its missionary role to develop cricket abroad, by continuing to arrange tours and coaching to Associates and Affiliates of ICC, and by taking an active interest in the development of cricket in Europe through coaching, touring and hosting competitions
- To maintain an Indoor Cricket School of the highest standard, and to provide MCC Young Cricketers with coaching of the finest quality combined with first-class vocational training for their future careers
- To maintain and encourage the use of the Tennis and Squash Courts
- To exercise the guardianship of the Club's artistic and literary treasures and to enhance the content of the Museum
- To continue as the home of Middlesex County Cricket Club

The Report clarified for me that MCC was still primarily a membership club but had to be run in a business-like way. It was independent and should concentrate on the game of cricket in all its different forms and activities locally, nationally and internationally. Also clear was the willingness to work with other bodies in the game and to maintain and speak without fear or favour about the traditional values of cricket. MCC Committee meetings came and went, and Steph produced immaculate minutes, which I checked, seldom amended substantially and passed on to the President. The sub-committees met and provided the expertise and experience in the different areas that they covered. The outdoor nets were set up, the squares received much attention and the season approached.

John Jameson, the Assistant Secretary (Cricket), oversaw the fixtures on the main ground and on the Nursery Ground as well as keeping up with the laws of the game, all the cricket activities that the Club undertook and the MCC Young Professionals, who had arrived back for their season. His career record in cricket as a forceful opening batsman, who played in four Test matches for England, became county coach for Sussex, national coach for Bangladesh and a first-class umpire for three years, meant he was perfectly suited for the role. Nobody could have been more supportive than John, if he agreed with a suggestion or any proposed changes. On the other hand nobody could have been more stubborn if he thought the changes were inappropriate. He worked slowly but methodically, had his own well-tried systems and was the perfect man to oversee the Laws of Cricket and queries that arrived at the Club on those Laws. He and I got on well, and both of us enjoyed discussing all aspects of the game.

John Smith, the Assistant Secretary (Estates), oversaw the running of the ground, any building or maintenance work, anything commercial such as catering or ticket sales and issues directly affecting the membership. He briefed me whenever I asked about these different aspects of the Club. He had been chief executive of Luton Town Football Club, so had experience in running a sports ground. He was an extremely well-organised administrator and arrived early at the ground and left before the bus lanes closed at 4pm whenever he could. He had a clear mind, and I always knew that I could rely on him to get things done.

The third member of the Secretariat and my deputy was Mike Blow, the Assistant Secretary (Finance). He and John Smith worked closely together on the financial areas involved in running the estate, and all heads of department produced their budgets and discussed them with Mike before we submitted them to the Finance Committee and the MCC Committee. He also oversaw personnel matters. He was a most adept accountant and also very aware of the inner politics of MCC, so a valuable deputy when I arrived. It was a tight group and, for the first year, I was very reliant on their skills and experience. I learnt on the job.

The MCC staff was very able and, apart from day-to-day minor decisions, which were always taken competently and confidently, was clearly capable of more. I remember Mike Blow and John Smith asking me, when I first started at Lord's, whether I was on the side of the Committee or the staff. In other words, did I see the staff as having a kind of Civil Service role or an executive function? A difficult question to answer early in a new position, but my response was that it was my responsibility to find a way to manage the aspirations of both executives and non-executives and to pull them together to produce and agree a strategy, which should dictate the way forward.

I believed that the strategy should evolve from committee discussions based on papers prepared by the executives, after consultation, where appropriate, with the membership. All three groups, the membership, the committees and the staff, were important parts of the Club. The actions should be the responsibility, on a day-to-day basis, of the employed staff. However, no matter what governance model is in place, its success depends to a large degree on the personalities involved and whether they can work together.

It was Fred Allen, the American comedian, who delighted in absurdist comments, who memorably once said: "A committee is a group of people who individually can do nothing but as a group decide that nothing can be done." This recipe for stalemate needed to be avoided, if MCC was to utilise its many strengths and retain its position as the pre-eminent club within cricket.

6

My Role in the House of Lord's

Once the 1994 season started, I was astonished early on the first day of the Test match to come through the gate from our new home in Grove End Road to see a policeman running from the Tavern Stand to the pitch, looking at his watch, walking back and running again. I went to meet him on the outfield and the red-faced policeman introduced himself, saying he had been involved for years with the Club. He explained that one of his roles was to protect the batsmen at the end of the match, because spectators rushed on to the outfield and tried to pinch a memento. He was timing himself to see how long it would take to get to the wicket. It was all pre-planned, so that the wicket-keeper would grab the stumps at the batsman's end, the umpire picked up the stumps at the other end and everyone ran off to the safety of the pavilion. It had, over the years, become quite a tradition, but safety eventually prevailed a few years later and the crowd was kept off the ground, unless specifically invited on, which occasionally happens at a calmer pace during the tea interval of a county match.

Preparations for a major match began weeks in advance. The staff all knew what needed to be done and put in place. The Head Groundsman, Mick Hunt, was the key figure, because without a top-class pitch the game might be over far too quickly or might end in a tame, boring draw after five days. The Estate Manager, Gareth Williams, had everything under control round the ground. He knew where everything was and where additional stalls and coffee outlets could be safely placed. Tickets had been sold in advance and security measures were all checked. In 1994 security was much more relaxed than it was post 9/11 and is today. Sports grounds are now much more conscious that large crowds can attract the wrong kind of attention.

On the day before the match I used to walk round the ground, checking that all the staff felt prepared for the influx of about 28,000 people. On the morning of the match there was a similar route march to see that everything was ready before the signal could be given that gates could be opened and the crowd allowed into the ground a couple of hours before the start of play.

Mick Hunt confided to me that he often stole out of his house within the grounds and crawled under the covers during the night before the match to check that the pitch was OK. Practice on the main ground had seen fielders running on the square and players and media representatives walking across to inspect and dig their keys into the pitch, and he was always nervous. His nerves went away once he had seen the first over bowled and assured himself that the ball was carrying evenly to the keeper. There was a buzz and a tension as the gates were opened, but it was a well-tried system and everything usually worked like clockwork. If issues arose, our loyal and thoroughly committed maintenance team, led by Gareth Williams, Jonathan Hawke and Dave Inman, could turn their hands to most problems and fix them.

There was a group of members who loved queuing from very early in the morning at the Grace Gates or the North Gate. They enjoyed the camaraderie of others in the queue before occupying their favourite seat either in the Pavilion or one of the Members' and Friends' stands. When the gates were opened there was an unseemly rush, and the TV cameramen were always asking permission to be there to film it, which we denied.

There were older and younger members, members with sticks, members with large ice boxes, those with physical disadvantages, but that did not seem to prevent them joining the 'Lord's Grand National', as one of the staff called it. Once, when we suggested that a couple of elderly, infirm members might come and sit on chairs inside the ground before the gates were opened, there was an outcry, with complaints that they would have a ten-yards' head start to reach the Pavilion. Admittedly, they did not seem to be slowed by their infirmity. Fortunately nobody fell at any obstacle, but out-of-breath members, having claimed their seats, then went to find a coffee and a bacon roll. There are usually plenty of seats for the membership, but some wanted to sit in exactly the same place for every day of the match.

As the matches and the years progressed, I became much more aware of what needed to be properly discussed and where issues might arise, but in the first year it was all a learning process. When John Smith retired, I took over the final pre-match briefings of the staff, and we produced a comprehensive check-list, which was covered methodically. There was a surprising number of action points every time but, as was put to me by a meticulous member of staff: "If we did not run a ground properly, we would run aground completely."

For every major match the senior staff members took responsibility for all the documentation that needed to be circulated. A complete list of Major

Match Day Instructions included ground regulations and accreditation for entry to Lord's and access to different parts of the ground, including the outfield and pitch, the pavilion, the media centre and other buildings. The ground map was computerised, updated for each match and made available on the Club's intranet for all staff.

One of the issues that occupied my thoughts was the greeting at the gates round the ground and the atmosphere within the ground. Neville Cardus was not in the least complimentary when he wrote: "Unless one happens to be definitely of Lord's, and a member of the mighty MCC, one is outside the pale here. You are inexorably kept at a distance. The place is a mass of signboards, teaching you your manners and position in life. A man from the unfashionable north, carrying with him a suggestion of real industry, feels that Lord's is all the time eyeing him curiously from a safe point of vantage. It is hard to imagine there is any place in the world where class distinctions are so firmly stressed."

By the 1990s things had substantially changed, but there was still a certain sense of austerity and solemnity about the ground. More needed to be done so that everyone attending a match or one of the many other activities at Lord's felt welcome. There is a story that is often told about Sebastian Coe, the winner of two Olympic Gold medals, arriving at the Grace Gates with an invitation to the President's Box; the ticket instructed the guest to enter via the North Gate. When Lord Coe asked whether he could be allowed to enter via the Grace Gates and walk round inside Lord's, rather than having to go right round outside the ground, the steward said that he could not make an exception and apparently then said it should not take such an athlete long to run round the 400 metres to the correct entry gate.

The welcome at the gates did improve. The often, not always unfairly, criticised gate stewards smiled more, there were discussions about maintaining security without being overbearingly negative and aggressive, and I believe we started to see a lighter but no less efficient approach to the very important security of access control.

We still required clear ground signage for our relatively small site to accommodate the multitude of additional booths that appeared for the major matches. There was a ground plan for the Nursery Ground and outer concourse, a site plan for advertising boards, a plan of the Harris Garden layout, a media guide of MCC regulations and a number of protocols relating to security. There was a document entitled Emergency Procedures, which included the numbers of the phone radios carried by senior staff in all departments and a list of public address and replay screen messages, which would be heard or seen in the event of an emergency. There was a Duty Officer's folder, which detailed the responsibilities of senior staff on match days and the days leading up to a match, role descriptions for the stewards and catering staff who were supplementing the full-time employees in these departments and others' responsibilities.

Finally there was a plan for the presentation ceremony, so that both the paying spectators at Lord's and the television viewers could see and hear any interviews and this included where the table and trophies would be stored during play and where they would be positioned. As the crowd was on the outfield at the end of a match in 1994, the presentation of medals and trophies took place on the middle balcony of the pavilion. Stewards had to move members so that the table and microphones could be set up. Once we had changed from the presentations taking place on the pavilion balcony and moved them to the outfield, we had to find a storage area for a much larger podium, which could be set up so that most spectators could see what was happening. It was helpful that Bob Willis, the former England captain, had large hands because, when interviewing captains after the match, he had to hold two microphones for a while. The broadcasters wanted one particular volume level for the television, and the ground needed a louder level for spectators.

Timings on the days preceding the match were precise. Teams practising did not want to be disrupted by advertising companies putting signage on the outfield, and the groundsmen had to continue with pitch and outfield preparation. Net facilities had to be allocated at different times between the two teams, who increasingly found the Nursery Ground too small for their fielding practices. For the first few years we did not allow football on the main outfield, mostly because it cut up the grass, which had been immaculately mown by our groundsmen. I have never understood why top cricketers think that playing a contact sport on the morning of a Test match makes any sense. Recently it has led to injuries to Jonny Bairstow and, in a recent series in South Africa, to Rory Burns, who needed an operation and was unable to continue the tour. Footballers, rugby or hockey players concentrate on preparing themselves physically and mentally and honing their skills for the game ahead. Injuries can still occur in these warm-ups, as when Glenn McGrath trod on a cricket ball before one Test match and was unable to play, but football played by competitive sportsmen with good hand-eye coordination but less skill in their feet makes little sense.

Broadcasters did not want delays in introducing miles of cabling and their cameras in the short period between the preceding Test match and the Lord's Test. Caterers had to stockpile food and drink for visitors to the ground, our shops had to find time for merchandise to be brought to the ground. We insisted that all contractors and suppliers had to have set up or delivered and left the ground two days before the match, with the last 24 hours reserved for access by suppliers of perishable goods and the vital final checks.

Deadlines were in place for setting up temporary stalls and premises, checking that licences were up-to-date, ensuring that safety and security matters, which were legal requirements, were properly in hand. There needed to be communication with the police, fire brigade, St John Ambulance, Westminster Council, the St John's Wood Society, the governing bodies and management of the two teams, MCC members and ticket purchasers, hospitality providers, the broadcasters, sponsors, box-holders and many others who would play a part in making the match a successful event. Last-minute maintenance had to be completed, scoreboards, CCTV and communication channels around the ground had to be tested to ensure they were functioning properly.

There were always last-minute glitches that needed to be addressed. Perhaps a telephone or television monitor was missing from one particular location, numbers on the seats in the stand were missing, when the painters or those replacing seats had done their work, or signage had been moved. One day the paper provided by a sponsor for scorecards was too thin; a water fountain was not working properly; some cables had not been fully secured; an advertising board left in an exit route from the outfield posed a potential hazard; an unauthorised tent had appeared by the Grace Gate, a programme seller had moved a booth into an exit gap, causing a potential blockage in an emergency, and the public members of the gymnasium in the Indoor School had not been notified that they would be unable to use it over the five days of the match. The staff took all of these matters calmly, and the ground was always ready on the day.

Although most of these matters were delegated to others, occasionally I would ask to see messages including the minutest details which were passed on to relevant members of staff. Details are a key to an efficient organisation and, whilst it was more often than not external contractors who caused or exacerbated a problem, it was the MCC staff's responsibility to spot the issue and put it right, because complaints from the public and members would, rightly, come to us as ground owners.

In one match later in my time at Lord's there was a clash between the ICC Security Manager and the MCC Safety Officer at a World Cup match. The former insisted that a back door to the pavilion, which provided access to the Secretariat offices but also led to the visitors' dressing room on the first floor, must be locked to prevent unauthorised access to the players. The latter insisted that, as a fire door and emergency exit, it must remain unlocked. As this was raised on the morning of the match, I decided that safety overruled security and that we would have a steward permanently on duty there to prevent anyone coming in without accreditation, but the door would remain unlocked. A push-bar on the inside, with an automatic locking to prevent access from outside, provided the solution before the next major match.

Running a sports event is a complex affair. There are always pressures from broadcasters who want to try new angles, place cameras in different places and intrude into parts of the ground, which they insist viewers want to see. Sponsors want to assure themselves that they were getting their fair share of exposure through advertising boards, on the replay screens and in the hospitality facilities that have been allocated to them. The governing body sometimes wants to involve itself in areas of the operation that we, at MCC, believe are our responsibility. Players, managers and coaches of the home team wish to persuade the groundsman to prepare a pitch which suits their team. The MCC Tours Manager does not want to miss out on days when he can bring tourists to see the museum and the ground. Stewards and caterers have to be interviewed and employed to supplement the full-time staff in those departments. There were over 1,000 people employed at Lord's on a big match day.

It is easy to feel beleaguered as the match day arrives. There will have been many meetings with all the key stakeholders, there will have been arguments and disagreements but, once the day arrived, everyone forgot their differences and pulled together.

Before anyone spoke of having red lines in negotiations, MCC had a number of things which would not be accepted. Security and safety remained the responsibility of MCC. My name was on the Ground Safety Certificate so I was not prepared to surrender that duty, although there were always lengthy debates on what we should, legally and practically, be doing. We did not allow cameras into the dressing rooms, believing that these were the players' sole places of refuge and parts of the ground where nobody else should intrude. There is still a notice on the dressing-room door to say that access is only allowed by permission of the captain or manager. Gradually the advertising areas have been extended, although there was one MCC President who said that sponsors would put advertising on the outfield "over his dead body". In the end he relented, and I can confirm that his ashes are not strewn on the outfield as some notable cricketers' ashes have been.

One television company wanted to place a manned camera at mid-wicket in front of the new Grand Stand. As it would have blocked the view of about 200 spectators, I refused. I suggested that an unmanned camera could be attached to the central pillar of the stand and operated remotely, which would not block any views. The programme manager declined to take this up because he said it would not be able to follow the flight of the ball once it had gone above 40 feet, as the balcony level would prevent that. I had little sympathy as the broadcasters already had another 20 or so cameras in the ground, and this was an unnecessary addition at the expense of a good view for 200 paying spectators.

We always insisted that the head groundsman knew his job best and that was why we employed him. We were not prepared to allow anyone else to dictate how the pitch should be cut and rolled or whether it should be left ready for seamers rather than spinners or vice versa. It was his job on the line, and determined amateur administrators and professional cricketers, who believed they knew all about ground preparation, were kept at bay. In any case, as I pointed out on numerous occasions, Law 6 states explicitly: 'Before the match, the Ground Authority shall be responsible for the selection and preparation of the pitch. During the match, the umpires shall control its use and maintenance.' There is no mention in the Laws of either of the competing teams being able to decide on the state of the pitch.

It was always handy having an office which overlooked the playing area. It was definitely the best view in cricket. During the Middlesex matches and games other than internationals or domestic finals, it was a good vantage point when I had work to do. On major match days I was very seldom there. There were endless places around the ground which I wanted to visit. Managers always speak of management by walking around, and at a sports venue that is vital. The Control Room covered everywhere by CCTV and monitored what was happening in the crowd and outside the ground. There were police, fire and safety officers, the head steward and security manager present in that room in the Warner Stand, all of whom were alert and ready to intervene if anything was spotted that might disturb the smooth running of the match. I called in there regularly, as well as visiting many other parts of the ground.

A Test match is scheduled to last five days so at the end of each day there was a cleaning-up operation which was overseen by the same staff who had arrived at the ground very early in the morning. It was important to welcome spectators on the next day to a ground free of litter and other debris from the previous day. They were long days.

Non-major matches, as they were termed, did not require so much monitoring, although there were still match-day regulations issued internally. That was where it was helpful to look occasionally from my office window. We hosted the Under-15 World Cup Final between India and Pakistan, and security was more relaxed than it had been at the Test match, a week or so earlier, between England and Pakistan. That proved a great mistake.

We had 7,000 spectators on the day and, towards the end when the Indian boys, who were batting, were clearly going to win, there was an invasion of the outfield. The two batsmen ran for the pavilion, the fielders, less hurriedly so, followed, and the umpires held their ground uneasily guarding the wickets and the pitch. The limited number of stewards available could not persuade the crowd to move off the outfield so I called the police, who arrived very promptly with dogs. It was an amazing sight to see how quickly the ground cleared as the dogs and their handlers moved in a line across the outfield. One of the ring-leaders was arrested and turned out to be the same Pakistan supporter who had been evicted from the ground at the Test match. Eventually the match was completed, and the Indian Under-15 team duly won. It showed that we should never take security arrangements for granted.

Lord's, even then, was used for lunches, dinners, receptions, wine tastings, net practices in the Indoor School, group tours of the ground, business meetings and other commercial activities, so there was always plenty to do on non-match days.

The role of Chief Executive, though this was not officially my title for some years, included responsibility for Lord's with all its activities. It was once rated as a venue second only to Madison Square Garden. This was, though, only a third of my job. All the commercial events had to be scheduled into an annual calendar in which there were also activities for members, for whom I was the Club Secretary: cricket matches, committee meetings and an AGM, tennis and squash matches, chess, bridge and backgammon evenings, lunches and dinners, concerts and lectures, carol concerts and films in the Brian Johnston Film Theatre. There was plenty to oversee, and it was just as well that Chris and I lived in the Lord's house, once owned by Gubby Allen, located behind the pavilion with a back gate into the ground. We had a wonderful 'back garden', but on some days there were 28,000 others who shared it with us!

I always enjoyed meeting members. I grew to know a large number of them. There was the strong cricket-playing group, older members who valued the chance to keep in touch with friends from their playing days, golfers, real tennis players, a lot of schoolmasters who coached cricket, members who had travelled from long distances by public transport, those who stayed in London for the duration of the match and many others who loved the game and supported their club fully. Longer-serving members, who had reached a certain age, were allocated pre-booked seats in the back row of the Pavilion just outside the Long Room. They were always grateful to have a set seat in 'death row' as they all called it. There was a noisy group who met on the upper balcony of the Allen Stand and still called it by its former name, Q Stand. There were others who populated the Long Room Bar, the Members' Bar on the top floor of the Pavilion and the Bowlers' Bar, next to the Writing Room and close to the bell rung five minutes before each session of play. At start of play the Long Room was packed to see the teams go out on to the field and applaud both batsmen and fielders. The support for the home team was always rousing.

It used to take me a long time to circumnavigate the ground during major matches, because so many members wanted to chat. I met different groups at matches at Lord's, at out-matches, at dinners and lunches in the Long Room or the Committee Dining Room, at committee meetings, on the tennis courts and, of course, at the AGM. It was always a joy to meet the vast majority of them, though, like the painful pupil in a class, who takes up an inordinate amount of your time as a teacher, there was a small minority who always had a moan or complaint or criticism. They seemed to find ways of catching me at the busiest times and getting away was not easy.

One member accused me of being 'only a schoolmaster', but when I pointed out that he was 'only a dentist', he was furious and went into great detail about his experience in business. In one AGM he stood up and said I should resign. I once saw him in a team photograph when I visited a friend with whom he had apparently opened the bowling. My friend's only recollection of this man was that he was an aggressive and unpleasant fast bowler, so little appeared to have changed over the years.

top: My parents, Cheryl and me at Knollys Road; Cheryl and me in our Graham of Montrose tartan kilts; *bottom:* batting in the garden; off to play for Dulwich Prep School

Dulwich College 1st XI, 1963
standing: RCW Wood, RDV Knight, NPR Wall, NJ Cosh, J Destefano, MJ Ross
sitting: J Dobson, JS Bottle, HJ George (capt), CA Jones, NB Bennett

Cambridge University XI, 1967
DR Aers, CP Pyemont, MK Whitaker, RDV Knight, CEM Ponniah, DWW Norris
DL Acfield, VP Malalasekera, SG Russell (capt), GA Cottrell, NJ Cosh, AB Palfreman

Two successes at Lord's

above: Gloucestershire win the Gillette Cup, 1973 – *(from left)* Andy Stovold, John Mortimore, Jack Davey, Mike Procter, Sadiq Mohammad, Roger Knight, Tony Brown, David Shepherd, Jim Foat, David Graveney, Zaheer Abbas

left: Captain of Surrey with the NatWest Bank Trophy, 1982

Sussex 1976

Back: Arnold Long, Paul Parker, John Spencer, Paul Phillipson, Mike Buss, John Barclay, Chris Waller, Javed Miandad;
Front: Peter Graves, Tony Greig (captain), John Snow, Roger Knight

Surrey, with the NatWest Bank Trophy, 1982

Back: Kevin Mackintosh, David Thomas, Graham Roope, David Smith, Sylvester Clarke, Ian Payne, Graham Monkhouse, Monte Lynch

Front: Geoff Howarth, Alan Butcher, Roger Knight (captain), Micky Stewart (manager), Robin Jackman, Jack Richards

Bowling was a useful second-string to my bow
with 369 first-class wickets and 297 in one-day games, but ...

I am confident that, if I had faced my own bowling,
I would have scored a stack of runs!

Wedding day, 27 March 1971

top: Housemaster at Cranleigh
bottom: Headmaster at Worksop, with the prize winners and guest speaker Tim Rice

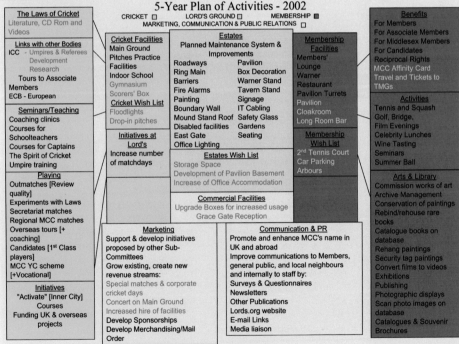

5-Year Plan of Activities - 2002

CRICKET ☐   LORD'S GROUND ☐   MEMBERSHIP ▣
MARKETING, COMMUNICATION & PUBLIC RELATIONS ☐

The Laws of Cricket
Literature, CD Rom and Videos

Links with other Bodies
ICC - Umpires & Referees
    Development
    Research
Tours to Associate Members
ECB - European

Seminars/Teaching
Coaching clinics
Courses for Schoolteachers
Courses for Captains
The Spirit of Cricket
Umpire training

Playing
Outmatches [Review quality]
Experiments with Laws
Secretariat matches
Regional MCC matches
Overseas tours [+ coaching]
Candidates [1st Class players]
MCC YC scheme [+Vocational]

Initiatives
"Activate" [Inner City] Courses
Funding UK & overseas projects

Cricket Facilities
Main Ground
Pitches Practice Facilities
Indoor School
Gymnasium
Scorers' Box

Cricket Wish List
Floodlights
Drop-in pitches

Initiatives at Lord's
Increase number of matchdays

Estates
Planned Maintenance System & Improvements
Roadways   Pavilion
Ring Main   Box Decoration
Barriers   Warner Stand
Fire Alarms   Tavern Stand
Painting   Signage
Boundary Wall   IT Cabling
Mound Stand Roof   Safety Glass
Disabled facilities   Gardens
East Gate   Seating
Office Lighting

Estates Wish List
Storage Space
Development of Pavilion Basement
Increase of Office Accommodation

Commercial Facilities
Upgrade Boxes for increased usage
Grace Gate Reception

Membership Facilities
Members' Lounge
Warner Restaurant
Pavilion Turrets
Pavilion Cloakroom
Long Room Bar

Membership Wish List
2nd Tennis Court
Car Parking
Arbours

Benefits
For Members
For Associate Members
For Middlesex Members
For Candidates
Reciprocal Rights
MCC Affinity Card
Travel and Tickets to TMGs

Activities
Tennis and Squash
Golf, Bridge,
Film Evenings
Celebrity Lunches
Wine Tasting
Seminars
Summer Ball

Arts & Library
Commission works of art
Archive Management
Conservation of paintings
Rebind/rehouse rare books
Catalogue books on database
Rehang paintings
Security tag paintings
Convert films to videos
Exhibitions
Publishing
Photographic displays
Scan photo images on database
Catalogues & Souvenir Brochures

Marketing
Support & develop initiatives proposed by other Sub-Committees
Grow existing, create new revenue streams:
Special matches & corporate cricket days
Concert on Main Ground
Increased hire of facilities
Develop Sponsorships
Develop Merchandising/Mail Order

Communication & PR
Promote and enhance MCC's name in UK and abroad
Improve communications to Members, general public, and local neighbours and internally to staff by:
Surveys & Questionnaires
Newsletters
Other Publications
Lords.org website
E-mail Links
Media liaison

top: In the MCC Secretary's office at Lord's, 2002
bottom: A demanding five-year plan starting that year

top: A historic moment: Anthony Wreford (Working Party Chairman), Colin Ingleby-Mackenzie (President) and RDVK with the 1998 report proposing the admission of women to MCC membership

left: RDVK as MCC President in 2015, under the watchful eye of Lord Harris, President in 1895

left: A family picnic at Cranleigh, 1984

below: Mariella, Meredith, our son Graeme and Alex

above: Anna, Roy, Jonah, our daughter Katie and Danny, with Reg their dog

right: Sitting on the garden bench given by Katie and Graeme for our golden wedding in March 2021

The third part of my role was less easily defined but was, in some ways, the most varied and interesting. There was travel to the other cricket countries, which helped to build relationships with their administrators who came to Lord's and also to sound them out on the Laws of the game. There was a huge amount of hospitality and entertaining, when Chris and I travelled overseas, which we reciprocated at home and in the Secretary's Box at Lord's. I was a member of various ICC committees, in particular the Development Committee. This committee oversaw an increase of countries where cricket was played to over one hundred and introduced many exciting initiatives. There were numerous speeches to be made, dinners to attend and people to meet at home and overseas, all of which was intended to maintain MCC's influence round the world.

Distinguished guests to Lord's had to be met and shown to where they were awaited. The Royal Family usually arrived by car at the back door of the pavilion, where I met the Queen and Prince Philip and introduced them to the President in the Committee Room. When South Africa was readmitted into Test cricket, President Mbeki insisted on being met at the Grace Gates, where he said he had once been refused admittance when demonstrating against apartheid in the past. Prime Ministers usually arrived into Car Park 6, where I would escort them to the Box to which they had been invited. Visiting dignitaries were greeted. Lord's was MCC's home, and it was seen as an important symbolic gesture for me to welcome the leading guests of the day to the ground.

It was always a joy to meet the Duke of Edinburgh. He loved cricket and came mostly to the Committee Room with the Queen. On one occasion, though, he arrived on his own with his protection officer just before the lunch interval, and I met him to escort him to the President's Box in the Grand Stand. He had always made it clear that security should be as inconspicuous as possible, so we had moved away uniformed police and stewards but asked a couple of stewards in plain clothes to walk ahead of us to the lift. It was threatening to rain, so Prince Philip and I both carried rolled-up umbrellas. The lunchtime rush to the food outlets had started, so our two stewards had to move the oncoming crowd aside to create a pathway and acted rather forcefully, which Prince Philip saw. He poked one steward in the back with his umbrella and said: "It's OK. They're only people."

In the year when I was President-Elect, I was in the Committee Room to be introduced to the Queen and Prince Philip. As he came opposite me he said: "Are you still here?" On another occasion the Committee suggested that I should ask him to wear an MCC tie when he came to Lord's, which I did. He said that I would have to send him a new tie, which he wore on the next occasion, with a smile and the comment: "Is that alright?" He was aware and alert and loved cricket. The royal visits were usually fairly short, but Prince Philip was always rather reluctant to leave and once asked the Queen, who was keen to travel to Ascot, to wait for an over, so he could see the start of Joe Root's innings.

Match-day hospitality in the Secretary's Box was overseen by Chris, my wife. I was out and about during the match, appearing briefly at lunchtime to welcome the twenty-four guests who had been invited to spend the day in the Box in the Grand Stand. Knowing the overseas administrators made it much easier to introduce them to other guests and make them feel comfortable. We were privileged to host and get to know many well-known former cricketers and other sportsmen, politicians, television, film and stage personalities, local councillors and a variety of other guests.

The President's Box, at that time, was in the Tavern Stand, but the new Grand Stand in 1997 provided an opportunity to locate both boxes next to each other, available as a very large box, when the interconnecting doors were opened up. Sir Oliver Popplewell, the President that year, was keen to move across the ground and have a box which the sun reached early in the day. For Test matches we kept the two boxes separate, but for limited-over matches they were often open and shared. We did have an occasional person who tried to bring an uninvited guest, which upset the numbers for lunch, and one President was embarrassed on the first day of a Test match to find that a guest and his wife had given the tickets to their son and his partner. This famous former Test cricketer and his wife then talked their way up to the box for the day. Space and two extra chairs were found, but it was a crush at the lunch tables. The following day they were due to be in the Secretary's box so, forewarned, I met the son and his partner when they arrived, welcomed them, took two Tavern Stand Rover Tickets from my pocket and ushered them to the stand reserved for members and their friends. I explained this to the cricketer when he arrived a little later. I think the message was received because it did not happen again.

Sometimes, after the day's play, we would invite guests back to our home for a drink or snack before leaving. Once I overheard one of the Prime Minister's protection officers tell him that his wife had gone out for supper and had suggested that he should get something to eat on his way home. I asked John Major, whom I knew from the Oval, whether he would like to join us at home, where we were going to have a take-away curry with the President and Treasurer and their wives, a couple of overseas guests and my parents who were staying with us. When he accepted and mentioned that his four protection officers would have to come with him to our garden, where we were intending to eat, I immediately rang home and asked Chris to order five more curries. It made for a most entertaining evening, much enjoyed by us all. It was noticeable that the protection officers took a quick look around the garden when they arrived, and the Prime Minister deliberately sat with his back to Century Court, the multi-storey apartment block along the road, which was the only vantage point that overlooked the garden. Security is always an issue for people in top positions.

Any discussion about security reminds me of a visit to Dhaka, where John Jameson, Chris and I were guests of the Bangladesh Cricket Board. We were given seats next to the President of the country's box, which was separated from ours by a low wall. A sofa was brought into the President's Box, thoroughly searched and an immaculately dressed soldier was placed close behind it. A temporary airport-style metal-detector gate was erected at the entrance to the row of boxes in the section labelled VVIP, but it promptly fell over and needed to be put up again. At that stage another more senior soldier came and searched the sofa again, putting both hands down under the cushions. Next the caterer arrived with the lunch in a huge metal cooking pot, and the alarm on the gate screamed at everyone around. It brought several other security officers to the area, and the armed guards strategically placed on the adjacent buildings just outside the ground turned to see what was causing the alarm. It was amusing, but Chris and I agreed wholeheartedly when John Jameson said that he hoped those marksmen were accurate in the event of a genuine intruder coming in. By the time the President arrived, wearing trainers and a baseball cap, everything had been reset, the sofa checked for the third time, and she enjoyed the match surrounded by other politicians and smiling at us, the guests from England.

Wherever we went, I learnt how others approached the running of a ground, the security and safety measures inside and outside the ground, access control, how the grounds were used when there was no cricket and how pitches were prepared. The Melbourne Cricket Ground (MCG) was a great example of a sports stadium that doubled as a cricket ground and an Australian Rules oval by using drop-in pitches. The Cricket Club of India (CCI) had accommodation, restaurants, other sports facilities and set out tables and chairs on the outfield on non-match days for members to have tea and cakes. Most grounds we visited were in operation in some way throughout the year, usually for the benefit of the members of the club that was based there.

In the UK I met people in the equivalent position in the All England Lawn Tennis Club, the Royal and Ancient Golf Club and the Rugby Football Union, and we shared our experiences of operating at Lord's, Wimbledon, St Andrews and Twickenham. We also built up close relationships and friendships with each other, finding so many aspects of our roles in common. It was all broadening for me as a person, providing opportunities to visit different places, meet many new people and learn about the best ways to be an ambassador for my sport and my club.

One wonderful opportunity was a trip to the Royal and Ancient Golf Club at St Andrews, hosted by Michael Bonallack, who had called me to say it was his turn to invite the four secretaries to lunch and discuss security issues at our grounds. Chris Gorringe from the All England Lawn Tennis Club at Wimbledon, Dudley Wood from the RFU and I accepted the invitation and were asked whether we would like to play a round of golf on the Old Course. Chris Gorringe and I both answered that we would love to accept but that neither of us was a regular golfer. Nevertheless we had a wonderful round together, while Dudley and Michael decided not to play. Neither of us went into one of the many bunkers because we failed to reach those placed to catch a wayward drive, fell short of those round the greens and somehow managed to avoid them with scuffed pitch shots. A great experience!

It was a real pleasure to get to know Dr John Lill and his wife, Rosey, at the Melbourne Cricket Ground. He was the Secretary of the Melbourne Cricket Club, and Chris and I learnt a lot from their way of making guests feel completely at home and welcome. We have remained firm friends ever since and have recently spent a week with them near Perth, where they now live close to their son and his family. They have also stayed with us in the UK and in New Zealand. Their successor, Stephen Gough, and his wife, Dianne, have also become good friends, and we have spent a couple of New Year's Eves enjoying a party and watching the fireworks from their apartment overlooking Federation Square in Melbourne.

The relationship between the two MCCs is strong and important. So too is the link with the Cricket Club of India, which has the real atmosphere of a members' club at the Brabourne Stadium. The Secretary when we stayed there, Rupendra Renjen, and his wife, Malti, have also become good friends. The role of Secretary has brought us all together and given us so many opportunities to spend time in different countries.

It was one of the inevitable roles and responsibilities of the MCC Secretary & Chief Executive to attend memorial services of Past Presidents, distinguished cricketers and senior members of a club where the average age was close to 60 and is forever getting higher.

What will always be a wonderful memory for me was being in St Peter's Cathedral, North Adelaide on Sunday 25 March 2001 for the Memorial Service for Sir Don Bradman. Speakers at the service were Sir Donald's son John, Governor General Sir William Deane, former Australian captain Richie Benaud, and Jill Gauvin, a personal friend of Sir Donald. Cricket Australia was well represented. A mention was made of his first Test match, when Australia were caught on a 'sticky wicket' and were all out for 66 in the second innings losing by 675 runs, which is still a Test record. Sir Don made 18 and 1 and was dropped to twelfth man for the second Test, though he came on the field as a substitute because of an injury to Bill Ponsford. In this Test match England scored 636, to follow their 863 runs in the first Test. He certainly came back with a vengeance over the years scoring 19 centuries against England in a career lasting from 1928 until 1948, interrupted by the Second World War.

Less than a week later, on Saturday 30 March 2001 I attended Westminster Abbey for the Memorial Service for Lord Cowdrey. Colin died of a heart attack on 4 December 2000, aged 67, having suffered a stroke earlier that year. He was the third and latest sportsman to have a memorial service at the abbey, the others being Sir Frank Worrell and Bobby Moore. It was a privilege to be there and to hear John Major give the tribute and say: "He left us too soon, but it was a gem of an innings. He lived life with a clear eye, a straight bat and a cover drive from heaven. He was a true Corinthian." It was John Woodcock who wrote the epitaph on his simple headstone, which reads: "... some journey, some life, some cover drive, some friend."

It was a poignant moment for me, having played against Colin in my early days as a professional. He usually greeted me on the field of play by saying: "Good morning, schoolmaster." He was a marvellous man of Kent, England and MCC, with a career record of great distinction. He played in 114 Tests with a batting average of 44, scored 107 first-class centuries, 22 of them in Tests. He was the first cricketer to play 100 Tests, and he marked the occasion with 104 against Australia in 1968. He was a highly respected giant of the game who was called back to Australia to represent his country at the age of 41, four years after his previous Test, and when Lillee and Thomson were at their peak. His cheerful greeting to Tommo of "How nice to meet you", when he went out to face the fast bowler, was not reciprocated with quite the same friendliness!

It was a chance to say farewell to two great cricketers, both of whom scored over 100 first-class centuries, one probably the greatest batsman of all time. Certainly nobody is close to Sir Don's Test career average of 99.94, with a 36% ratio of centuries per innings played. There were only a handful of people who were able to attend both services, and it was a privilege and a wonderful memory to have been there on both occasions.

7

Changes at Lord's from 1994 to 2006

One of the comments made by Stephanie Lawrence, my PA nearly throughout my time as Secretary & Chief Executive, which I took as a great compliment, was that I was always prepared to consider change.

Two leading people made persuasive statements about change. The Dalai Lama said: "Open your arms to change, but don't let go of your values." President Jimmy Carter said: "We must adjust to changing times and still hold to unchanging principles." Both comments left a lasting impression on me. I had started at Lord's by saying that I was a great supporter of tradition but that I was keen to strip away some of the folklore that seemed to have grown alongside it. Tradition is a strong platform on which to build future thoughts and ideas. Folklore grows from custom and practice, sometimes initially unintentionally, and may easily become restrictive.

It was often expressed in the media that MCC was thoroughly opposed to change. In reality, although there were inevitably some amongst the membership who wished to retain everything as it had been when they joined the Club, the MCC Committee and the vast majority of members wanted to see progress and greater opportunities to use the Home of Cricket more widely. In the years from 1994 to 2006 there were numerous changes to the ground at Lord's, and many more activities became available to MCC members and the local community. I feel proud to have overseen these improvements which benefitted spectators and increased opportunities for members of the Club.

The main building changes started in 1994 when the Duke of Edinburgh opened the new Indoor School, designed by the architect David Morley. The innovative practice facility used outdoor light without the glare or shadow from the sun. Most indoor nets were artificially lit at that time. The lanes provided a proper run-up for bowlers, with shock pads to lessen the chance of injury. It was possible to play a full game of indoor cricket by pulling all the netting back. Cameras were installed to allow batsmen and bowlers to analyse their techniques. Modern equipment has been added as technology has moved on, and it is now possible for umpires, or indeed anyone interested in trying it out, to use Hawkeye to test themselves and see how accurate their decision-making ability really is. It is very salutary for bowlers, who suddenly realise that some appeals may be not out, and for batsmen, who have to accept that on occasions they are rightly given out lbw. It is a fine centre, now called the MCC Cricket Academy, and it remains a first-class facility for the MCC Young Cricketers and for any teams or individuals who wish to practise there. It stands next to the Nursery Ground, another vital part of the cricketing facilities at Lord's. The Nursery Ground is small but large enough for many games of cricket to be played, especially by youngsters and Cross Arrows who have a full fixture list against clubs, who are delighted to play at the Home of Cricket.

Alongside the Indoor School are the offices for ECB. At the East Gate the Lord's shop has replaced the cottage which originally handled all the merchandise for sale at the ground and also served as the home for the Head Coach.

By 1998 Lord's had a new Grand Stand, which was a much lighter building with infinitely better views for spectators. Before Nicholas Grimshaw's design with open seating, hospitality boxes, the three columns and two-storey spine beam, which increased the seating capacity by a third, spectators sitting in the back rows of seats next to the scoreboard were only able to see half the ground because of the central structure, housing the scorers and one of the two giant scoreboards.

The MCC Secretary's hospitality box was always located on that side of the ground, but lunch and tea were served in a small room at the back of the stand, with no view of the cricket. The President's and the Secretary's boxes were now alongside each other centrally on the north side of the ground. Both hospitality double-boxes provided greater flexibility and, although not located behind the bowler's arm, they were as close as anywhere on the ground to the action. There were two knock-on effects of the new facility: a need for a new scoreboard and scorers' box and a new home for Father Time, the iconic weathervane, which had overseen the ground from the solid roof of the old Grand Stand. The scoreboard, which by then needed to be capable of showing replays, notices and advertising, took its place in front of the Clock Tower. Father Time has taken up residence on the south side of Lord's above the new scorers' box.

As always with buildings, the deadline was tight and there were huge concerns whether the outfield, where heavy cranes and lorries had driven during the two winters, could be re-turfed in time. The new turf fortunately settled very well with constant rolling, though it was in place only a week before the first major international match. Until that game Mick Hunt and his ground staff had prepared non-major match pitches on the lower side of the square.

On the first day of the Test in 1998 there were still some notices missing, in particular the signs for the ladies' and gentlemen's lavatories. One of the guests in the Secretary's box was Ali Bacher, the South African cricket captain and now administrator, who left just before lunch to find the lavatory. He had just locked the door to a cubicle, when he was horrified to hear women's voices outside. He stayed in place for twenty minutes until he could not hear any more conversations and then returned to the box late for lunch, much to the consternation of his wife. He arrived back at the table just as I was welcoming all the guests and giving a brief introduction of each one. Chris and I were always keen to make these introductions, so that, after lunch, guests knew who was there and could chat with those they wished to meet. Whenever we went to Sydney Cricket Ground, Alan Davidson, the great Australian fast bowler and chairman of New South Wales Cricket, welcomed us and spoke about all the guests. We were impressed at how he seemed to remember the names and background histories of over seventy guests without notes. I was relieved that we were limited to twenty-four.

At the same time as the Grand Stand was being built, a decision had been taken to build a new Media Centre between the Compton and Edrich Stands, to be completed in 1999, in time for the Cricket World Cup. The logistics of materials arriving during the winter, when the final parts of the Grand Stand were also arriving, were brilliantly managed by the MCC Estates staff and also by close cooperation between the teams of the Grand Stand's architect, Nicholas Grimshaw, and of the architects of the Media Centre, Future Systems, where Amanda Levete and Jan Kaplicky produced a wonderful facility for us that won them the RIBA Stirling Prize for architecture.

This building was not universally popular, particularly amongst some members of the cricket press and, in particular, *Test Match Special*, whose base had been on the north turret of the Pavilion for many years. Henry Blofeld once remarked that he loathed the new facility and yet thought that the best place to be at Lord's was inside it because it was the only place in the ground where one could not see 'the monstrosity'. Amazingly, much to the surprise of the President, Sir Oliver Popplewell, and me, permission was granted by all the necessary bodies in almost record time.

There had been a competition amongst architects and three were selected by the working group, passed through the Estates Committee, the Cricket Committee, to ensure it would not adversely affect the cricket in the middle, the Finance Committee, who had originally agreed a budget of £1.7 million, the planners, Westminster City Council and the local St John's Wood Society. Once all these bodies had accepted the design, the cost, by now considerably higher, as the first draft from Future Systems was already at £2.3 million, and the pressing timescale, which had to have a deadline of the start of the 1999 season, the project was put to the membership at an SGM and passed with a large majority.

As becomes apparent from the list of consultations above, turning an original decision into reality is not an easy task at Lord's. At the same time that the Media Centre was being accepted by all these influential bodies, the new scoreboard had to go back to the planners for appeal, having been turned down after a complaint about light spillage from one of the neighbours. Once again, there was a very tight deadline for this innovative building to be tested and ready on time, and even more important was the fact that there would be no shortage of criticism if the area where the world's cricket writers and radio and television commentators were located revealed any shortcomings.

As the first ever all-aluminium, semi-monocoque building in the world, with no builder prepared to bid for its construction, Future Systems had to go to two shipyards in Cornwall and one in the Netherlands, because of the similarities to boat-building technology. The front glass screen, which is part of the structural support of the facility, has only one opening window. This was inserted at the insistence of *Test Match Special* commentators, who wanted the atmosphere of the crowd. Originally the idea was to pipe the ambient sound of the spectators into the cricket writers' parts of the Media Centre, but the microphones were very close to the Compton and Edrich Stands and the speakers were soon switched off.

The Media Centre is, in the eyes of most visitors to Lord's, a great triumph. It stands directly opposite the Pavilion, built in the nineteenth century, and contrasts the old with the new architecture of the ground. It is self-supporting on two columns, which house the lifts and stairs. It has allowed the new Compton and Edrich Stands to be put in place without demolishing the building. It stands fifteen metres above the ground and is roughly the same height as the Pavilion at the other end.

The cost of the building rose astronomically, partly because the boat-builders were able to ask a high price, as there was no competition to build it, and partly because, to fund the original target expenditure, a sponsor was sought. The NatWest bank was the first sponsor to lend its name to the Media Centre but wanted two hospitality boxes, one at each end of the building to entertain guests. This entailed extending the length of the building and, inevitably, increasing the cost.

Nevertheless, the final cost of over £5 million, although considerably more than was originally budgeted, has produced another iconic building at Lord's, a landmark for British Airways pilots as they come into Heathrow Airport from an easterly direction. It has received acclaim worldwide and is a very useful additional facility for dinners and receptions in the restaurant overlooking the Nursery Ground, as well as proving that modern and more traditional architecture can be mixed to produce an interesting and distinctive backdrop to the cricket. It helps to maintain the feel of Lord's as a cricket ground, with separate buildings, as opposed to a stadium, which has always been the intention of generations of committees and members.

These three buildings were the major development projects within the ground during my years. However, countless areas of Lord's underwent change before I retired in 2006. Indeed, the development of the ground has continued and even increased in pace since then. Spectators and visitors to the ground rightly expect top-class facilities, and MCC members expect their club to be kept up-to-date with their own facilities.

As new buildings have been erected, MCC departments have moved around the ground. It would be ideal if the people working for the Club or ECB or Middlesex CCC at Lord's could all be housed in a purpose-built block of offices, but that is perhaps for the future. In the meantime, the Printing Office, the Finance Office, the Control Room, housing the police and heads of safety and security, the Tours Department and the Ticket Office were all relocated. Extensions were built to the Museum and Library, which included the new Film Theatre, named after the much loved Brian Johnston. A third electronic scoreboard/replay screen was installed at the back of the Edrich Stand, and a new scorers' box and smaller scoreboard between the Tavern and the Mound Stands.

Every year there was a comprehensive programme of redecoration and renovation. The Tavern Pub and the Banqueting Suite, now the Thomas Lord Suite, once inside the ground but now available to the general public from St John's Wood Road without having to enter Lord's, were fully refurbished. The Nursery Pavilion was erected next to the Nursery Ground, running along the Wellington Road, as a temporary structure, expected to stand for ten years, but still in place in 2019. Directional signage round the ground was much improved. More attractive landscaping was carried out and railings replaced external walls in some areas, so that the ground became more visible to passers-by.

The members of MCC contribute a large sum each year in subscriptions, which provide them with free access to cricket matches. Their own facilities were also kept up to date and the activities available increased. The real tennis court and the squash courts are constantly in need of an upgrade. The pavilion was totally renovated in 2004 at a cost of £8.2 million. This listed building originally cost £21,000 in 1890. It has seen many changes to the game and has hosted many very important people. The renovations and redecoration were extensive. A lift was installed, and a terrace at the top with more seating was introduced along with bars on the South and North turrets. All the exterior of the building was repointed and repaired. Inside, the whole place was refreshed and turned into a building fit for the 21st century. It was a massive task, led by David Batts, the Deputy Chief Executive, whose background in hotel management made him the ideal person to take charge.

Apart from a cricket pavilion with the dressing rooms, containing the famous honours boards, officials' rooms and seats for viewing the cricket, the most famous room, the Long Room, is a multi-purpose area, which is popular with members and former players, who watch through the see-through sightscreens, introduced by Tony Dodemaide, our Australian Head of Cricket. It is an art gallery for some of the Club's paintings, a dining hall, reception venue and concert hall. The pavilion also provides offices for the senior executives of MCC. It is well used and a very good source of much-needed income, particularly during the winter months.

More activities for members have been organised, and there are supporters of the golf days and tours, the bridge, chess and backgammon evenings. There were several highly successful Long Room concerts held in conjunction with the Lord's Taverners' music committee, sponsored by Classic FM. The first of the Cowdrey Spirit of Cricket Lectures was given in 2000 by Richie Benaud, and there has been a long list of experienced and distinguished speakers, mainly cricketers of note but one or two others who have not played at the top level but love the game. They have all contributed their thoughts about the game of cricket and their love of it. Those able to attend or listen as the lecture is streamed live have enjoyed what has been said. Afterwards, Mark Nicholas has expertly chaired a panel of three and has brought out the best in some top cricketers with his lively questions. Now held in the Nursery Pavilion to accommodate more members, it is followed by a dinner in the Long Room, attended by members of the Cowdrey family. The Film Society, the museum exhibitions and the winter dinners and suppers are well attended. Cricket tours overseas have remained popular for the active cricketers within the Club and have visited many cricketing countries amongst the ICC Associate and Affiliate members. All these additional cricket opportunities have been added to the ongoing out-match programme which reached over 450 matches against schools and clubs.

MCC has remained primarily a cricket club, much to the relief of the vast majority of members, but other activities have been introduced and will continue to be enjoyed.

Lord's is one of the best-known cricket grounds in the world and can justifiably continue to be called the Home of Cricket. In the period of my tenancy as Secretary & Chief Executive there were many changes and improvements to the playing area, all overseen by the cricket department.

The innovative hover-cover, which is over thirty yards long and has side covers attached to be unrolled across the square, has allowed the pitch to be protected from the rain very quickly and has avoided the wheel marks that were often to be seen when the ground was soft. Sponsored by Amlin Insurance in conjunction with their chosen charity, Macmillan Cancer UK, there was nearly a row when Benson & Hedges and ECB requested that the Macmillan wording should be covered during the Benson & Hedges matches. We were very reluctant to agree and Macmillan refused absolutely to lose their sponsorship rights, so the wording remained.

The complete relaying of the outfield, to stop the pooling at the lower side of the ground in front of the Tavern Stand after heavy rain, was an immediate success. For years, to the frustration of spectators, the rainwater took an inordinate time to drain away, and the crowd grew restive in the sunshine, as much of the top half of the ground was drying quickly and the players were practising above the square. The logistics for relaying all the turf during the winter were fraught with concern. It was unthinkable that the ground should not be available for the season, but there was a huge amount of earth and rubble that had to be removed before the new base and drainage could be laid. That necessitated a lot of digging and lorry-loads of the old, thick, clay-based soil leaving Lord's with the possibility of wet weather intervening, making it impossible for work to continue.

Fortunately September and October were fine and so the first part of the work went very well as we cleared down to the solid London clay. The next concern was frost or cold weather while the foundations for lighter soil were installed, but again we were fortunate. At the beginning of the year anyone standing in the pavilion saw a green square surrounded by brown soil on top of the pebbles, shingle, sand and irrigation system, which were laid ready for the new surface to appear. The final worry was whether the grass would grow sufficiently in the spring. The contractors had arranged for the whole surface to be grown in East Anglia, ready to be rolled up and transported in lorry loads to St John's Wood. In case of any unforeseen difficulties, exactly the same amount of turf was also being grown elsewhere. One way or another the grass would be laid, and the pieces of turf allowed to unite so that fielders would be safe from turned ankles in the early matches.

It worked. We were indebted to Dr John Lill, the former Secretary of the Melbourne Cricket Club, who had experience of similar re-turfing on the MCG after the AFL season, and he was a reassuring presence at crucial times. Tony Dodemaide took responsibility for this whole enterprise.

Tony also took charge of the see-through sight-screen in front of the pavilion. Members in the Long Room had, for years, been faced with a solid screen, which blocked their view. The solution, which still provided and increased the background that the batsmen needed to sight the ball, was a screen that was transparent from inside the building. Lights in the Long Room were visible through the screen but, with these switched off, everyone was content. That is until the white ball matches needed a black sightscreen! We never found a solution to that problem.

Tony Dodemaide's time at Lord's, before he returned to Australia to become the Chief Executive for Western Australia Cricket Association and subsequently for Cricket Victoria, oversaw these very important changes at Lord's, allowing more cricket to be played and enhancing the members' view from the pavilion.

Throughout all these changes, nothing improved more than the IT provision, as capability grew. Technology and its uses have always fascinated me. In 1994 MCC possessed two word processors and only one computer in the Assistant Secretary of Finance's office. Minutes, notes and instructions were routinely sent round the ground on paper in orange envelopes. The envelopes were used several times and the intended recipient's hand-written name was always the last on the list. It was clear that we needed to modernise and enter the world of the internet and emails. There was a certain amount of trepidation and resistance amongst the staff, so our IT consultant, Stephen Wilder, suggested that I should take the lead and use a desktop computer. I opted for a laptop so that I could practise at home. Slowly, communication round the ground and outside changed, and the staff embraced the new methods.

Technology has been introduced into cricket on the field, but that is something that I shall return to in another chapter.

As MCC became more commercial in its approach, a Marketing Committee was set up and, with the appointment of a Communications Officer, members received regular newsletters and surveys asking for their views. Computerisation of many areas helped, and those on our enormous ticket database were contacted more regularly through emails. Merchandise in the newly-built shop, replacing the old cottage at the East Gate, was increased, and more sponsorship was sought. Following NatWest and Amlin, British Airways provided sponsorship for tour parties and coaching trips overseas, and Buxton Water helped us start the MCC Spirit of Cricket Challenge, which was, perhaps, a precursor to the activities of the Chance to Shine charity. Our initiative consisted of visits to school assemblies, cricket lessons during PE periods and cricket camps during the summer holidays and was well received by the pupils and the school teachers.

An important sponsorship was the Waterford Crystal replica of the Ashes Urn. For years and particularly after several Australian victories in the Ashes, there had been requests for the Urn to be retained in the country of the winning team in any Ashes series. On one occasion even John Howard, the Australian Prime Minister, wrote a letter to me suggesting that, in the spirit of cricket, it was time for MCC to let the Ashes out of its museum. My reply was straightforward and explained that the Urn was not, and had never been, the trophy for the Ashes series. It emanated from a joke when a bail was burnt after a country house match down under, placed in the Urn and given by a group of Melbourne women, amongst them Florence Morphy, to Ivo Bligh, the England captain, who later became Lord Darnley. He subsequently married her and, on his death, his widow presented the Urn to MCC as a gift. The Ashes Urn has resided in the MCC museum since then and is owned by the Club.

This story is not as well-known as the origination of the term. This occurred in a satirical obituary published in *The Sporting Times* immediately after Australia's first Test win on English soil in 1882. The obituary stated that English cricket had died, and 'the body will be cremated and the ashes taken to Australia'. The mythical ashes immediately became associated with the 1882/83 series played in Australia before which the English captain, Ivo Bligh, had vowed to "regain those ashes". The English media therefore dubbed the tour 'the quest to regain the Ashes'. The presentation of the Ashes Urn to Ivo Bligh after the light-hearted match was in response to this comment but never a trophy for winning the Test series.

After John Howard's letter MCC spoke with Waterford Crystal and a suitable trophy was struck, an exact replica of the Urn but about two feet tall, which would be presented to the winning captain after the Sydney Test. England agreed to this, and Australia rather less enthusiastically accepted it, too. Tony Lewis, the MCC President, made the first presentation of this trophy to the Australian captain on the outfield after the last match of the series at the Sydney Cricket Ground in 1999.

In addition it was agreed that the actual Urn, which is extremely frail, could be flown to Australia for a series of exhibitions at museums and cricket grounds, which it did in 2007. Virgin Atlantic sponsored the trip and the Urn, safely packed in a box and strapped to the wrist of the assistant curator of the MCC museum for security and insurance purposes, set off for only the second time that it had ever left Lord's. Despite the existence of the larger trophy, there is still a desire by the winning captains to display a life-sized replica of the actual Urn for photographs, so the myth continues.

Advertising hoardings, sponsors' logos or names on hospitality boxes, the hire of boxes, debenture seats and many dinners and receptions in the Long Room and other buildings round the ground have increased the revenue of the Club substantially and, in turn, allowed the building development work to be completed without recourse to public money. Cricket may be the primary focus for MCC and its members, but income generation to sustain the development programmes and the many activities that take place and need funding is vital. However, the members will soon remind the Secretary & Chief Executive, the staff and the Committee if the balance between Club and business alters unacceptably.

What Else Might Have Been Done?

Having had the great opportunity of visiting other clubs around the world, there are just a couple of regrets that still linger about the changes and development that might have taken place.

Outside the cricket, Lord's has never really become a club where members meet during the day for coffee or lunch or in the evenings for an informal drink or a meal. The Lord's Tavern does provide a venue, but there is no semblance of a London club as a social centre. Lord's is quite central and does benefit from plenty of parking when there is no cricket. Several of the newly-elected women members and some longer-standing men members have mentioned that they would like that.

There is no overnight accommodation for members, as there is at the Cricket Club of India, although consideration was given to building a hotel with subsidised accommodation. It would allow more reciprocal links with other clubs, aside from the cricket. With the covid-19 problems, a hotel within the grounds of Lord's would have allowed a safe environment for the competing teams in the international matches being played in 2020.

The stands have no central heating and are not ideal for winter events, as the OCS stand at the Oval is and as are so many stands in Australia. Eventually, when the Tavern Stand is redeveloped, there will be an opportunity in a members' area for many of these facilities, though the cost may well remain prohibitive unless there is some prospect of a return on the investment.

MCC has always encouraged children by offering much cheaper tickets to matches. I would have liked the museum to have become more child-friendly, but space is at a premium and there is not enough room for more interactive display screens. Equally, I should like there to be some kind of junior membership club, centred on the website, with more interactivity and with opportunities for youngsters to come to Lord's on the less busy days. All cricket administrators have a responsibility to attract the younger generation to our game, and watching cricket is only one aspect of encouraging them to love it as so many of the older generation do. MCC could contribute hugely to this. At the Oval I introduced the Captain's Club and youngsters under sixteen were able to come to certain days of county championship cricket free of charge and meet the players, speak to the groundsman on the square before the match or at lunchtime and meet a celebrity.

Less importantly, but nevertheless something that could be considered, would be to move the ticket office somewhere on the site where there is access directly from the street. This would make security easier to manage within the ground. I was always envious of Melbourne Cricket Ground, where all the service vehicles entered below ground, avoiding the problems of pedestrian and vehicular access being together. At Lord's all the outer roadways are narrow and it is a relatively small site.

Underground entrance points for vehicles would be a great improvement. Parking would also be made easier and more spaces could be available.

There are disused tunnels underneath part of the Nursery Ground, and MCC pays rent to use the strip of the land above them along the Wellington Road. When Railtrack put the head lease of the top 18 inches of land above the tunnels up for auction, it was an opportunity for the Club to take control of the whole of its site. Although MCC made two offers direct to Railtrack, both were rejected and, subsequently, MCC was outbid at the auction. The sub-lease, which extends for well over 100 years, continues to be paid.

My memory of the time leading up to the auction is sketchy, because I was not involved in any conversations with Railtrack. I do remember the Committee taking advice from Gardiner & Theobold about the value of the land and agreeing an upper figure that the Chairman of Estates, Maurice de Rohan, and our professional advisors could offer at auction, which I did not attend. I have become aware many years later that Maurice was prepared to put up some money himself and requested permission from the Club that he should be able to make use of another £1 million from the Club's reserves but, at that time, MCC had just completed the Grand Stand and the Media Centre at a cost well over the original budget and the finances were not robust.

It is easy in hindsight to say that MCC should have done more to acquire the only part of Lord's that does not belong to the Club and that the Club should have increased its borrowing, but Charles Rifkind told me afterwards that the Rifkind Levy Partnership (RLP) was always intent on outbidding the Club no matter how high we were prepared to go, as he saw tremendous development potential.

Since my time at Lord's, RLP has put several development proposals to the Club involving large blocks of residential accommodation. There have been time-consuming arguments and costly and very unpleasant negotiations. My successors and the MCC Committee have been at the forefront of this, and the MCC members have taken sides leading to the high-profile resignation of Sir John Major, a member of the working party set up to consider the opportunities of maximising income from any commercial development.

Initially the Committee decided that all contact with the RLP should be via the Chairman of Estates, and I was told not to have any contact with their partners. I did attend a meeting at Lord's in November 2001 and a presentation by Charles Rifkind in January 2002, with Maurice de Rohan and David Batts. He had introduced himself to me at Newlands cricket ground two years earlier and, after his presentation, I was invited to his home to see the architectural plans and a very detailed model, which were most impressive and covered many of the ideas, which had been discussed in the early stages of the exercise undertaken by the Estates Committee to create a masterplan for Lord's.

There would have been many enticing advantages in accepting the RLP's 'Morley Plan'. The increasing sums of money being offered plus a number of new facilities for our use within the development seemed attractive. However, when the proposal was eventually put to the MCC members, they voted by a huge majority not to allow development along the strip. The Club has never chosen to do anything purely on the basis of money and has always put cricket at the head of its priorities.

In their determination to keep Lord's as the Home of Cricket, members agreed that it was essential to retain the Nursery Ground for matches, some of them as local community or charitable events, practice off the main ground and circulation and picnics on match days, which the buildings would have prevented. It is a facility not available at all Test Match grounds and, if it were possible to increase the grassed area, it would be an even greater asset. The dimensions of the outfield for all nine pitches on the square are suitable for Under-15 teams. Under-17 and women's cricket can be played on five pitches. There is space for 42 net pitches, plus any drop-in or hybrid pitches that might be in preparation in the future. Broadcasters park their lorries and vans next to the Indoor School, which is adjacent to the ECB offices and the MCC shop. That end of the estate is very well used, and apartment blocks may be the most lucrative but are not the best use of limited space at the cricket ground.

Advice from the police and our security advisor was that shared access with apartment owners to the parking beneath the Nursery Ground and new access points might bring additional security issues. In addition we would still have to pay a rent for use of our new facilities. It was thought likely that any development at the Nursery End of Lord's would come up against numerous planning obstacles, not least the proposed height of the buildings, the relationship with existing buildings and the possibility that the Media Centre might become listed. St John's Wood Churchyard is an important, historic space and the views from Regent's Park are very important. Permission for residential development would be very much dependent on the scale. Now that MCC has gone ahead with its own masterplan for development projects in all areas of the ground and has built the new Compton and Edrich Stands, there is even less scope for any buildings along the Wellington Road.

We must never forget that the RLP are property developers and that their main purpose is to make a profit from their investment in speculative land acquisitions. MCC is primarily a cricket club, which owns the world's greatest cricket ground and will always strive to preserve the character of Lord's. As arguments continued to rage less publicly, the RLP purchased a long lease of the tunnels below the land, although the Railways Act contains a provision whereby the authority which controls the live tunnels, now Network Rail, has a pre-emptive right to acquire the land back if it is required for operational purposes. The partnership has also bought some properties in Grove End Road, backing on to Lord's, so any relationship between the Club and the developers has deteriorated further.

I still hope a way can be found for MCC to acquire the land at the Wellington Road end of the Nursery Ground and avoid the five-yearly rent reviews, which lead to more costly and disagreeable negotiations, but the situation appears intractable at present. Unless some agreement can be reached, nothing will change for several generations, when the lease expires eventually.

8

Matters Arising and Relationships

Matters Arising

In a club of 18,000 members, all with an opinion and often a totally individual view on every decision taken, it is inevitable that there will be frustrations, pressures, disagreements about the way forward and resistance to some changes.

In fact, MCC has evolved over the years and it is not true, as once mentioned by one critic, that MCC members believe that 'change is something which people keep in their pockets'. There are some members who will seemingly never support the Committee's decisions, but the vast majority accept that the Committee, more than half of whose members are elected by the membership, does its best and leads the Club in the right direction.

Timely communication remains a key element in retaining the support of the membership. There has been a relatively small group of members unhappy with the governance structure of MCC but, as with any structure, it works provided the occupants of the senior positions have the ability to lead in the right direction with openness and transparency. There have been numerous doubts expressed by a vociferous minority, papers on governance have been produced by working parties that have proposed changes, and MCC has grown from a cricket club, run by committees and determined individuals, to a highly competent cricket and business organisation overseen by committees and managed by a skilled executive staff. The senior employee, now named the Chief Executive & Secretary, sits at the centre and has to weld together all the executives and non-executives, much in the way that the Secretary and then the Secretary & Chief Executive did.

One of my abiding memories from my time at the heart of MCC is of the member who wrote over 180 letters or faxes to me in the first three months of one year. As the artistic director of the Welsh National Opera, he was articulate, intelligent and initially made some excellent points but, as each piece of correspondence was often several pages long, contained numerous,

149

detailed questions which demanded answers and usually impugned the integrity of the MCC Committee, he caused huge interruptions to the normal running of the Club. I answered many of his points, but it took a lot of time and research, and each response was met with yet another long-winded letter. At one stage in the middle of this barrage, one of our barristers on the MCC Committee suggested that I should take him on as a vexatious litigant, but that would not have helped the situation when there were other pressures from all sorts of different areas and he had some support from a group who loved to bash the Committee whenever they could.

At the AGM, following this mass of paperwork, he stood up and said that he wished to complain about the Secretary, who did not answer his letters. When invited to respond by the President, my reply, that I had received 182 letters or faxes from this member and had answered most of his many questions in 90 of my own letters, was greeted by applause and a collective laugh from those present.

This particular member started with some valid points, but his insistence on endlessly repeating the same points in letters and at AGMs did not help his cause. There was an adverse reaction whenever he stood to make another point at AGMs and he became a laughing stock, which was unfortunate, because he had started with the best of intentions.

He was not alone in banging on about the Committee's or individuals' failings and it is a time-consuming exercise, which has to be managed. To this day it continues, though, fortunately, it appears that the majority of members have little appetite for constant carping, particularly when some of the gripes and criticisms go back as far as 1987 and often further.

The AGMs highlight the maxim that 'A wise man is someone who has something to say. A fool is someone who has to say something.' Undoubtedly the majority of views expressed and questions asked are wise, sensible and well thought through and are rightly put to the Committee and others at the main annual meeting. However, there is a small group of members, who see it as necessary to promote their ideas, criticisms and seemingly their own self-importance at the AGM. They are convinced that they have better opinions on all sorts of matters than those who have been elected or appointed to oversee the running of the Club.

A touch of justifiable and constructive criticism can be helpful, but the fundamental criticism from these members always seems to amount to lack of transparency, lack of consultation, personal agendas and a revolving-door approach within the Committee, with the same old names reappearing time after time. There is an element of truth in this. Committee ballots tend to favour famous cricketers and well-known members, which makes it difficult for new, fresh faces to be considered.

Unlike decisions taken in the confines of a school and most of those taken in a cricket team, MCC's major decisions are almost always exposed to public scrutiny. Opinions from disenchanted members are often aired in the media, with one or two journalists, sadly MCC members themselves, rubbing their hands in glee while expressing their own negative views and, frustratingly, perpetuating the outdated view of some detractors that the Club is still firmly rooted in the last century or even the one before.

MCC is an international institution and an influential part of cricket's establishment. Over the years it has been faced with many challenges, many changes and some criticism, but overall there has remained a respect, somewhat begrudging in some parts, for what the Club has managed to achieve. New approaches to the game have challenged the traditional views, increased demands from television companies, who have paid large sums into acquiring broadcast rights, have put pressure on ground owners, and governing bodies have become more aware of the commercial opportunities of cricket.

During the twelve and a half years that I was in post at Lord's a large number of major matters had to be faced. The continued need to maintain and improve the Home of Cricket has been documented already. There were quite a few vitally important debates that took place in the MCC Committee, where papers had to be provided, recommendations put and decisions taken and other matters that had to be dealt with immediately.

I shall deal with only eight of these here: the introduction of women members; the charging of members for access to Lord's; England's matches in Zimbabwe; the alcohol policy at Lord's; the relationship with ECB; the Laws and the new Preamble in 2000; MCC's reaction to the tsunami disaster of 2004; and the Test match versus Australia in 2005.

There were other matters, some covered extensively in the media, some remaining under the radar, which were equally time-consuming and all demanding the same attention to detail and good communication. I shall mention these briefly later, but they should probably be the subject of a separate book, concentrating on the Club.

MCC MEMBERSHIP FOR WOMEN

The debate about the momentous decision to admit women to membership in 1998 was possibly the most important. A change of Club Rules has always needed a majority of two-thirds of members voting and, although there was nothing in the wording of the Club Rules which actually prevented women from becoming members of MCC, attempts had been made in vain on a couple of occasions to introduce women onto the waiting list.

The Committee decided that a rule change would clarify the situation once and for all. Custom and practice had ensured that it remained a club for men only, despite numerous calls from inside and outside the Club for that to change. There had been two votes in the past on whether membership should be extended to women, but in 1997 a decision was taken that it was time for a third vote, because it was felt by the Committee that the mood had changed amongst the membership and also there were increasing pressures from outside.

A vote was held in February 1998 during the presidency of Colin Ingleby-Mackenzie. Once again, although there was not a large enough majority in favour of a change of rule, 56% of the members who voted were supportive of the Club opening its doors to women. This was problematical, given that there were now more in favour than against and, it was assumed, those who did not vote were probably either undecided or unconcerned. The President was keen to hold another vote quickly, although there were other voices proposing a wait of a few years. After lengthy discussions the Committee took the decision to forge ahead and see whether another vote, almost immediately, while the debates were still fresh in members' minds, would provide a sufficient majority. It was clear from correspondence from members that many did not appreciate how much this issue impacted on MCC's public role.

For the second vote a Mori survey was conducted to gather opinions, a brochure was sent to all members, and the President and the President Designate, Tony Lewis, signed a joint letter. Informal meetings were held at Lord's and around the country. Opinions were widely expressed and over 10,500 members responded to the survey, which made it clear that members wanted MCC to play a strong and broad public role and wanted to see that supported by commercial sponsorship or other external sources.

There were four factors, which had caused concern at the first ballot and which the Committee clarified. It was agreed that women would join the end of the waiting list as they were nominated, in the same way as men wishing to be nominated. This would entail a wait of around 19 years, unless they were elected as Playing or as Honorary Members. The Club did not propose to organise any mixed matches, but there would be a women's fixture list. As a narrow majority of responses to the survey was in favour of retaining a men's bar, the Bowler's Bar would remain for men only on all match days. (This decision was reversed after only a couple of years.) Fourthly, given the proximity of the Allen Stand Upper Tier to the home dressing room and its showers across a corridor, there was a view that this area should also remain as a men-only area when access for major matches was via the bridge from the pavilion.

The Committee put forward in the brochure 'MCC and the Future. Women Membership?' eight compelling reasons why it was recommending that members should vote 'Yes' so soon after the last ballot:

1. Attention will focus on Lord's with a World Cup in 1999.
2. MCC's ability to fulfil its public role depends on its reputation in cricket and business circles.
3. 82% of members agreed that MCC should work with other cricket bodies, all of whom wished the Club to admit women as members.
4. Commercial sponsors have already declined sponsorship opportunities with MCC purely on the grounds that the Club is not open to women. 76% of members believe that MCC's public role and new initiatives should be financed mainly through sponsorship and external funding as against increased subscriptions.
5. The Committee believes that MCC should recognise the growing interest amongst schoolgirls in the game. 374,000 primary schoolgirls and 83,000 secondary schoolgirls now play cricket.
6. Women also play an important part in cricket as supporters of the game, as sports teachers in schools, as coaches and as mothers encouraging children to play.
7. Virtually all major cricket clubs, at home and abroad, are now open to both sexes. The Committee does not believe that MCC should be an exception.
8. The Committee is concerned about the Club's potential vulnerability to future legislation in the area of discrimination.

But perhaps what best encouraged support was the question of whether MCC should be a gentlemen's club or a cricket club. If the latter, it was obvious that anyone, male or female, who played or watched and loved cricket should be eligible for membership.

It was far from an easy time, because there were members, who had voted against the proposition in February, who were extremely unhappy that the Club was to hold another vote, so that, as they put it, 'the Committee can get the result it wants'. There were some, who had voted in favour, who thought that it was wrong to be asked to vote again so soon.

However, the vote went ahead, and in September 1998, before the end of Colin Ingleby-Mackenzie's presidency, the membership delivered a majority above the required two-thirds and so women became eligible for membership.

The appropriate rule change was accepted and preparations were put in place for this major change to the Club. Decisions can take a long time, but implementation and realisation of them can take even longer! The first small group of women who graduated to full membership from the waiting list arrived in 2018, Chris, my wife, among them.

MEMBERS' ACCESS TO LORD'S

There was further unrest, which arose at the same time, because of the ICC World Cup in 1999. Members had never paid to enter their own ground to watch cricket but ICC, working closely with the England and Wales Cricket Board, which had recently superseded the TCCB, made it clear that every seat had a price and all spectators, including members, would have to be in possession of a ticket.

Rightly, in my view, the MCC Committee thought that it was wrong for all 18,000 members to subsidise the cost of tickets allocated to the 8,500 members able to occupy the number of seats available in the members' areas of the pavilion, the Allen, Tavern and Warner Stands, so the recommendation was to be that individuals attending should pay for their ticket.

The real problem was that ECB released the news of all tickets having to be purchased before the Committee had had the chance to communicate this or discuss it with the membership. We always did our best to ensure that the membership was informed before the general public or the media, but here we were caught unprepared and it unleashed a furious reaction.

As a former President, Lord Bramall, said to me: "In the army we always consider it unwise to fight two wars at the same time." Here were two major issues which had arisen at the same time, and the Committee and staff were drawn into two battles with quite a number of members. It was a very difficult period, especially at a time when there were buildings to complete, preparations for major matches to be overseen and the changes that were necessary for the admission of women members. There were endless letters and telephone calls from members to be answered.

In the short term, with the successful second vote on women membership, one of the key issues of 1998 had been addressed. However, the World Cup tickets continued to be a very contentious point, and various members raised any number of objections in preparation for what was to prove a most unpleasant AGM in April 1999. Colin Ingleby-Mackenzie had moved on by then, and Tony Lewis, his successor as President, bore the brunt of the wrath of a sizeable number of members.

Most AGMs until then had been held in the Indoor Cricket School. On this occasion the meeting was held in the Nursery Pavilion, which is a long and not very wide building. It might have been a lot easier if the podium had been placed at one end of the building, as has happened subsequently, but the AGM took place in theatre style, with the top table halfway along one of the long sides. Inevitably this led to a much more difficult room in which to chair an extremely fractious meeting.

Despite the lengthy preparation, it became impossible to conduct the business of the meeting. The top table consisted of four officers of the Club facing the massed members: the Chairman of Finance at outside right, the President at inside right, the Secretary at inside left and the Treasurer at outside left. To our left, but lower and slightly behind the podium, sat the Club's legal advisors. Immediately in front, facing us, sat the Committee with the membership stretching away into what seemed vast distances to our left and right.

From the start it was a nightmare, and the whole proceedings seemed to be orchestrated so that someone would spring up far to the left to claim a point of order, followed almost immediately by someone from the far right of the room. Some of the points of order were valid, others were not and were merely complaints about any and every thing that was on the agenda. For example, one man stood up and said that the AGM could not vote on the previous year's minutes, because there might have been different people present at the two meetings and therefore there could not be genuine questions or points raised as matters arising.

I was continually turning to the legal team for advice and to ask whether the points of order were valid, which in most cases they were deemed not to be. In the continuing chaos, I turned back to convey the response to Tony Lewis, who was on his feet trying to chair the meeting and being bombarded from every side. It would probably have made a wonderful comedy sketch, were it not such a ghastly experience for those on the top table.

However, after attempts to move through the agenda were delayed by these interruptions, including a refusal to vote in favour of the minutes, nothing else was put to a show of hands, which was the customary method of getting the agenda items accepted. It became apparent that the more vociferous members at the AGM were not in the mood to be appeased or reasoned with. After various attempts in vain to persuade these members to calm down and allow the business of the AGM to be conducted, the President rose to his feet again after about an hour and closed the meeting, stating that, as allowed in the Club Rules, he would reconvene the AGM at a future date. The Annual Dinner that evening was a welcome relief after the aggressive interventions of the afternoon. We all knew that the explosion had been coming, but it had been much louder, more confrontational and more sustained than expected, so a respite was welcome, but it was only temporary.

The AGM was reconvened within the three months that were allowable in the Club Rules and, in order to widen the number of members who would be able to vote on the various items, a postal vote was introduced. This decision was met by a small group with the complaint that it was unfair on those who had 'bothered' to attend the meeting. It did not seem to occur to the disgruntled group that not all members live close enough or have the time to be at Lord's on the first Wednesday in May.

As a result of allowing the vast majority of supportive members to cast their postal votes, key matters were duly passed, and the Club rallied round the Committee. There were still a number of furious speeches from some members who were extremely unhappy with the decision to charge for entry. A members' resolution that stated that the Committee would never again charge MCC members for entry to the ground without consulting and obtaining agreement from the membership in advance was passed.

Fortunately, this agreement has subsequently been given on a couple of occasions for ICC fixtures, such as the 2019 World Cup matches, without which the games would conceivably not have been played at Lord's. Since that AGM, the resolutions have all been subject to postal voting to allow every member the chance to take part.

ENGLAND'S MATCHES IN ZIMBABWE

Fiduciary duty could always cause a potential conflict of interest for MCC's nominee as a director of ECB, which I had been since 1997. Perhaps the most difficult decisions arose twice over the question of whether England should tour Zimbabwe.

The first occasion was a match scheduled to be played in Harare in the ICC World Cup in 2003. Because of political pressure and safety concerns, both England and New Zealand declined to play in Zimbabwe. England's players, backed by the ECB, refused to travel to Zimbabwe because of serious security concerns. The ECB had hoped that the death-threat letter they received from an organisation called Sons and Daughters of Zimbabwe would act as the key evidence to support their case, but the ICC Technical Committee ruled against the ECB after considering a legal submission from them in a seven-hour meeting. The ruling was a huge blow to England's chances in the competition as they went forward having effectively lost the fixture against Zimbabwe, who had been awarded all four points. They still had to face defending champions Australia, Pakistan and India with just three teams set to qualify for the Super Sixes stage. As well as missing out on vital points, the ECB risked a huge claim for compensation for cancelling the match.

The second moment arose in 2004 when England were due to play five one-day matches in Zimbabwe in October and November, as scheduled in the ICC Future Tours Programme Agreement (FTPA), which had been accepted by all the ICC Full Members. Robert Mugabe's regime was at its worst, and safety was not guaranteed. Several Zimbabwe cricketers had been sacked by their Board. The Australian Board was considering not playing a Test series there in May of the same year. The debate in the media and within the MCC Committee was intense, and opinions were split about honouring the fixtures.

This issue was one of the most difficult for me as a director of ECB. I was present on the Management Board and was expected to put MCC's view, which was not a united one. My own inclination was that England should not travel to Harare, and yet I had to take a decision bearing in mind my fiduciary duties as a director of the governing body.

Legal advice had been sought by ECB. Failure to proceed with the tour without an acceptably valid reason would result in ECB being found non-compliant under the FTPA. If ECB were to decide to proceed with the tour, the Board would not suffer any adverse financial consequences. Taking this decision, however, the risks would be commercial, political and of a public relations nature. The FTPA permitted a country to withdraw from a tour only on safety or security grounds or if its Government directed it not to tour.

The legal advice received made it clear that there were currently no grounds for non-compliance with the FTPA acceptable to ICC. The lawyers concluded that the current government advice did not constitute a valid force majeure. In addition, failure to comply with any ICC Regulation or Resolution could lead to suspension from membership of ICC, which could mean the immediate cancellation of incoming tours to England. This would potentially be a financial disaster, leading to insolvency. The lawyers emphasised that: 'A Director's principal fiduciary duty is to act in good faith in the best interest of the Company. When the Company is solvent the best interests of the Company equates with the best interests of the Company's shareholders as a general body. If the Company faces insolvency then those best interests equate with the best interests of the Company's creditors as a general body.'

It was confirmed that individual Board members were not obliged to vote either for or against the tour and were free to determine subjectively what they believed to be the best interests of the ECB, having considered all the issues, facts and advice. However, the legal advice taken on behalf of the ECB recommended that directors should honour an oral contract with ZCU by the ECB Chairman, David Morgan, who had said in Harare that, provided Zimbabwe toured England in the summer of 2003, England would tour Zimbabwe in October 2004, barring any safety or security concerns.

It remained unclear when the ECB Management Board would need to make a final decision. The Chairman was expecting to call for a vote on 8 June, but the ICC Executive Board was due to debate the Zimbabwe tour at the Conference in early July and the ICC President, Ehsan Mani, had asked David Morgan to delay any vote until after that meeting. Unless ICC decided to omit Zimbabwe from the Future Tours Programme or to suspend the country's membership from ICC, the One-Day Internationals between Zimbabwe and England would remain in the list of fixtures to be played in October/November 2004.

The Management Board was to meet Jack Straw, the Foreign Secretary, who it was hoped would clarify the government's thinking and possibly direct the tour not to go ahead, and so it was likely that the debate at Board level would be delayed again. With other Full Members of ICC not supportive of ECB's withdrawal from the tour and having recently introduced the FTPA, the sanction of suspension was a realistic possibility. Seven out of the ten Full Members would have to vote in favour of a suspension and a reliable friend, who attended the ICC Executive meetings, confirmed that only New Zealand was likely to support England.

MCC debated the matter on more than one occasion, and views were being forcibly expressed by members. At the MCC Committee meeting on 10 December 2003, the Committee was firmly of the opinion that the tour should not go ahead as a matter of principle. No public statement was made, but ECB was informed. A second discussion at the Committee meeting on 21 April 2004 resulted in a change of opinion amongst those same Committee members. A vote on this occasion took the more pragmatic decision that MCC should support the ECB view that the tour was becoming inevitable in order to avoid a sanction being imposed by ICC, which might lead ECB into a financially unsustainable position. This decision led to the resignation of Robert Griffiths from the Committee, stating that he believed that ICC would be acting unlawfully if they suspended England. In his view as a QC it might be legally argued that it was an 'abuse of a dominant position'.

At the MCC Committee meeting immediately preceding the AGM on 5 May, there was a strong feeling that the members at the AGM should be told of the Committee's recent thinking and that there should be a debate at the AGM. However, it was eventually decided that there would not be a vote or even a straw poll. Although it was clear that the situation changed on an almost daily basis, the MCC Committee was moving against the views expressed by the membership at the AGM, which were clearly that it was a matter of principle and that England should not tour Zimbabwe.

Since that discussion the Zimbabwe versus Australia Test series had been postponed, although Cricket Australia had made it clear that it was unlikely to be able to reschedule the matches in the next four years. The One-Day Internationals were played, but the Zimbabwe team, without many of the contracted players who had been sacked, was extremely weak, making it a ridiculously one-sided series.

In the circumstances I requested assurance from the MCC Committee that I was free to make an appropriate decision, with which I felt comfortable, at the time that any vote was taken within ECB. A mandated decision does not fit easily with the fiduciary duty of a director, as was highlighted at that time in the Carpenter Report reviewing ECB's corporate governance. Equally, I was personally unwilling to vote in favour of the tour going ahead when all three main political parties, our membership and public opinion were firmly against England playing in Zimbabwe.

There were strong arguments for making a stand against a regime that had been heavily criticised and which constantly made threats against any opponents, of which England, as the former colonial power, was seen as one. There was little doubt that the integrity of cricket at the highest level was being compromised after the sacking of the contracted players by ZCU, which was seen as a racist move. Also there could be no guarantee that the cricketers, the officials, the supporters and the media would be safe in Zimbabwe. In fact, journalists had been expelled quite recently from the country.

As could be seen from the two conflicting votes in the MCC Committee, the views expressed at the AGM and the diversity of opinion put forward in the media, this was not an easy decision to make. As a member of the ECB Management Board, I would have to bear in mind my fiduciary duty and also my duty of care to the players and then decide how to react if the other directors voted differently from me. I was conscious that any actions that I took would be taken as an ECB Management Board director but, as Secretary & Chief Executive of MCC, I did have to consider carefully my position and any major steps, which might affect the relationship between MCC and ECB.

There were a number of aspects that I needed to address. First the moral question. I believe that cricket should be played in nearly all circumstances as a means of building bridges between people. Occasionally, however, there are circumstances which make it unpalatable for a national team to play in another country.

Personally, I did not accept that England should play in Zimbabwe where there were clearly many instances of appalling intimidation, political interference, rape, torture and murder being reported. Robert Mugabe had recently been quoted as saying: "Our opponents already smell their demise. They now fear elections and are giving all sorts of lame excuses for boycotting elections. We dare them. Boycott or no boycott, they are ripe for burial and we will put them to eternal sleep in March next year."

I believed that general sanctions should be applied against the Zimbabwean regime. Zimbabwe had resigned from the Commonwealth, had banned 119 prominent Englishmen and Europeans from entering the country, in response to the ban on its own government members from visiting Europe. The European Community had asked member countries to avoid sporting contacts with Zimbabwe. Zimbabwe had lost the support of the IMF and had been severely criticised by Amnesty International. Britain, other EU members, the United States, New Zealand and Australia had in the past imposed sanctions on senior government and Zanu PF officials as well as businessmen and bankers considered to have links with the ruling party. All UK political parties were opposed to the tour, though the Government was not prepared to ban the team from touring. The media were for once united on an issue. The issues at stake were much greater than a cricket tour.

I have never taken a decision not to play a fixture lightly. The ZCU brought their team to England the previous summer, and I was happy to stage a Test match at Lord's. I would have been happy for England to play matches against Zimbabwe on neutral territory, because the world had no quarrel with the Zimbabwean cricket team, even though their Board was politically influenced. As I was not personally prepared to travel to Zimbabwe in the current circumstances, I was not prepared to say that an England Team should travel there. If others wished to take that decision, it was up to them. I thought the ECB Management Board would be wrong to make the decision to tour and effectively leave the individual players to make their own decisions based on morality and conscience. The players might have been prepared to go to Zimbabwe, but I questioned whether it was entirely safe for players, officials, spectators and the media if they expressed their own views. I asked Peter Chingoka, the Chairman of the Zimbabwe Cricket Union, this question at the ECB Management Board meeting and did not receive a satisfactory reply.

The second consideration was the threat to the integrity of cricket. The Zimbabwe Cricket decision to sack players was based ostensibly on racist policies, unacceptable in the game and not dissimilar to the South African apartheid position before South Africa was excluded from international competition. Political interference in the affairs of the national cricket boards was not acceptable to ICC. Already some England players had said they would not join the tour for personal reasons. It did not help that the London Olympic bid for 2012 made it more difficult because the government needed the votes of the African nations and also the relationship between ECB and the other ICC Boards was at its lowest ebb.

It was a great pity that any commitment was given to reciprocate and play in Zimbabwe if that team played in England in 2003.

The most distressing feature of this sorry saga, though, was the way that an excellent paper produced by Des Wilson was mishandled. He had been elected as chairman of the ECB's Marketing and Communications Advisory Committee on the recommendation of MCC in June 2003, having joined the ECB in the autumn before. This was after England's shambolic boycott of its World Cup fixture in Harare, when ECB had delayed and not worked closely with the England players over the decision whether to play the match in Zimbabwe, before pulling out. He was asked to take responsibility for the Board's approach towards Zimbabwe in an attempt to avoid a repeat of that episode, with a brief to form a strategy that would allow the ECB to set its own course on overseas tours and provide English cricket with a viable get-out clause to avoid the impending tour to that country. His paper was a serious attempt to fulfil that responsibility.

Des, who played an increasingly central role on the issue, argued that the ICC would never have carried out a threat to 'ban' England because it would have been internationally criticised as a moral loser and also an equal financial loser, but he argued also that, if ECB directors cancelled the tour, the Board would not necessarily be ignoring its 'fiduciary duty'. His point was that the best interest 'of any Company' did not always lie with financial issues alone but included the value of its ongoing relationships, reputation and many other factors. He also argued that there was never a threat of insolvency as, should England be denied a year or so of international cricket, activities could have been organised to reduce at least part of the loss.

Des Wilson's paper was widely praised within the MCC Committee, within the game and in the media as being well balanced. He spoke to the England team on the issue, and ECB director Dennis Amiss, who was present, told the ECB Board that in no way did Des seek to force his views but simply presented the players with both sides of the question. His paper identified the six points he believed should be considered in such situations and ended there. He would rightly argue that those six issues led to only one conclusion, but he did not take the opportunity to say so, allowing them to speak for themselves.

I was concerned about my position, but I felt sympathetic towards the ECB Chief Executive when he resigned. I did not always agree with the policies being implemented by Tim Lamb, on behalf of the Board, but he was a man with whom I had a good working relationship. I did not know whether this episode brought about his resignation, but the article by Matthew Engel in the *Financial Times* on Friday 28 May 2004 raised that possibility. The article summarised the situation very accurately, as one might expect from a writer with his finger on the pulse and a genuine love of cricket. It also gave me hope that there might actually be a sound reason to vote against the tour going ahead.

As MCC Secretary & Chief Executive I now had a changed mandate to support the ECB Management Board majority decision, instead of the earlier decision of the MCC Committee to vote against. As an ECB Director, I was being told that legally the tour should go ahead. Should I abstain? Even if I voted against the tour, once a decision was made I was bound by collective responsibility for that decision. Personally I was not prepared to accept that situation and so I thought that I should resign from the Board before the vote. Looking back, I think that I should have done that, even though there would have been repercussions within MCC.

When Des Wilson resigned from the ECB Board, he wrote to David Morgan stating that he had presented a report to the Board earlier in the year saying moral considerations should be taken into account before touring and said he could no longer share the Board's collective responsibility should they decide to tour. 'My differences lie with where we go from here,' he wrote in the letter that was reprinted in the *Guardian*. 'I do not claim superiority of judgement or greater moral virtue – we just differ, but the differences are so profound that my position is I believe untenable.'

The media were full of the story. He was quoted: 'I am unable to share collective responsibility for the ongoing strategy in relation to the Zimbabwe tour. I have no desire to offer succour or support to the ECB's critics at a difficult time. This is not an 'I'm right, you're wrong, I'm off' resignation. We simply differ, but the differences are profound. It is right, therefore, that I should go and thus enable the Board to unite around the course it believes to be right.'

He added: 'The fact is the ECB has been placed in an intolerable position by the ICC's inflexible and, in my view, malevolent enforcement of its international tours programme with draconian penalties that would devastate the English game, forcing the ECB into insolvency and bankrupting up to a third of the first-class counties. In the short term, I believe the ECB should make such a tour only under protest. Even if this tour goes ahead, I believe the ECB should commit itself to fight for as many years as it takes to change the protocol so that no other country can be coerced in this way. Alas, there appears no appetite for that course of action, either.'

Writing in the *Guardian*, he described the ECB management as 'buffoons', their counterparts on the International Cricket Council as 'charlatans' and said, 'Whatever happens now, it is clear this tour should have been called off a year ago.'

'In the paper I wrote for the ECB at the beginning of the year I identified six justifications for abandoning an international sporting tour,' he wrote. 'At least five of the six have come to pass. The ECB did not even discuss my paper. The ICC rubbished it.'

The ICC response to the paper was: 'Mr Wilson's attempts to pressure people were naive and ill-considered. The paper he leaked at the outset of this issue highlighted the fact that while he sought to force his own view of the world on others, he lacked the ability or willingness to listen and understand the views of people who did not share his perceptions. His comments today will only reinforce this perception among other boards.'

As mentioned above, the paper Des Wilson produced did not, in any way, seek to impose his personal views on the ECB Board.

The media coverage made the point that the ECB would avoid punishment if the Government ordered it not to tour, but senior Foreign Office sources had ruled out any hardening of the existing line, which was that the Government had no power to prevent the tour taking place, prompting criticism from the Conservative party.

At the Management Board meeting Des proposed that if the tour went ahead it should be completed 'under protest' to signal disapproval of the Mugabe regime, that the ECB should campaign to change ICC regulations, which take no account of political or human rights conditions in its members' countries, and that it should address his proposal that moral considerations should be taken into account when considering where to tour. All three of these proposals were rejected, prompting his resignation.

One article continued: 'The ECB was set to adopt his proposals, but in March the ICC president, Ehsan Mani, persuaded Mr Morgan to hold off ahead of the ICC annual general meeting in March. Instead of helping Mr Morgan find a solution, however, the ICC passed a new regulation under which the ECB would face a one-year ban from international cricket if it did not fulfil the tour. This prompted Mr Wilson's most stinging criticism yesterday: "No one should have the power to force anyone else ... to suspend their moral judgment. The proposition that maintenance of an international programme of cricket tours matters more than any other consideration has to be contested."'

Eventually, on the eve of England's Champions Trophy match versus Zimbabwe being staged at Edgbaston, the ECB decided that the tour must go ahead, subject to it being safe and secure to do so and in the absence of firm instruction from the government not to tour. The fear of financial loss and suspension was too great.

Whether Peter Chingoka's letter to all the first-class county chief executives was instrumental in persuading the Board to vote in this way is doubtful, but the counties were definitely concerned about possible loss of revenue from ECB. His letter made strong arguments: the commitment from the ECB Chairman David Morgan would be viewed by the ZCU's lawyers as legally binding; Zimbabwean cricket would be compromised by the loss of TV rights and other commercial contracts, foreign currency and ticket sales, for which he would seek compensation; faith, respect and trust had been severely undermined in the ECB Chairman and Chief Executive, as ECB was considering reneging on the agreement without the courtesy of ZCU being given notice or consulted in any way whatsoever; England were currently very unpopular within the world game, as there was lingering resentment among several Boards by the way ECB had disrupted the World Cup the year before, which cost the ECB £1.5 million in revenue.

Michael Ancram, the shadow foreign secretary, called for the foreign secretary to step in, saying: "The ECB has been left in an impossible position over the tour to Zimbabwe. Jack Straw knew what was required of him but he failed to be sufficiently robust. The government must now make its views absolutely clear." Richard Caborn, the sports minister, said the government would prefer that the tour did not go ahead but that the decision was down to the ECB. "Obviously, they've had advice that England men are unlikely to opt out. We don't think it's in the benefit of cricket to tour, but at the end of the day it's a decision for the governing body to make."

Ultimately there were a couple of players who opted not to tour and ECB omitted a couple of others, but the tour went ahead.

It was not long afterwards, in 2006, that Zimbabwe decided that it would not play Test cricket. Peter Chingoka, chairman of Zimbabwe Cricket's new interim Board, said the decision to withdraw from Test cricket was made after "consideration of the recent performances by the national and A teams". This was the second time in 20 months that the country had been forced to cancel its Test commitments.

Stuart Carlisle, the former Zimbabwe captain, said: "The whole situation could have been avoided with action a year and a half ago. In April 2004,

ICC chief executive Malcolm Speed travelled to Zimbabwe to talk to the country's cricket chiefs about a boycott by the country's top white players. He was forced to return home after the Zimbabwean officials refused to meet him. Instead of sending Speed, they should have sent a committee. They should have sent a three-man research team and spoken to players and administrators. They always get one side of the story. They could have sorted this out a long time ago. Zimbabwe will not be able to return to the Test arena until deep-seated problems are resolved."

In July 2019 Zimbabwe was suspended and funding was stopped by ICC as the actions of the Sports and Recreation Commission were deemed to constitute government interference in Zimbabwe Cricket's affairs. ICC Chairman Shashank Manohar said: "We do not take the decision to suspend a member lightly, but we must keep our sport free from political interference. What has happened in Zimbabwe is a serious breach of the ICC Constitution and we cannot allow it to continue unchecked." This was the first time that a Full Member had been suspended by ICC.

It was an extremely divisive period and might so easily have been better managed if the ECB Management Board had been given Des Wilson's paper and the opportunity to discuss it at length. If ICC had been more understanding and supportive this situation might and should not have arisen.

THE ALCOHOL POLICY AT LORD'S

Safety and security at sports grounds have become ever more important as threat levels have risen and incidents have been recorded. MCC, as an unincorporated club, took full responsibility for Lord's as the Ground Authority, and my name was on the safety certificate. ICC was concerned about some aspects of safety at a number of grounds around the world and issued a blanket policy for each national governing body to implement, which would ban all bottles and cans from being brought into a ground by spectators. This threatened to enforce a change to our Ground Regulations, which had been in place for many years, so I was given the task of writing a paper for ICC and speaking to this paper at the ICC Chief Executives' meeting at Lord's in June 2005.

I went to the ICC meeting soon after there had been an incident at Lord's. One of the Australian team, Michael Bevan, was hit by a beer can, whilst standing on the middle balcony of the pavilion for the presentation ceremony. I argued that there were two issues to be faced: drunken behaviour and objects that could pose a threat if thrown. I suggested that a drunken spectator constantly visiting the many beer, wine and champagne outlets in the ground was probably more likely to behave badly than someone drinking one bottle of wine with his wife or a friend on the Nursery Ground, in the Coronation Garden or in a stand. Licensing hours were controlled by the local councils in England, but at Lord's we retained the right to close bars at any time during the permitted hours and did so.

I stressed that MCC put the safety and security of players, officials and spectators at the head of its list of priorities and worked extremely closely with Westminster City Council in agreeing the ground's safety certificate, without which the ground would not be allowed to operate, and with the police in stewarding the ground. The Lord's Ground Regulations were supported by a clear Alcohol Policy and a clear Policy on Access Control.

Clearly, every international cricket ground needed an effective policy in place to monitor, control and, if necessary, to limit the amount of alcohol consumed by individuals. It had always been MCC policy to allow a very strictly controlled amount of wine (1 x 75cl bottle), beer (2 pints), soft drinks or water to be imported in cans or bottles by members of the Club and the general public for use on the Coronation Garden or the Nursery Ground or in the stands. It had been the deliberate intention of the MCC Committee over many years to encourage the 'atmosphere of the village green' and a 'culture of picnic baskets on the grass areas' surrounding the main ground. This had been thoroughly successful in preserving a unique atmosphere at Lord's, where there were relatively very few incidents of drunkenness during international matches. There was great concern in the MCC Committee that a new policy would adversely change this atmosphere and would not improve the safety and security at the ground but might actually be detrimental to it. So, MCC was appealing to ICC to permit Lord's to be treated individually and released from the constraints of this regulation, which ICC had wished to see applied to all international grounds.

I mentioned that, after the Michael Bevan incident, MCC had changed the policy and no longer permitted spectators at international matches to enter the field of play even after the close of play. There were no other recorded incidents at Lord's where missiles had threatened the safety of players. Vast numbers of spectators had watched matches at Lord's over many years and the new ICC policy seemed to be an unnecessary additional constraint on hundreds of thousands of spectators, who came each year to Lord's.

I argued that many different articles could be thrown and referred to an article in the *Melbourne Age* [26/12/2003] where mention was made of empty water bottles and a chewed bone, presumably from a chicken leg, being thrown. Also, recently, spectators at a football match in Turkey had been prohibited from taking in mobile phones for fear of them being used as missiles. In addition, coins, fruit, small pebbles or something bought in the shop, such as a cricket ball, were all to hand in any cricket ground. In MCC's experience, bottles were not the most likely projectile.

I concluded that in all crowd management situations it was vital to put in place clear regulations to attempt to limit the potential dangers and then it was the responsibility of stewards to ensure that these were upheld and that their own areas remained safe. Ultimate responsibility must lie with the Ground Authority and not with the bodies promoting the matches or overseeing the global programme. It was helpful to have dialogue with both bodies, but different circumstances prevailed at different grounds and, in MCC's view, it was not appropriate to attempt to impose a one-size-fits-all policy for such an important issue as safety. Indeed such a policy flew in the face of established principles of safety management.

The Club believed that ICC and ECB should monitor the safety policies which were in place, make suggestions if there were recorded problems at particular venues, but not impose specific regulations, the breaking of which might bring severe penalties. For the players, officials and administrators at all levels the most important issue was to feel confident that any venue had policies in place for ensuring as safe an environment as possible for the staging of a cricket match. MCC believed that a more general requirement from ICC would achieve that aim equally as well in the case of Lord's, and possibly more effectively, than a specific regulation, which highlighted only one aspect of the potential dangers that existed.

In the case of Lord's the ground regulations were circulated with the tickets. The policy on the importation of alcohol, and of soft drinks, whether in glass bottles, cans or plastic containers, was known by the spectators and had been very much the same for the last few years with minor changes as appropriate. Altering the regulations would incur great discontent. The clear preference of MCC was that, at Lord's, the Club should continue to implement the policies that had evolved over the years. We were not convinced that the proposed requirement to ban the importation of alcohol in glass bottles or cans would improve the safety at Lord's.

I was successful in my attempt, and Lord's was granted an exemption for that year from the ICC regulation. However, following that meeting, there was an interchange of letters between Malcom Speed, the ICC Chief Executive, and me and also a lengthy telephone conversation. He was basically sympathetic towards what I had put forward. In his first letter he wanted me to explain further the Club's Alcohol Management Plan, referring to a couple of incidents when drunken spectators had been ejected from the ground. My reply satisfied him. I suggested that the very small number of ejections from the ground over the past few years supported MCC's view that the current alcohol management plan was proving effective. Stewards monitored the bars. It was their responsibility to remind the bar staff, if necessary, to refrain from selling alcohol to spectators who were clearly the worse for wear. In the Control Room police, stewards and the Safety Officer permanently monitored the CCTV system, which comprised 120 cameras round the ground. Towards the end of the day police took up positions in the stands, but the stewards were encouraged to move, at an early stage, into any group becoming disruptive. If a steward was concerned that any spectator might be aggressive or might antagonise other spectators, the steward was expected to remove the person from the stand, either individually or with the assistance of the police.

Malcolm made the point that other sports venues sold beer in disposable cups. He asked whether there were ways to sell beer in plastic containers or for bar staff to pour the beer into disposable cups. I replied that Lord's was a very small site compared to most others holding 30,000 spectators. At Lord's there were six permanent sites, situated behind or under stands where there was limited space for circulation. I confirmed that spirits were not available in public bars. Queues which were in place for too long created a Health and Safety problem. I promised to investigate with the breweries whether it would be possible to find a plastic container as an alternative to a can.

At the end of this drawn-out process, Lord's was granted an exemption from the ICC regulation for each year, so the mission was achieved and the regulations were added to the tickets just in time before applications began. The exemption continues to this day. Safety and security issues remain the highest priority for the ground owners, and it is very hard to see any valid reason for allowing anyone else to take on that responsibility.

THE TEST MATCH GROUNDS CONSORTIUM AND ECB

When I first arrived at Lord's I could not understand why so many antagonistic comments were made about the other body by both MCC and TCCB. It was a situation that I had inherited, and it continued throughout my time in the post. I got on well with Alan (AC) Smith, its Chief Executive, and on the face of it the individuals all related amicably, albeit with an underlying mistrust on both sides.

The longer I was in the position, the more I realised that there were two different agendas and a lot of historical baggage. There had been various spats over the years since 1968, when the changes to governance were put in place, but I hoped that the poor relationship might be repaired. For the most part these conflicts were overcome, but there were times when feelings ran high within MCC and in the newly created ECB under its first Chief Executive, Tim Lamb.

The dispute over staging agreements for international matches was one conflict that escalated into a real battle. The five other Test Match Grounds (TMGs), the Oval, Edgbaston, Trent Bridge, Headingley and Old Trafford, were as discontented as we were at Lord's over the high-handed approach from the governing body. ECB expected to dictate how the surplus from matches at our grounds was divided up, and the TMGs wanted a proper contract to be agreed. We could not accept that all decisions regarding the game's finances should be dominated by the non-Test Match Grounds, who had the majority vote in the Board and an interest in receiving a share of the revenue. It was a most unpleasant couple of years where relationships between the Board and the Test Match Grounds Consortium and between the TMGs and the Non-TMGs were very strained.

All six grounds felt that we were not receiving our fair share of the surpluses, especially now that there was considerable money coming in from the broadcasting deals. MCC and, separately, the other five Test Match Grounds as a group, had been seeking ways to ensure that there was a fair distribution between the Board, the grounds and the constituent parts of the ECB – the players, the non-Test Match Grounds, the Minor Counties and the Recreational Game.

Ironically, there had been a detailed written agreement in place one hundred years before, when MCC ran the game in the UK. In 1898 there was a Board of Control of Test Matches at Home, chaired by the President of MCC. Everything regarding the staging of the matches was clearly specified.

The 1898 Staging Agreement for Test Matches

1. **Umpires** – Umpires shall be appointed by ballot and shall be paid £10 per match.

2. **Distribution of profits** – All monies taken at stands and enclosures at the Test Matches shall, together with the gate money in respect thereof, less the Opponent's half of the gross Gate Money and less such expenses as are authorised by the Board, be placed in the hands of the Board for distribution as follows: 30 per cent to the grounds where the matches are played, in equal shares; 10 per cent to the counties that take part in the Second Division of the County Championship and 60 per cent to be divided equally among the First-Class Counties and the MCC. But should there be a loss on these matches such loss shall be divided among the said First and Second-Class Counties and the MCC in the proportion of their respective interests.

3. **Expenses** – The expenses to be deducted from the gross Gate Money (or in Test Matches between Australia and South Africa from the stand money) shall include players (including reserve men), police, umpires, scorers, gate and ground attendants, printing, advertising, luncheons, match balls, and any other items specially sanctioned by the Board.

4. **Players** – The remuneration of players shall be £20 per match; of reserve men £10.

5. **Amateurs** – Amateurs' expenses to be allowed are railway fares and a sum at the rate of 30 shillings per diem, not exceeding five days for each match.

6. **Luncheons** – The amount to be allowed for luncheon will be £10 per diem.

7. **Scorers** – Scorers shall be paid £5 per match.

8. **Advertising** – The sum to be allowed for advertising shall not exceed £30 for each match.

As we could not persuade the governing body that a mutually agreed written contract was required, the only action that seemed appropriate was for MCC to join with those other five grounds and form the Test Match Grounds Consortium which, with Robert Griffiths, a feisty Welsh barrister and MCC member, as its chairman, proceeded to lead negotiations with ECB in the persons of Lord MacLaurin, its chairman, and Tim Lamb.

Robert researched fully and clarified that, in English law, there were two major sets of rights that were important in sporting events: the access rights to the venue and the image rights of the people participating. ECB had its players under contract, as did other national bodies, so players' image rights had been conceded to the Boards. Access rights to all the grounds belonged to the clubs or counties who owned them or, in the case of Surrey, leased the Oval from the Duchy of Cornwall. Once this could be accepted, the distribution of revenue from broadcasting rights, advertising rights and ticket sales could be split in an equable way, which appeared reasonable to us as the landlords.

We produced contracts for the Board's use of our grounds. Initially the Board responded that this was unacceptable, and various threats were issued about taking Test matches to other grounds such as Chelmsford or Worcester, which was palpable nonsense given the capacities of these other grounds. Comparisons with the Brabourne Stadium in Mumbai, which lost its international matches to the Wankhede Stadium, built only one mile away, had been made before as a warning to MCC of the consequences of its perceived reluctance to conform to ECB's guidelines, edicts or directives.

Robert Griffiths was bright, a competitor and, as an experienced senior Queen's Counsel, not used to losing cases. I had been told very clearly by Lt Col John Stephenson, when he briefed me before retiring, that there was likely to be a battle with the governing body on this topic but one that I must win on behalf of the MCC Committee and the members.

The ICC World Cup was imminent in 1999, and there was a Test series against New Zealand later in the summer. The vagueness of the Staging Agreement issued by ECB on behalf of ICC for the World Cup had raised the hackles of ground owners, but it was the New Zealand series that became the centre of the negotiations between ECB and the TMGC.

The TMGC emphasised that there was a need to plan ahead to maintain and develop the grounds for international cricket. All the Test Match Grounds needed constant updating and renovation, and the return from international matches was essential for that work.

There was no intention to challenge ECB's position as the governing body of cricket in England and Wales. It did seem odd, though, that the Board should try to persuade the TMGs to accept its own alternative version of a Staging Agreement. ECB was told in no uncertain terms that it was customary for a contract to be drawn up by a landlord for the tenant to negotiate and then sign, not vice versa.

The key elements of the Staging Agreement, as far as MCC was concerned, were clearly outlined. A guarantee of continued major matches was vital for the Club's business plan (at that time Lord's staged two Tests and one or two ODIs as well as a domestic final). My name was on the ground's safety certificate, and I was unwilling to compromise on safety and security matters and hand over any responsibility to ECB's executives. MCC would continue to act as the ground authority, to protect the commercial opportunities, the retention of the atmosphere of Lord's as the Home of Cricket and to safeguard our financial needs, as the Club looked towards the development and maintenance of Lord's.

There were some most unpleasant moments during the negotiations, especially when I was told in an ECB Board meeting that I was a disgrace as a director. I had not been on the receiving end of such a tirade since the 4th form at school! It lasted for several minutes, and coupled with me in the criticism by the Chairman was Tony Cross, the Deputy Chairman of Warwickshire CCC and also an ECB Board director. Fortunately he was not there, because he was a fiery character who would have responded entirely differently. He would have returned fire with fire and the meeting would have become a slanging match. There had been more than one of those in the past few months.

I sat and took the onslaught and then calmly, and I hoped reasonably, explained how and why the situation had developed and why a staging agreement was essential for all concerned. I was surprised that other members of the Board seemingly were not fully in the picture. At the end of my explanation I was asked (or rather told) to leave the meeting while the Board discussed further. I walked around awaiting the outcome of the Board's deliberations. It was, though, reassuring when the Deputy Chairman of the Board came outside and told me that my comments had been well received and that it was important that they had been made.

It may have been a turning point. Eventually something had to give, and finally one or two senior members of the ECB Board sat down with our negotiating team to discuss the situation in a friendlier and more receptive manner. Suddenly there was less heat and more light in the negotiations.

The staging agreement was a complex document which encompassed many different aspects: cricket operations, financial, branding, legal, presentational, commercial and political issues. The final draft agreements were produced and signed to come into effect in time for the New Zealand series and last until 2002, when a new broadcasting deal was due to take place.

During my time as Secretary & Chief Executive there were more staging agreements to be negotiated and signed. They were marginally less contentious and the TMGC disappeared, as the six Test Match grounds, soon increased to nine International grounds, dealt individually with the governing body.

SHOULD MCC EVEN BE A MEMBER OF ECB?

There has inevitably been the potential for a conflict of interest for the MCC director on the ECB Management Board and the disagreement over the staging agreement led to questions about the Club remaining part of ECB. In advance of a Committee debate in 2004, I provided a paper detailing the perceived advantages and disadvantages of membership of the Board and the pros and cons of leaving.

Historically there had simultaneously been a number of different relationships: MCC acted as landlord in leasing a building at Lord's to ECB for its offices. MCC was a business partner with ECB in the original Lords.org internet website. When international matches and domestic cup finals were played at Lord's, some rights were contractually licensed to ECB under the terms of the Staging Agreement. The Club funded the ECB Under-13 club competition and aspects of the University Cricket Centres of Excellence as a sponsor of the Board. MCC has always retained a position within the governing body of the ECB and been a constituent member of it. Originally an MCC initiative, the Club now assisted in European development as service provider through a mandate from ECB, acting, as the Full Member in the region, on behalf of ICC.

MCC was internationally accepted as guardian of the Laws of Cricket. ECB, as a national governing body, played all its cricket under these Laws. MCC's ownership of Lord's Cricket Ground provided opportunities to stage its own matches. There was also a role with ICC, without our being a member of that body, as I sat on the ICC Development Committee.

As an independent private members' club, MCC employed the Young Cricketers, who played in ECB competitions with County 2nd XIs and other teams. MCC members sat on several ECB Advisory Committees as individuals but not ex officio. None of these needed membership of the governing body for them to continue.

There were obvious advantages in our being a member of the governing body. MCC had a direct link with the English game with an opportunity to participate in ECB meetings, to influence discussions on topics raised at these meetings and to cast a vote. ECB benefitted from the independent views, authority and experience which MCC could bring to the meetings. The Club could approach discussions from a different perspective from the first-class or minor counties.

On the other hand there seemed to be some disadvantages of membership of ECB. There was an inevitable conflict between the desire for independence and the requirement to accept collective responsibility. MCC was bound by the rules of ECB membership to accept the decisions of the First Class Forum and the Management Board. ECB was reluctant to treat MCC differently for fear of upsetting other members of the FCF, yet we were a different entity. MCC's presence in ECB perpetuated the misconception, including in the rest of the cricket world of ICC, that it still ran English cricket.

Were there risks in leaving the Board? The extent to which ECB would continue to value Lord's was unknown. Was there a potential risk that the Board might feel obligated to allocate more matches to the grounds of its members? This would clearly affect MCC's revenue streams although ignoring the ground with the largest capacity would also substantially reduce ECB's income from matches. In addition it would possibly reduce ECB's ability to attract sponsors, who generally entertained more at Lord's because of the facilities and because of the ground's location in London.

Would ECB mind losing the independent views that MCC could bring to discussions on matters involving counties, players and the relationship between the professional and the recreational game? Some senior ECB officials saw MCC's independence as a threat rather than a strength to be used by the Board, and it would be easier for ECB to establish its position as the governing body without our presence.

Some of us saw appealing advantages of being outside the Board but still working with them either contractually or as partners. The proposed objectives listed in the Griffiths Report of 1994 were all achievable whether MCC was a member of ECB or not. Point 3 of the report had strongly indicated that MCC should retain an independence to enable it to speak publicly in order to uphold the standards of the game. There was no mention of membership of the governing body. It would undoubtedly be easier to speak independently, as many members wanted, if the Club were not a member of the Board.

From a Secretariat point of view, the executive time preparing for and attending ECB meetings would be reduced. With one vote in nineteen at the FCF and one vote in fifteen at the Management Board there was seldom a decision in which MCC could play a decisive part.

If MCC and ECB were able to come together as equal partners, an extremely powerful unit could be created for the benefit of cricket in England and Wales. Commercial negotiations between MCC and ECB should ideally have been handled at arms' length. Negotiation of the staging agreement was much more complicated with the Club being a member of the Board, because 'conflicts of interest' of individuals on both sides were difficult to avoid. For the overall good of the game it might be better for MCC, as the guardian of the Laws of Cricket, to retain its independence rather than to be swallowed up within one of the ten Test-playing countries. Some members of ICC in their minds still linked MCC entirely with English cricket.

We were aware that there would be no advantage to cricket if MCC's role failed to complement and assist both ECB and ICC and was in any way divisive. The biggest disadvantage, though, seemed to be that leaving the governing body would be seen negatively by the English media who would probably portray it as a major rift in English cricket. MCC and Lord's were based in England and had always been firmly entrenched in England's cricket.

Invited to an MCC Committee meeting, the ECB Chairman, David Morgan, had stated clearly that he believed it was advantageous for ECB to have MCC as a member of the Board. The relevant minutes of David's presentation and the ensuing discussion were included with my paper. There was a lengthy debate. It was pointed out that, although my paper appeared to state that the advantages of remaining a member of ECB were fewer than the advantages of leaving the Board, some of the arguments in favour of staying might be considered stronger.

It was and is a much-debated and sensitive subject which continues to be alluded to by some MCC members on their independent website. In 2004 the final decision was that MCC should not, at that time, leave ECB. That did keep open, though, the possibility that leaving might at some time in the future become a sensible or necessary option. In my view it should not be feared, particularly now that the Club has no representative on the ECB Management Board, and the decision should only be taken after further discussion with MCC members and ECB. I remember the extract from the minute of the October meeting:

'The Secretary said he had no doubt that MCC could contribute as much whether or not it was a member of ECB. He thought there was a slight fear in withdrawing of the Club being marginalised. In the past, working with ECB had been very difficult, but that was not so much of an issue now. MCC worked closely with ICC but was not a member of that body. He thought it would be possible for MCC, if it was independent, to have representation on some of the ECB committees. He thought the Club should be talking to ECB about its independent stance, which was an important factor. He was of the view that at some time MCC would probably decide to leave the Board, but that it might not be the right time at present.'

Perhaps the analogy of Britain's membership of the European Union is an accurate description of this dilemma for MCC. Many of the Club's members, if given a referendum, might well decide that independence and neutrality would be preferable, whilst many in the Committee, in the same way as a large number of parliamentarians, believe that inclusion is safer and more beneficial. Time will tell in both cases.

THE LAWS AND THE NEW PREAMBLE IN 2000

As the MCC Laws Working Party set out to revise the Laws of Cricket for a new code in 2000, there were some fundamental principles to be examined. Cricket is the only game in the world in which the captains are responsible for the discipline of their team. In all other team sports the umpire or referee has a whistle to control and stop the game and the ultimate sanction of sending off a player. In cricket, umpires are the sole judges of what constitutes fair or unfair play and are given authority to impose sanctions in several specific cases, but they have to refer to the captains, who are responsible at all times for ensuring that play is conducted within the Spirit of the Game as well as within the Laws.

At that time advanced technology had been questioning many of the umpires' decisions and finding that, with the benefit of countless TV replays and slow-motion-magnified images, some of those decisions were at best doubtful and on several occasions clearly wrong. This not only made life embarrassing for some of the best umpires in the world but also publicly undermined their authority. It was not so much the players who showed dissent but the commentators, as all the viewers on television and the spectators watching the giant replay screens found the umpires wanting. It was noticeable, however, that the outgoing batsmen were beginning to take longer to walk back to the pavilion and constantly looked over their shoulder at the screen. The unwritten rule that the umpire is always right was being sorely tested.

There had been calls for technology to play a greater part in decisions during televised matches. Run-outs, stumpings and boundary decisions had already been accepted from a third umpire with a television screen. It had been suggested that radar could decide on lbw decisions and close-up, slow-motion photography could cover catches and near misses close to the wicket. Modern scoreboards now showed the overs and individual balls as they were delivered, so it might soon no longer be necessary for an umpire to have coins or counters in his hand. One international umpire made the point that he could well become an animated coat hanger, where players leave their sweaters, caps, sunglasses and even mobile phones. However, he did also say that if every appeal were to be referred to the third umpire there could be a problem in keeping the over rate above nine or ten an hour.

The first decision for the Laws Working Party was whether the umpires should be given a red or yellow card and the authority to take control of all discipline. There were many different views expressed, ranging from the necessity and inevitability of umpires having to take this ultimate sanction to the desirability of the status quo. The clear view of the Working Party was that the Laws of Cricket were written for all cricketers throughout the world at every level of the game and that should remain the case. In many instances the umpire might be the number eleven of the batting team; often only one of the umpires, sometimes neither, might have qualifications for the role other than their readiness and willingness to stand and officiate. International and first-class cricket were already played with additional regulations, in which the Match Referee had become an important figure. Perhaps it was important for these matches to be treated separately from the recreational game, although MCC was very keen to retain one set of Laws for all cricket matches.

Umpires themselves were not keen to see a change in the ethos of the game, and Test captains felt that they could control the situation. Nevertheless we had seen some areas of the game where self-discipline and fairness had become less apparent. Catches on the half-volley had been claimed, sledging had become more personal, abusive and calculated, appeals more orchestrated, and pressure put on umpires at every opportunity as fielders ran to congratulate each other and the bowler before the decision had been given. Batsmen looked away after nicking the ball, showed their bat when hit on the pad, rubbed their forearm when the ball had flicked the glove and ran down the middle of the pitch to rough it up for their bowlers. This had been apparent at all levels including at schools. So much for the expression "It's not cricket"!

For former cricketers the Spirit of the Game was, for the most part, accepted without question, and umpires generally knew who was likely to test the system in English first-class cricket or on their circuit in club cricket.

Now there were different views on this unwritten code of conduct, which was not surprising as attitudes had changed in the eyes of the world. It was not so much a question of whether a batsman was in or out as whether the batsman could get away with a decision either from an umpire's mistake or from an attempt to mislead the official.

Until 2000 the term 'the spirit of the game' was included in the Laws of Cricket without any definition at all. There was an assumption that it was a concept understood and accepted by all those who played the game, although it was interpreted differently in different parts of the world and at different levels of the game. The earlier MCC Laws of Cricket stated that 'Cricket was a game to be played within the Laws and within the Spirit of the Game' and left it at that.

With the new Code of the Laws at the start of the new Millennium, MCC felt it right to put into words some clear guidelines, which would help to maintain the unique character and enjoyment of cricket. Everyone in the Working Party was aware of how difficult it would be to attempt to define the aspirational term. It was easy to say of some action "It's not cricket", but nobody wanted this to be a negative Preamble.

After several lengthy discussions, it was decided that the key word was 'Respect'.

The four fundamental principles were based on Respect for:
   a) Your own captain and team
   b) Your opponents
   c) The role of the umpires
   d) The game's traditional values

It was not too difficult for players of all ages to accept that they should display respect to their captain and their own team. It was not quite so easy for players to show respect to the opposition, especially in teams where 'banter' had declined into 'sledging' over many years. In many cases, and particularly when decisions had gone against the player, respect for the umpires and the Laws of the Game was much more problematical and easily forgotten or ignored. The final sentence, which asked for respect for the traditional values of the game, merely showed that there should be a traditional approach, without defining those formerly unwritten 'values', so this sentence has since been abandoned. When the Preamble was still in draft form, the captains from all the Test match countries came together at Lord's and agreed that they were supportive of this new written code and would attempt to follow its principles.

Whether it is the Queensberry Rules in boxing, the Spirit of the Game in cricket, fair play or sportsmanship in any sport, which is best defined as 'ethical, appropriate, polite and fair behaviour while participating in a game or athletic event', it remains extremely difficult to find succinct wording for any guidance. The Laws of Cricket 2000 made a start and the Preamble was introduced.

Attempts have been made over the years to provide more detailed guidelines, but an aspirational concept is impossible to define conclusively and the fewer words to express it the better. The Spirit of Cricket touches on numerous aspects of the game and is worthy of a book on its own, as Mike Brearley has recently shown.

MCC'S REACTION TO THE TSUNAMI DISASTER IN 2004

The Club has a history of successfully staging matches of its own at Lord's. There had been previous matches between MCC or England and the Rest of the World at Lord's and, in 1998, a match was staged in memory of Princess Diana, who had died in a road accident on 31 August 1997. The date coincided with the 150th anniversary of the birth of WG Grace on 18 July 1848 in Bristol, so the memorial match was a celebration, not only of the Princess's life but also of WG's.

The match was very well attended, and television viewers were treated to a spectacular game played by most of the top 22 cricketers in the world at that time. Michael Atherton captained MCC and Sachin Tendulkar captained the Rest of the World team, which won the match.

There was during my time another MCC match to raise money after the devastation caused by the tsunami on Boxing Day 2004. Sri Lanka was the chosen beneficiary, and MCC played a televised match against an International XI in 2005. Stephen Fleming captained MCC and Brian Lara the International XI. On this occasion MCC amassed a formidable total of 327 for seven in the 50 overs, with the runs shared mainly by Stephen Fleming, Jacques Kallis, VVS Laxman, Andy Flower and Kumar Sangakkara. The International XI's reply tailed off quickly despite 68 from Graeme Smith and 42 from Brian Lara. Three spinners – Anil Kumble, Harbhajan Singh and Chris Gayle – took the wickets after Shaun Pollock had removed the dangerous Virender Sehwag early in the innings. It was another spectacular occasion, especially while Graeme Smith and Brian Lara were adding 75 in just eight overs as the asking rate was kept within reach, but once they both departed the rest of the International XI's wickets fell in something of a rush.

It showed how generous cricketers can be with their time in a good cause that again most of the world's top cricketers accepted the invitation almost by return of email. The money raised was spread between the Red Cross and Leonard Cheshire, who were immensely helpful in setting up the match with their fundraising ideas, with a further large sum left for a worthy cause of MCC's choice in Sri Lanka.

I was given the task of visiting that country and making a recommendation to the MCC Committee of how the sum of money could be best spent. I knew Sri Lanka well, and two very close friends from my Cambridge days lived in Colombo. I took their advice and also guidance from Sidath Wettimuny, a former Test captain who had become a friend, and was introduced to Kushil Gunasekera, an inspiring man who was devoting his time to improving the lot of the villagers in Seenigama, where he owned an ancestral home. He was the driving force behind the Foundation of Goodness, a charity which he had developed exponentially after the tsunami hit the area of Hikkaduwa, where a thousand people died on a train hit by the wave, and Seenigama.

He had been in Seenigama on that fateful Boxing Day and had been alerted by the local village people running and shouting: "The sea, the sea!" He looked out to see the onrushing wave and took flight along with all the others who were streaming past his villa. Fortunately he and others were able to reach a mound on which there was a Buddhist temple and where they took refuge as the first wave came in, retreated and the second wave arrived and went out again. When he returned to his home the water mark was a foot from the ceiling and he realised that, if his elderly mother had been there, as she had been due to be, she would not have been able to escape the force of the water.

There was little doubt in my mind, and the MCC Committee took little persuading about supporting the Foundation of Goodness. I set up an MCC bank account in Colombo, and Vijaya Malalasekera, a lawyer who was a Cambridge Blue in my first year, and Mano Ponniah, an architect, who had spent three years with me in the Cambridge team, agreed to oversee and authorise the expenditure that Kushil spent in setting up an MCC Centre of Excellence based on his ancestral villa and at a school in Sri Sumangala. They brought in an experienced businessman, called Ajith Dias, and so was put in motion a lot of support for the Centre.

MCC received regular reports, and in 2019 there were still some funds remaining to be spent. It is well worth visiting the Centre and many cricket teams and several MCC Presidents have been welcomed there and have been impressed with the outstanding work that Kushil and his team have done. For those unable to visit in person there is an excellent website:

http://unconditionalcompassion.org

THE TEST MATCH VERSUS AUSTRALIA IN 2005

MCC has always attempted to maintain a balanced fixture list at Lord's, providing cricket for schools, clubs and counties, but the international matches and domestic finals were the major matches. The week before a major match saw the security ramped up, an increased number of stewards recruited and trained, the safety of the ground checked and last-minute maintenance conducted in all areas. The teams practised for two or three days before a Test match, the pitch was prepared with the greatest of care and the catering and hospitality organised. The television crews arrived to install their cables and the many cameras that now cover the matches. Advertising boards were moved to accommodate ECB's sponsors. Accreditation was tight.

No matches attract more support than the Ashes Tests on the first few days. They are special days, but I remember one Ashes Test match in particular. On the opening day of the Test match in 2005 we had put additional security measures in place, and dogs trained to detect explosives had searched every nook and cranny of the ground before the gates were opened. London was on high alert for terrorists, so we made sure that our security was at top level. All spectators had to pass through scanning gates, similar to those employed at airports, and stewards were alert, checking entry tickets and passes assiduously as the crowd arrived.

The game started well with hostile bowling by England. Steve Harmison hit Justin Langer on the elbow second ball and, five overs later, he hit Ricky Ponting on the helmet and drew blood. At lunch Australia were 97 for five. Although Australia went on to win by 237 runs, events off the pitch remain in my memory rather more than the cricket.

Two weeks before the match four bombs had been detonated in London, killing 52 people, and on the first day of the match, Thursday 21 July, four more bombs were set off. The explosions occurred around mid-day at Shepherd's Bush, Warren Street and Oval stations on the London Underground and on a bus route on Hackney Road in Bethnal Green. A fifth bomber dumped his device without attempting to set it off. Connecting lines and stations were closed and evacuated.

The news was not broadcast over the public address at Lord's until an hour or so later, by when we had ascertained which underground lines were still operating. We told the Australian manager, and we agreed that it made sense for the players' families to stay at the ground and return to the hotel with the team. Several wives and children were taken into the Committee Room at the close of play to wait for the players to change. The Committee members responded warmly and welcomed the families to the Pavilion.

After they had all finally left the ground along with the players, I sat down with the tour management, and we spoke at length to administrators in Australia. They were anxious to know whether there was any danger in continuing the match and wondered whether the tour should be aborted. Eventually we managed to make them feel more confident and comfortable, and it was agreed that the match would continue. The events of the day had not interfered with the match in any way, yet we were all concerned at the uncertainty that terrorism is bound to bring.

The cricket on Friday was like any other Ashes Test – competitive and hard fought. Australia started to dominate as they bowled England out and began to put together a large third innings total. At close of play they had added 279 for seven to their first innings lead of 35. At the end of the day there was relief that the decision to continue had been taken and that there had been no further scares in London.

Saturday started in the same vein with Australia scoring well and beginning to look as though they were building much too large a score for England to beat in the fourth innings. Everything was going well until 11.50am, but then the day changed quite dramatically. An anonymous caller telephoned the Middlesex office and warned that there was a bomb set to go off at Lord's at 12.30pm. A similar call had been made to Rotten Row police station and also to a newspaper.

This is any ground administrator's nightmare. It was not the first time that it had happened at Lord's, but the circumstances of the last two days made me particularly concerned. The protocol for such a threat was for the two senior police officers at the ground, the Gold and Silver, to meet my security officer and me in my office. The four of us came together within five minutes, but that left us only half an hour to decide what to do.

Evacuation of the ground was one option. The police said that, as there had been no warning given and they had received no intelligence of any threats, it was more likely to be a hoax. They also said that our security measures before and during the game were very good and that the bombs two days before had been set off on the transport network and it would be unusual for a specific event to be targeted by the same group of terrorists. Finally they said that, if they thought it was a genuine threat and definite emergency, they would take over the ground, but Lord's was a privately-owned ground and the decision lay with the ground authority. Thanks!

That narrowed the decision down for two of us to make. My security officer, who was extremely experienced both in cricket and football ground operations, made two very persuasive points. He said that, in the time remaining, it would be impossible to evacuate the ground completely, and there was a danger that spectators might be going towards any danger, as there had been no notification of where the bomb was supposed to be. Secondly, he said that, as it was the first Test match of the series, copycat calls to disrupt other matches throughout the summer would almost certainly follow. The police officers agreed with both points and so I made the decision that we should not interfere with the cricket. It certainly was a risk, but it was agreed by all four of us. It was a ghastly decision to have to make, and the repercussions, if it turned out to be the wrong decision, were unthinkable.

The only additional thought from the police was that we should ask the stewards to look out for suspicious packages. I said that I was not prepared to send any messages out to stewards on their walkie-talkies, because someone might well overhear what was said and that might start a panic. I also pointed out that nearly every seat had a bag underneath with sandwiches and a drink, so it would be a futile exercise. It was tense as 12.30pm approached, came and went.

We were all mightily relieved when lunch was taken at 1pm and nothing had happened to disrupt the cricket or endanger those in the ground. The vast majority of the crowd, the media and the staff knew nothing about the incident. It was kept to a very small group. It was probably the most unnerving moment of my time at Lord's.

It was not the first bomb hoax, and I do not suppose it will be the last. It did ensure that the security was kept tight and that all the protocols were revisited. The rest of the match and the series passed without such an unpleasant incident and ended with the marvellous match at the Oval, where England won the series by two victories to one.

Was it the greatest Ashes series ever? It certainly was up there with the best and the spectators at the grounds and on television watched the fluctuating fortunes of the teams throughout the summer. But there might not have been a series at all if we had evacuated or if Australia had decided to return home.

IMPORTANT RELATIONSHIPS

Apart from relationships with ECB and Middlesex CCC, the county based and playing its home matches at Lord's, MCC has strong relationships with the world governing body, European cricketing countries and its own charity, the MCC Foundation. I was involved with them all.

INTERNATIONAL CRICKET

MCC is not a member of the International Cricket Council, though until 1993 the Club provided the Secretariat for the Council and the President of MCC was the Chairman of ICC. Things changed when the ICC appointed its first chief executive. My relationship with David Richards at ICC was strong, and we both fully understood how we might work together to the benefit of cricket around the world.

From 1993 until 2004 the offices of ICC were in the Clock Tower at Lord's and it was then obvious that increased office space was becoming essential. ICC considered the possibility of relocating away from the UK, which they subsequently did, but MCC did its utmost to find the required additional space in order to keep the world governing body at Lord's.

UK Sport had offered to approach the Treasury to gain permission for ICC, as an international governing body, to benefit from exemption from corporation tax and reduced rates. In addition ICC suggested a move to the larger space in the ECB offices in September 2005, as ECB had expressed a willingness to consider it, on the assumption that most of the Board's offices might relocate to Loughborough, leaving a few senior employees' offices at Lord's in the Clock Tower.

UK Sport had offered to fund up to one-third of the rental cost for ICC and had requested that MCC review the total rent for the ECB offices. Despite all these efforts, ICC moved to purpose-built accommodation in Sports City, Dubai.

We still worked closely as organisations. I was a member of the ICC Development Committee on behalf of the Club. The ICC Umpires' Manager attended the MCC Laws, Spirit and Ethos Sub-Committee. MCC received the agendas and minutes of the ICC Cricket Committees. MCC overseas tours to ICC Associate Member countries were organised after consultation with the ICC World Development Manager and the Regional Development Managers, in order to assist with their development strategies, and tour reports were copied to ICC.

From its long association with the international cricket world, MCC was closely linked to many of the Full, Associate or Affiliate members of ICC. MCC had given substantial support specifically to many developing countries within Europe and had assisted some of the best Associate members to become full Test-playing countries.

ICC Development Committee

Initially chaired by Ali Bacher, this committee was an outstanding example of what could be done to help develop the game and to encourage the spread of cricket globally. Ali was an experienced cricket administrator, an excellent chairman and someone who believed fully in the globalisation of cricket. It was a pleasure to be involved with such a forward-thinking group of former cricketers. Although the financial and political considerations were never far away in any discussions, the emphasis was definitely on what was best for cricket and how we could encourage more players to take up the game in countries with no existing cricketing culture. My experience in European cricket stood me in good stead, and other administrators also had ideas about the way to enthuse, exhort and persuade the ex-pats from various cricketing nations, who played and administered cricket in most countries, to encourage and include the local inhabitants and indigenous population.

I was asked to write a report about the 1997 ICC Trophy in Malaysia and recommend how the 22 competing countries could be divided into two divisions in the future. Although the best two teams, Kenya and Bangladesh, reached the final, some of the earlier games produced distorted results, because of rain and the influence of experienced cricketers enlisted to represent some countries. There was little doubt that there were seven countries which stood out ahead of the others: Kenya, Bangladesh, Ireland, Scotland, Holland, Denmark and Canada. Equally there were six countries which were definitely weaker than the others: Argentina, West Africa, Gibraltar, East & Central Africa, Israel and Italy. The potential growth of indigenous cricket was important to my recommendations for other positions in the first division as well as results in this particular tournament.

I travelled to all games in a coach with Papua New Guinea, who were a delightful group of people. They all sang wherever they went, accompanied by a guitar played by one of their team. Their cricket was rustic but quite effective against bowlers who did not have great control over the ball.

I had already spent a weekend in Port Moresby, the PNG capital, inspecting the pitches for ICC. I was welcomed at the airport by the chairman of cricket, a politician, and his Australian chief executive. On dropping my luggage at the hotel, I was greeted by a notice prominently displayed inside the room. Rather ominously, it listed ten essentials points, including to keep the door and windows locked at all times, not to answer the door without checking with hotel reception that it was a bona fide member of staff, not to wear valuable watches, rings or jewellery outside the room and to remember the 10pm curfew, which had been imposed by the government.

As we drove around, I was impressed by the large number of youngsters playing impromptu games of cricket in the street or on wasteland. I spotted a lot of houses built on poles over the sea and asked my host if that was to keep the homes cool. His slightly disconcerting reply was that it was for safety and security reasons, because the raiding parties that sometimes came down to the town from the hills did not have boats. The PNG chief executive worked extraordinarily hard to oversee the different grounds, one or two of which had barbed wire round the pavilions to restrict the 'rascals', as he called some locals who tried to live in them. It was a pretty lawless country at that time but, by contrast, the PNG players seemed almost the most gentle of all the teams in the ICC Trophy.

After a day of visits to the grounds to inspect pitches and net facilities, if there were any, the chief executive took me to the local men's bar for the evening, where most of the socialising seemed to happen. It was a friendly place, mainly filled by Australians working in PNG. At about a quarter to ten, I asked the CEO about the curfew and how long it would take to get back to the hotel. I was more than concerned when he said it would be about twenty minutes, but that he would take me via various back roads to avoid any police presence. He assured me that, even if we were stopped, the only likely outcome was that we would spend the night in a police cell and be released the following morning. I was not impressed and said that I did not think the ICC representative should find himself in prison for the night. In the end we saw nobody on our way home so I locked my door, as required by the hotel, and slept rather uneasily in a stifling bedroom. The trip was an interesting experience and another chance to see how cricket can enthuse people in different parts of the world.

Malcolm Speed, the second ICC Chief Executive, later took on the role of chairman, and we met twice a year, once in Dubai and once in different countries to monitor development. One of the meetings in 2001 was held in Kathmandu, where we were entertained in the royal palace by King Birendra of Nepal. It was inconceivable to read, a few months later, that the Crown Prince Dipendra had shot his father and eight other members of the family, in that same palace, before shooting himself.

The Development Committee was stimulating for us all, discussing high performance coaching methods and umpire training, recruitment of youngsters into cricket and support for fledgling administrations amongst other topics. We introduced a second tier of multi-day cricket below Test matches, the Inter-Continental Cup, and a series of leagues for one-day matches. The committee contained several distinguished cricketers as well as experienced administrators. It was fascinating to learn about their own problems in their countries and how they went about encouraging people to play the game. ICC was doing its best to coordinate cricket round the world, and we were part of that exercise.

EUROPEAN CRICKET

Cricket has been played in Europe for many years and, indeed, France was the winner of the silver medal at the Olympic Games in 1900 on the only occasion that cricket featured in the Games. There was only one cricket match played, won by Great Britain.

Following a meeting in Germany, the European Cricket Federation (ECF) was founded in 1989 and had as its first President Simone Gambino of Italy. The ECF comprised the European Affiliate Members of the ICC, who had no representation at the ICC conference and no funding from the world's governing body. The Federation organised tournaments, helped countries to administer the game with their limited resources and encouraged the expatriates to help in the development of facilities and indigenous players.

Simone was a dynamic personality who had driven forward Italian cricket, concentrating primarily on the local population and insisting on high standards. Italy's clubs were fined for arriving late, for not fielding eleven players and for not providing adequate facilities; even, it is rumoured, for wearing grey socks. No two non-Italians could bat together and non-Italian players could not bowl consecutive overs. He showed the same drive within the ECF, and his effervescent personality was persuasive and instrumental in increasing the profile of the Federation.

I succeeded Simone as President. The ECF's committee structure, over-complicated and very bureaucratic, was too reliant on MCC staff at Lord's.

There had been successful and enjoyable competitions in 1996. The Indoor Tournament at Lord's gave seven teams the chance to play at the Home of Cricket. Austria, who hosted the 1995 competition in Vienna using an indoor sports hall on a boat moored on the Danube, were rewarded with a victory in 1996. There was a Clubs' Championship in Bologna and a European Nations Cup in Osnabrück, on the British Army base in Northern Germany.

Don Oslear, the English Test match umpire, acted as the Nations Cup Referee in his usual robust way. A stickler for discipline and following the Laws to the letter, he had to remind everyone that the Laws and the Spirit of the Laws, which were somewhat difficult for some players to understand and accept, were an essential framework to all cricket matches.

The attitude of most players and administrators had been excellent, but in an indoor tournament when Greece were playing Italy, both fiercely and vocally competitive teams, there was an incident. The Greek batsman who had nicked the ball to the keeper went through every emotion ranging from disappointment, anger, sorrow, despair to acceptance that he was out before he dragged himself off, but not before turning to congratulate and shake the hand of the wicket-keeper, who had sprawled full-length to make an outstanding catch. At the dinner that evening I publicly congratulated the batsman on his display of sportsmanship. It was very unfortunate, therefore, when he was given out caught behind in the next round, he refused to walk off, gesticulated and shouted that he had not hit the ball and accused the keeper of cheating and the umpire of being incompetent. He was banned from the final for dissent, which rather contradicted his earlier display of the Spirit of Cricket. These contests were often volatile affairs.

MCC, as part of the new structure of ECB, was mandated to co-ordinate the ECF with the ICC European Associates and appoint a European Development Officer, as ICC started to organise world cricket on regional lines. The European Cricket Council (ECC) was set up in 1997, initially chaired by Doug Insole, a most experienced cricket administrator, who had played an enormous part in the growth within England's cricket through his many past roles, especially as England's representative on the ICC. Nigel Laughton was appointed as the first European Development Manager in 1997 and his salary paid by MCC. The seven ICC Associates welcomed assistance from ECB. ECF, which still included Italy, by now elevated to one of the ICC Associates, saw the advantages of being included. France and Germany were keen to join the list of Associates.

In the next ten years growth continued, as ICC created a stronger regional structure, based largely on the way ECC operated. The Asian Cricket Council, with its 21 countries, had developed with financial support from the revenues from TV rights attracted by Indian cricket. European cricket had 34 countries playing cricket but only had one ICC full-member country. The ACC had India, Pakistan, Sri Lanka and Bangladesh, with Afghanistan, and more recently Nepal, developing quickly. The 22 countries of the African Cricket Association (ACA) had beneficial links, both financial and in competitive cricket fixtures, with the ACC. The Americas Region, with 16, also only had one full-member country, the West Indies, but there was hope that the USA and Canada, where cricket had been played for a long time, might adopt the sport more wholeheartedly, despite the current TV sports continuing to dominate airtime. The East Asia Pacific, the smallest region with 11 countries, had support from Australia and New Zealand. EAP had benefitted from the strong Australian and New Zealand administrative expertise, and Japan appeared to have the most potential.

I took over from Doug Insole as Chairman of ECC after my retirement from MCC in 2006. As cricket was not an Olympic Sport, governments were not readily persuaded to offer financial assistance, so even limited funding from ICC was a bonus. As the ECC grew, there were now 10 ICC Associates in Europe, 17 ICC Affiliates and another 10 ICC Prospective members, all of which were encouraged to grow the number of clubs, tournaments and coaching courses.

There was a major step forward when three European countries, Scotland, Ireland and Netherlands, qualified for the ICC World Cup in 2007 in the West Indies.

By 2010 there were concerns about the legal status of the ECC. It was not incorporated, as were the Asian Cricket Council and the African Cricket Association, and there was no chance of recognition by the European Union because of its non-EU members. It was not a formal part of ICC, and there was growing uncertainty about the distinction between ECC and ICC-Europe, which ICC recognised as the regional body and through which European countries received any funding.

ECC had become little more than a talking shop. The constitution was based on a paternal and supportive approach from both MCC and ECB. ICC was now providing most of the funding and running the development programme. Things had to change. There was no longer a need for an ECC Chairman, so I stood down. The ECF, and then the ECC, had kick-started a unified effort to develop cricket in European countries, but now that ICC had decided to oversee the regions, it made sense for Europe to work more closely with the others.

The most exciting proposed innovation had been a cricket equivalent of golf's Ryder Cup. It would have provided an opportunity for the best players in ICC Associate countries in Europe and in the Americas. There might have been an opportunity to increase the revenue streams to benefit the development of cricket in both continents. A European XI had already played two one-day matches, one in 2006 in the Netherlands and the other at Lord's in 2007, both against MCC. Very sadly, though, it did not get off the starting blocks because of lack of funding and an already crowded competition programme. In addition ICC wanted competitive cricket to be played between individual countries and not regions.

The growth of cricket in Europe has undoubtedly been encouraged by the ECF, the ECC, by MCC and by the ECB and the later establishment of the ICC Development Department in 2001, which brought professionalism and very welcome funding to the countries. The main hope for future growth may be cricket's appearance in the Olympics, which will enable all cricket countries to access government funding and supplement the money received from ICC. This may be getting closer now that England and India have overcome apprehension about allowing the Olympics to be seen as a possible competitor to the World Cup and the other ICC tournaments.

THE MCC FOUNDATION

It was only in 1993 that MCC decided that it needed its own charitable foundation. David Hudd, the MCC Chairman of Finance, was the first Foundation chairman, and it was still in its infancy when I arrived in January 1994. Over many years the Club had provided financial support for small projects such as the provision of sightscreens, scoreboards, rollers, mowers and bags of cricket kit. Now it was the Trustees of the MCC Foundation who were asked to continue with this tradition.

David stood down after several years, and Charles Fry took on the chairmanship, appointing our first paid director, Sue Brealey. Before that, all the administration had been undertaken by a member of the MCC staff in addition to her normal workload for the Club Membership Office.

With increased income, the Foundation needed more focus. It was important to avoid initiatives already being funded by the national governing body or the counties or any other cricket charities such as the Lord's Taverners. The most glaring gap seemed to be for children in the first few years of state secondary school. Independent schools still coached cricket and arranged fixtures; Chance to Shine was making inroads into encouraging participation in primary schools. Little was being done, outside the county academies, which catered for the best cricketers of all ages, to help the talented children, boys and girls, aged between eleven and fifteen, who were in years 7-10 of state secondary schools. In fact, statistics showed that only 1% of state-educated 11-18 year olds regularly played cricket.

MCCF started by funding Hubs in seven areas of the country as pilot studies. A Hub consisted of indoor facilities, cricket clubs and young cricketers. The cricketers had to be at state schools and not receiving coaching through an academy. They were either in years 7 or 8 and therefore under thirteen, or in years 9 or 10 and so under fifteen. We decided that the GCSE year 11, might not appeal to some parents or teachers. I am sad to say this, because I feel it is important for children, even in the years of national examinations, to have exercise and sport as a break from study for their mental health and well-being.

Hub Managers were appointed. Advertisements in the local schools and trials were an obvious source of players; school or club nominations were another, word of mouth was helpful. Added to the ten weekly sessions of coaching from January to March was the encouragement of the cricketers to join a local club for the summer and enjoy matches. We sought schools where facilities would be provided free of charge, and we agreed to pay for the coaches and shirts and equipment for all those involved.

As Chairman of Governors, I was particularly pleased that King's College, Taunton was ready and willing to be one of the pilot studies. Richard Biggs, the Head, was keen on sport and accepted that the facility should be provided free. We asked Keith Parsons, a top-quality coach who had played first-class cricket for 16 years for Somerset CCC, to be our Hub Manager, and Dennis Breakwell, the College's groundsman and coach and another long-serving and successful county cricketer, joined him. What was important was that both had strong connections with local clubs and so the young cricketers were met by a friendly face when they first went, initially sometimes hesitantly, to the club to play in the summer. This and other Hubs were highly successful from the start, and we were all delighted to see, a few years later, five of the older Taunton Hub cricketers selected for the Somerset Academy squad alongside boys from King's College and Millfield School.

In 2019 the Foundation funded 50 Hubs across the UK for 1,900 young cricketers. Nearly all cricketers played at clubs and 19% went on to play representative cricket.

The MCC Foundation has followed the MCC's wish to support initiatives on a local, national and international basis. The Hubs are the main national project. Now with our third chairman, Phillip Hodson, like Charles a past President of the Club, there have been increased fundraising drives.

Abi Carter came as the director of the charity, replacing Sue Brealey, and helped to set up an initiative in Nepal. MCC has committed to three years of touring parties and the Foundation has funded a number of mat-covered concrete pitches as well as some cricket equipment and coach education. Nepal has the Asian instinctive love of the game and, between the Club and the Foundation, we hope that we can help raise the standard of the cricket sufficiently for Nepal to follow the example of Sri Lanka, Bangladesh and Afghanistan to become a Full Member of ICC.

MCC has a history of cricket development but also has donated funds in times of humanitarian disasters, such as in Sri Lanka after the tsunami. The MCCF is likely to be the vehicle for these in the future, if and when they arise. Recently, the Foundation successfully encouraged donors to contribute to an emergency appeal in response to the covid-19 pandemic, to fund meals for the most vulnerable in Westminster.

Also in Westminster, working alongside the MCC Community Development Department, we have funded a new tournament – the MCC Foundation Westminster League – to introduce local state secondary school pupils to the game, show that sport is fun and encourage them to play cricket.

New Trustees, a third director and the three other staff members are now looking to develop the fundraising efforts and continue to increase the amount available to put back into the game we all love. Our latest director, Dr Sarah Fane, has a distinguished track record in the charity world, having founded and led the Afghan Connection after working as a war-time doctor in Afghanistan.

As funding increases, there will be more opportunities for the MCC Foundation to continue to support local, national and international initiatives and projects. Some proceeds from sales of this book will go towards the MCC Foundation.

OTHER MATTERS THAT STICK IN THE MEMORY

Personal memoirs are not the place for lengthy descriptions of the many matters that arose at MCC during those years. We had a long battle with Kookaburra about the blades of their new 'Kahuna' bats, which were made of wood bonded with a graphite strip on the back. It took a long time to convince ICC and Kookaburra that the bats infringed Law 6.4 and 6.5 – The Blade and Covering the Blade – and should be banned.

There were numerous Committee discussions about management and governance. Most of them were based on reports all recommending that the executive staff at MCC should be given more authority to take management decisions, whilst the Committee should act in a non-executive governance role. The Senior Management Team agreed wholeheartedly. The best was the report by Sir Scott Baker in 2002, but it was not fully implemented by the Committee and so the governance structure did not alter greatly. This is an ongoing complaint by some members, though their solutions mainly attempt to retain membership control, which is right in a cricket club, but not necessarily helpful in what has become a medium-sized business. This remains a very contentious dilemma for MCC, though the changes in 2021 may move things forward and help the Chief Executive/Secretary and his staff.

The Club is rightly proud of its role, both historically and still today, in helping to develop and promote cricket around the world. I was delighted to be invited by Ehsan Mani, the ICC President, to address the delegates from twenty countries who were all attending the Asian Cricket Council seminar in Lahore in May 2004. The speakers included Clive Lloyd, Sunil Gavaskar, Ravi Shastri, Rameez Raja, Barry Richards and Bob Woolmer amongst others, and it was wonderful to listen to the combined wisdom of those gathered there to talk about many aspects of cricket, ranging from Asia's specific needs, global development, cricket education, coaching, high-performance programmes, development of umpires, grounds, pitches, physical fitness, media relations and cricket facilities.

I was scheduled for the second day to explain MCC's current role and the many activities it undertook locally, nationally and globally. My words and the PowerPoint presentation were well received, and Ehsan spoke for all the delegates when he said he had no idea how much MCC was doing to assist the development of cricket.

The Club made a successful bid to host the Archery competition in the 2012 Olympic Games. I had retired by the time the Olympics took place, but the process and contracts had been put firmly in place many years before. Arrangements were also put in place for the Ashes Urn to travel to Australia and to be placed on display in a number of different places. This trip took place in 2007, after the Urn had been repaired and all the appropriate security measures were confirmed.

Not every initiative worked. To celebrate the 100th Test at Lord's in 2000, we had organised a lunchtime concert, with the help of David English, the former manager of the Bee Gees. As it was a West Indies Test match we started with a Jamaican steel band, Third World, to be followed by Jools Holland.

Courtney Walsh and Curtly Ambrose gave lunch a miss as they moved to the rhythm on the team balcony, but box-holders, having their lunch, hastily closed their doors and the St John's Wood residents, also troubled by the volume, which considerably exceeded the permitted decibel level, made irate telephone calls. Several letters of complaint followed. It was a great shame, because the idea was excellent. As it happened, it probably put paid to amplified music at Lord's for some years, and we returned to the marching bands of Christ's Hospital School and military bands, interspersed with youngsters demonstrating their drills on the outfield.

A much more successful initiative was the appointment of a young artist to accompany the England team on overseas tours. This provided a source of paintings for the MCC collection and gave a number of artists a chance to show their talent.

Within MCC any decision needed to be debated through various committees and the outcome, ideally, explained first to the main Committee, next to the membership and the staff, thirdly to partners and the bodies with whom we had a close relationship and finally to the general public via a media release. Major decisions needed agreement at an AGM or SGM, some decisions needed MCC Committee approval and other day-to-day decisions could be taken at executive or senior staff level. The main point to remember was which decisions needed the approval of which level of governance or management. That was stated in the Club Rules, clarified by legal advisors and very much part of the Secretary & Chief Executive's remit, as documented in my lengthy Management Report in 2004. Outside factors could derail the order of precedence because of a leaked letter or comment, and that led to greater need for management of sensitive issues. That was exemplified by the early and unexpected announcement about the 1999 World Cup by the England & Wales Cricket Board.

9

MCC President 2015-16

Little did I think, even in my wildest dreams, that I would be invited to be President of MCC and I was thrilled when David Morgan asked me to succeed him. I accepted without a moment's hesitation.

The President Designate has plenty of time, from the AGM in May until October, to catch up on all the important topics within MCC, but we knew it would be crucial to organise our diaries well for the year ahead. Apart from the role of a grandparent, I had commitments as President of Cambridge University Cricket Club, Trustee of the MCC Foundation, Chairman of Governors at the King's Schools, Taunton, Chairman of the ECB Association of Cricket Officials and President of the Dulwich Preparatory School Old Boys' Association. Chris also had her roles within the local neighbourhood with the St Ebbe's New Development Residents' Association.

It was a relief to know that MCC had an arrangement for members to stay at the Dorset Square Hotel, which became a convenient base when there were commitments on consecutive days or to avoid driving home to Oxford after a late dinner. The staff were always welcoming whenever we stayed. Although New Zealand, where Chris and I had spent the winters since 2010, would not be on the itinerary, there were trips on behalf of the Club to Adelaide, Durban and Cape Town as well as numerous journeys to different parts of the UK.

On Thursday 1 October 2015 Chris and I drove to Lord's, and I was straight into the thick of it with a tour round the ground with Janet Fisher, the Chief Executive & Secretary's PA, who, with Emma Chambers, plays a very important part in keeping the President in the loop. She introduced me to several of the departmental staff, some new but many who had been there in my time.

That evening there was a Long Room dinner to thank and say farewell to the outgoing Club Chairman, Oliver Stocken. The next day, Friday, we attended a memorial service followed by a reception in the Long Room for Mark Williams, a hard-working Committee member, popular amongst the membership. Saturday was a good chance to snatch a day in Oxford, but a trip to the local farm shop brought a surprise encounter with Charles Rifkind, who called our meeting serendipitous and immediately dragged me into a conversation about various MCC characters who, he felt, had not handled well the negotiations over his development proposals for the Wellington Road end of Lord's. So much for a day away from MCC's politics!

What is so stimulating in this role is the variety of events which come your way. In the first few days, I was asked whether I could arrange a discount for a reception in the Long Room after a match between the Archbishop of Canterbury's XI and a Vatican XI. There was a graveside service at Elmers End Crematorium and a church service at St George's Beckenham to commemorate WG Grace's life. I was given a lift back to Dorset Square by John Fingleton, who explained everything about the MCC Independent Online Pavilion, which he claimed was viewed by 700 members although only 50 contributed.

I see from my diary that, in the year of my presidency, I hosted or was a guest at 72 dinners, 27 lunches, 14 receptions, 33 days of cricket, six memorial services and countless meetings of one committee or another, as well as chairing the MCC AGM. One dinner was to commemorate the 330 MCC members who died in the First World War (two VCs, three Test cricketers and 69 first-class cricketers) and the 286 who fell in World War Two. It was a pleasure to see many old friends again as well as coming into contact with so many new acquaintances at these events. It was extremely helpful to have key points to include in speeches, provided by Neil Priscott in the MCC media department and also some excellent drafted comments from Colin Maynard, still the fount of all knowledge at the Club.

I was keen to make time to keep fit, so a doubles on the Real Tennis Court with the MCC Chairman of Tennis & Squash was a welcome break from eating and drinking, of which there would clearly be no shortage of opportunity.

Janet Fisher was an excellent diary secretary. Emma Chambers organised the travel arrangements. Suzanne Robinson and Christine Hewitson helped to organise the details for the Cowdrey Lecture. I was delighted that Brendon McCullum, the New Zealand captain, whose manager, Garth Gallaway, is a friend of mine from Christchurch, agreed to deliver the lecture. Brendon was as outstanding as a speaker as he had been as a captain.

I sat down again with Suzanne Robinson to discuss names for hospitality in the President's Box in the summer, with Derek Brewer, the Secretary & Chief Executive, to hear his views on the way forward for the Club and its Foundation, Holly Roper Curzon, the Club in-house lawyer, Gerald

Corbett, recently appointed as the Club Chairman, and Robert Leigh, the Treasurer, to listen to their priorities for the year. There was also a Surrey Past Presidents' briefing at the Oval, so it was a busy first month.

The Club Winter Dinners were one of many highlights of the year. The President invites the guest speakers, and I chose good friends who would bring different topics of interest for those members gathered in the Committee Dining Room. Sir Scott Baker was my guest for October, and his comments about MCC's governance were very relevant as there were still discussions continuing about the recommendations from the Incorporation and Structure Working Party (ISWP) Report, presented earlier in the year. In November, the guest speaker was Nigel Wheeler, a former Eastbourne schoolmaster who ran the cricket at the College for thirty years, a recent High Sheriff of Kent, a man who loves cricket and has his own team called the Scorpions. The December Club Dinner was addressed by Des Wilson, the Club's former MCC media and PR consultant, who remembered as a 14-year-old playing in a cricket match in which John Reid, the great New Zealand captain, was also playing. At the fourth Club Dinner in January the guest speaker was Lord Boyce, the former Chief of General Defence Staff, now Warden of the Cinque Ports in succession to Queen Elizabeth the Queen Mother and a long-time friend from when we used to play squash on his return to Dulwich after three months in a nuclear submarine under the ice. He was always fit, having carried out a strict Canadian air force exercise regime (5BX) in a cabin of very limited dimensions. It was another fascinating insight into a different world for the members attending. In February everyone was captivated by our speaker, Sir Nicholas Young, who touched only slightly on his career as Chief Executive of Macmillan Cancer and then the Red Cross but spoke with passion about the spirit of cricket. The final Club Dinner, this one held in the Long Room, was addressed by Ehsan Mani, the knowledgeable and experienced ICC Chairman, who spoke extremely well to a packed room.

At the end of October I looked back at my diary and felt that quite a lot had been achieved. The ECB ACO AGM had accepted a new constitution for the Association; the dinners had gone smoothly; I had got to know Derek Brewer, Gerald Corbett and Robert Leigh, the three senior Club officers; the first Members' Forum of the year had been successful, punctuated by some amusing remarks, as always, by John Page; the debates at a post-Committee meeting dinner had identified several topics for consideration. I had even managed to watch some of the Rugby World Cup and hear the

Archbishop of Canterbury at a question-and-answer session at St Aldate's church in Oxford. I had conducted two tours of Lord's for four people, who had won the tours as prizes in auctions. It was lovely to be back in the middle of things at MCC after a gap of nine years.

There were ongoing Committee debates about how to deal with the unpleasantness that had not dissipated over the Wellington Road development suggestions. The new Club Chairman was all for facing the situation head on and proposed holding his own private meetings with the Rifkind Levy partnership and a couple of their associates who were MCC members. The Estates and Finance Committees and the Chief Executive were less inclined to start a new negotiation without the attendance of those who had been in discussions for several years. As a former Chief Executive Gerald Corbett was used to seeing a problem and addressing it. As a former MCC Chief Executive I could appreciate too the need for executives and non-executives to be on the same message, which would be difficult if separate groups were involved in different discussions or negotiations.

In November dinners continued thick and fast and provided the opportunity to meet again many friends and acquaintances. I explained to the Cricket Society that I was the 14th Knight to be MCC President but the only one who was a Knight from birth. I also welcomed Sir Tim Rice, a two-fold SLA of note: both a slow left-arm bowler and a king of Songs, Lyrics and Arias!

The highlight of November was undoubtedly the chance to attend the first ever day/night Test, played between Australia and New Zealand in Adelaide. The MCC World Cricket Committee arranged its meeting in Adelaide, as there would be many top cricketers in South Australia for the match and for other celebrations which took place. The match showed off the spectacular new stands that adorned the Adelaide Oval, lit up by the brilliant setting sun which went down behind the scoreboard.

It was good to see Keith Bradshaw, my successor for five years at MCC and now CEO of South Australia CC. The groundsman, by his own admission, had left a little too much grass on the pitch in fear of the ball going soft quickly. This altered the balance rather too much in favour of the swing and seam bowlers and batsmen's techniques, particularly just outside the off stump, were tested and found wanting. It was an exciting match and, although it ended in just three days, it could have gone either way. Sadly for New Zealand there was a DRS decision, which seemed to be wrong and went against them. ESPN CricInfo reported the incident as follows:

> Nathan Lyon top-edged an attempted sweep off Mitchell Santner into his shoulder and up to slip. New Zealand's appeal was denied on field by umpire S Ravi, and Brendon McCullum asked for a review, confident that Australia would soon be 9 for 118. But despite evidence that would have convinced most courts of law, the third umpire Nigel Llong was unswayed.
>
> After five minutes of replays, Llong upheld Ravi's decision. There was a clear Hot Spot on the top edge of Lyon's bat, and he had walked halfway to the dressing room. There also seemed to be a deviation in the ball's course. But nothing showed up on Snicko, which appeared to create enough doubt in Llong's mind. To add to the farce, he checked also if it could have been lbw off Lyon's shoulder, but seemed not to notice that the replay was of the previous delivery.

Australia thus went on to record a victory in the first Test match played with the pink ball that MCC had been instrumental in developing.

The atmosphere throughout the match was lively. There was a food village on the nursery ground and over 10,000 spectators were entrenched there with their beers, a rock guitarist and a sheep-shearing exhibition as the cricket continued on the large screen.

The MCC World Cricket Committee had a meaty agenda and there were presentations on Remedies for Enhancing Test Cricket (Rod Marsh), Women's Cricket (Charlotte Edwards), the Laws (Simon Taufel), Playing Regulations (Fraser Stewart and John Stephenson of MCC), Ideas for Restructuring ICC (Wally Edwards of Cricket Australia), Cricket Australia's Strategic Plan (James Sutherland, their CEO), Hong Kong, China, Asia and Underprivileged Cricket Countries (Rodney Miles, Chairman of Hong Kong Cricket Association) and Corruption in Cricket (FICA's CEO, Tim May). There were also lengthy discussions about the undesirability of preparing pitches with home advantage and the possibility of cricket in the Olympics. This committee is the only cricket group which does not contain cricketers mandated by their international board, and their own individual and independent views are always well considered and thoughtful.

Several of us in the MCC party found time to cycle 30km to West Beach and back. I talked with Derek Brewer about a successor as President. No sooner is the President in office than he is asked to consider who should succeed him.

The chance to spend time away from Lord's with the Chief Executive was very valuable. I always appreciated these opportunities to forge a closer relationship with the Presidents. Chris and I attended a Choral Eucharist at Adelaide Cathedral and visited the Yalumba Wine Estate in the Barossa Valley, before returning to the UK. Then it was back to more meetings.

December started with the MCC Tennis Finals weekend, continued with a Committee meeting and dinner, followed a few days later by the Christmas Lunch. The month ended with an England Test match in Durban against South Africa. We were entertained to supper by Mike and Maryna Procter, with two of their children, Greg and Jessica. We saw a couple of days of the Test at Kingsmead, then the England contingent flew to Cape Town for New Year and the Newlands Test.

Penny and Roger Prideaux, the former England cricketer, had arranged for Chris and me to stay in a friend's private home. They could not have been more hospitable and welcomed us with a braai at their home with Doug Insole and Norma before taking us to our house, which was about six hundred yards from them.

One evening, when we had arranged to meet other friends in a local restaurant, Roger suggested that we should borrow his car. He insisted that we parked in the multi-storey car-park directly opposite the restaurant, where there was an armed guard, and said the local security armed response group would meet us when we returned the car to his garage and then escort us back to our house. When we did return, the security vehicle, with yellow flashing light, was there and, although I said we were perfectly happy to walk back to our place, the security guard insisted on accompanying us. The following day, we learned that a couple of England supporters had been mugged at gunpoint at the end of our street by a man who jumped out of a car and escaped with all their valuables. In hindsight we were very relieved and much more wary for the rest of our trip, although it did not stop us enjoying Cape Town and catching up with more friends.

We had an entertaining lunch at Constantia Glen with Penny and Roger, Robin and Vonny Jackman, Bruce Jackman, Robin's brother, and Vintcent van der Bijl, where Robin was, as ever, full of good stories. We all appreciated his jokes and one, in particular, is well worth retelling here. "In the good times, our generation had Johnny Cash, Bob Hope and Steve Jobs – now it seems this generation has no cash, no hope and no jobs."

The Test was an entertaining match, despite ending in a draw. There was little chance of a victory for either side after England had scored 629 for six, with Ben Stokes making an incredible 258, looking at times as though he could smash any delivery over the boundary at will, and Jonny Bairstow scoring his maiden Test century. South Africa declared two runs behind on 627 for seven. Hashim Amla scored a superb 201, and Temba Bavuma became the first black South African to score a Test century. We were fortunate to be sitting next to Bavuma's parents, who were, understandably, extremely excited. We were well hosted by Andrew Golding, the President of Western Province Cricket Club and Tanya, his wife. We were delighted to catch up with Fritz Bing, the manager of the SA touring team to England in 1994, and Bruce Risien, whom I remembered well as the very efficient bagman for that tour party. It was also good to see Omar Henry, who had coached Scotland and whom I had joined for two weeks as assistant coach in 1985.

Before it was time to fly home, Chris and I had a chance to walk in Newlands Forest and to visit Kirstenbosch, one of our favourite botanical gardens, located at the eastern foot of Table Mountain. We also found time to visit an art gallery in Newlands Avenue.

Life outside MCC continued to be busy, with days given to my duties as a school governor and as Chairman of the Association of Cricket Officials, and I was invited to attend the opening of the Blavatnik building for the Department of Government in Oxford and to an entertaining interview with Andrew Marr at St Peter's College. Back at Lord's, an interview with Gina Kidd, a grand-daughter of Michael Melluish, made me think hard. She was writing a paper on how commercialisation had affected the traditions of cricket.

I visited the Archives at Dulwich College, where I had been asked to speak about a 1968 cricket bat for a podcast. A match was played in that year between the XIs of AER Gilligan and SC Griffith, respectively President and Secretary of MCC at the time. Both were Old Alleynians and their teams, which included a number of very well-known cricketers, all signed the bat. The signatures were mainly legible and I spoke about the players, many of whom I had met or even played against.

February is always a busy month at Lord's. In the tennis weekend my partner and I managed to reach the semi-final of our group. Isabelle Duncan spoke at the post-tournament dinner about her book on the history of women's cricket, called 'Skirting the Boundary'.

On behalf of the MCC Foundation, I met Luke Swanson, Director of Chance 2 Shine, to see whether we could work more closely together. Later in the month there was a meeting with the All England Lawn Tennis Club

Foundation, which was helpful to the MCC Foundation, although the funds to be distributed were vastly different. The Wimbledon Championships provide over £50 million each year to that foundation.

There were several days spent speaking individually to members of the Membership & General Purposes Committee, who were up in arms about the process and communication of the way their new chairman was named. Some were more incensed than others, especially as they had been members of that committee for some years, whereas the new chairman had not been involved. The antagonism took up considerable time and patience and led the MCC Committee to discuss it again. It reached the same decision, and Sir Ian Magee has done a good job since his appointment.

Between the 3rd and the 16th of March, travel plans seemed very like my days in county cricket. An ECB ACO meeting in London was followed by a dinner on High Table at St Peter's College, Oxford, then a train in the morning to Alderley Edge in Cheshire for the MCC North of England dinner, where I was given the hotel's bridal suite to myself. A train from Alderley Edge to Euston to pick up the car from Lord's and drive to Nottingham to stay with Bill and Jose Russell, who took me to Nottingham High School, the new venue for the local MCCF Hub. A quick drive to a Cambridge University CC committee meeting and AGM at Fenner's, and a night in Churchill College, were followed by an early drive back to Oxford for a day with the grandchildren, then another train journey for a Council meeting in Taunton. The MCC Finance Committee at Lord's was followed by a hasty return to Oxford to help our daughter and family pack up ready for a move to Dorset. Finally, back to London and the National Portrait Gallery for lunch with a headmaster to help him find a new cricket coach, followed by the playing members' dinner at Lord's and a night in Dorset Square.

Later in the month I had dinner with Matthew Fleming in London and asked him to succeed me as President. He accepted, although I knew that it was not an ideal time for him to be invited to take on the role because he was still working and would probably have preferred to wait a few years. However, I was keen to have a successor who knew MCC well, was an England cricketer and would not only be a very popular choice but also recognised as a man of strong principles, whose experience would be helpful to our new Club Chairman at a difficult time when the development of the ground and the recommendations of the ISWP were still causing anguish and argument in the Committee.

I strongly believed that there should be an MCC representative at the ICC T20 World Competition in Calcutta. I could have combined this with a trip to Colombo where I had been invited to open a new branch of the Foundation of Goodness in the north of the country. The Chairman of Sri Lankan Airways, Ajith Dias, one of the signatories of the MCC bank account in Colombo, had offered flights for Chris and me. It might have made sense for me to fly on to Calcutta, but I was conscious that I had already travelled to Adelaide and South Africa. It was most disappointing to me that there was no MCC presence at the final.

On 26 March Chris and I flew to Colombo to stay with Vijaya and Niri Malalasekera. It was another busy time with a series of dinners, meetings with the Sri Lanka Cricket Board, lunches and suppers with friends. We had a trip to the MCC Centre of Excellence in Seenigama, where Kushil Gunasekera, the founder, showed us the new pre-primary school uniforms, the local community workers operating an art database, tracking all major sales of art round the world, a group of local people operating the accounts back office for a Sri Lankan company, the women making lace tablecloths and cushions and those learning IT skills. I presented MCC certificates to boys to whom an MCC cricket scholarship had been awarded. There was a dance demonstration by a troupe whom we invited to perform on the outfield during a lunch interval at Lord's. I attended the opening of Murali's factory (Ceylon Beverage Can Ltd) and a tree planting ceremony.

A train journey to Killinochchi and the official opening of a new site for an extension of the Foundation of Goodness in the Jaffna area was an experience. The opening entailed a tramp along a narrow path that had been cleared to the centre of the 50-acre site, where a plaque had been temporarily erected. It was rather a shame that, when I pulled the string and a curtain fell away to reveal the plaque, the copy writer had misspelt Sri Lanka and added an extra 'a' so it read 'Sri Lanaka'.

It was on the way back to the road that one of our guides explained that the area had recently been cleared of mines after the troubles. He suggested that we should tread in his footsteps in case any remained. He also told us to look out for snakes. I am not sure why he kept this information to himself until we had already arrived in the centre of the site, but we reached the safety of the road with no mishaps. We spent the night with the rest of the group in an army camp and drove in the morning to Nilaveli, where another trustee of the MCC account, my Cambridge friend Mano Ponniah, had been the architect for a hotel.

Staying there for the night, we watched the T20 Final in which West Indies beat England. As will be remembered forever, Carlos Brathwaite needed 19 off the last over to be bowled by Ben Stokes. He proceeded to hit the first four balls for consecutive sixes and won the match. Quite an anticlimax for England supporters but a wonderful moment for cricket and for the West Indies, who had been in the doldrums for some time.

Back in England my former assistant housemaster at Cranleigh School invited me to deliver the Scholars' Lecture. It was a real pleasure returning to the school, meeting several old friends and colleagues and addressing the scholars, ranging from those in the Upper VIth to those in their first year, who had plenty of testing questions after I spoke about my chosen topic, which I entitled Choices, Values and Future Opportunities. I encouraged them to consider three key values for life: service, integrity and trust.

Reading a lesson at Tom Graveney's memorial service in Worcester Cathedral was an opportunity to join in the thanksgiving for a President, with whom I had enjoyed working at MCC in my penultimate year.

May Day was celebrated with friends in the Botanic Gardens in Oxford from 4am, listening to the choristers of Magdalen College sing from the top of the chapel and then watching the Morris dancers while enjoying coffee and croissants. The day ended in a game of bridge with friends where Chris and I succeeded in bidding and making a seven clubs contract. A day not to be forgotten.

Three days later was the MCC AGM, which the President chairs. After some of the more difficult AGMs of the past, it was a pleasure to find a meeting where there were no contentious issues and a very supportive group of members in attendance. The presentations all went well, and questions and comments from the floor were courteous and well thought out, so much so that the meeting ended at 6.31pm, one minute later than scheduled. The post-meeting dinner in the Long Room was a splendid occasion and the speeches from the President, the President Designate, Andrew Strauss the guest speaker and Nick Pocock, who gave a brief vote of thanks, were well received. There was a feeling of bonhomie, as everyone looked ahead to the cricket season. We were nearing the end of the winter engagements for MCC, and the delights of the cricket season lay ahead.

There was an excellent occasion when Mark Nicholas led a Chance 2 Shine Spirit of Cricket day at Lord's for youngsters with Charlotte Edwards and Matt Prior, who spoke of the importance of team-work. The only sadness was to see Charlotte upset, having just been told that she was to lose the captaincy of England Women's team after several successful years.

There was one piece of news, which caused shock horror at the Tennis & Squash Committee meeting. Rob Fahey had lost the Real Tennis World title, which he had held for 22 consecutive years.

Finally the first major international cricket match of the season at Lord's arrived. Leaving Chris to entertain the guests in the President's Box for the first hour and a half, which was no different from when I was Secretary & Chief Executive, I greeted the Duke of Edinburgh, who came to the Committee Room and thoroughly enjoyed, as he always seemingly did, his time watching the cricket and chatting knowledgeably about the game. The Sri Lanka Test was spoiled by rain, but we had an entertaining and interesting selection of guests on each day in the Box, so the hours passed quickly.

There followed, without doubt, one of the highlights of the year for me. MCC, in conjunction with the High Commissioner of Barbados and the Secretary-General of the Commonwealth, held a dinner in the Long Room to celebrate the 80th birthday of Garry Sobers and also the Barbados Golden Jubilee.

It was an evening that will remain for a very long time in my and the other guests' memory. I hosted the dinner and sat between Garry and the Secretary-General. There were 871 international caps in the room, a number from the West Indies and many from past England teams. The current Barbados team had been flown across for the occasion. Wes Hall spoke and was, as usual, when making a speech, off his long run! Garry kept telling me that he did not want to speak, but I persuaded him that the guests were expecting him to say something. In the end, and not surprisingly, he spoke brilliantly and held everyone's attention, speaking without notes and outlining his views on the game when he played and in the modern era. For someone who played against him in my early career, it was a magical occasion, and it could have gone on for much longer. The former international players really enjoyed renewing acquaintances and agreeing that this lasting camaraderie was the essential spirit of cricket.

As happened annually, we had invited the Chairman and Secretary of the All England Club to the President's Box, and they reciprocated by inviting us and the Chief Executive to the Royal Box at Wimbledon. It is always one of the best occasions of the year, and this was no exception when we went on the day after Chris's birthday. I still think that Wimbledon leads the way in staging an outstanding sporting event.

The second Test of the summer at Lord's was between England and Pakistan in July. It was a privilege to be able to invite the Archbishop of Canterbury and his wife to the first day. It was even more of a privilege to be invited to Lambeth Palace a few weeks later for a tour, supper and compline with a small, diverse group of very interesting people. There were two more days of entertaining in the Box before the Pakistan team won the match on the fourth day, and the whole team did ten press-ups on the square to show that their fitness regime had helped their performance. Two days later MCC staged a match against the Nepal international team and welcomed 250 guests to a reception in the Long Room.

It was a pleasure to meet MCC's oldest member, at 101, who attended the Inter-Services Tournament.

The Middlesex v Surrey T20 match saw David Cameron and his cricket-loving son, Elwen, in the Box along with three of our grandchildren and other youngsters. When I asked our granddaughter, Anna (10), whether she had enjoyed the game, sitting and chatting next to the former Prime Minister almost throughout the match, she said yes and then divulged that she had borrowed her mother's mobile and had taken a 'secret selfie' of herself and the ex-PM. It was good to be able to welcome the younger generation to Lord's and see how much they enjoyed the game.

A visit to the Scarborough Festival brought back special memories for me, having played there first as a Cambridge undergraduate, again for an England Under-25 team against an England team, captained by Brian Taylor, the Essex captain, and for a third time as captain of an MCC team against a Rest of the World team captained by Martin Crowe. In the England v Under-25 team, when the England team was fielding, there was movement behind the sightscreen. A policeman got the crowd to sit down but remained in front of the screen to watch the game until Brian Taylor cupped his gloved hands and shouted: "Get out of the bleeding way, Bluebottle."

On one evening during the Rest of the World/MCC match I had eaten at an Italian restaurant with Geoff Lawson, the Australian fast bowler, who was playing for the other team. As a trained optician he was forthright in saying that batsmen should not read before an innings but should get accustomed to the light and, as they went out to bat, should concentrate on the maker's name on the stumps at the bowler's end to prepare their eyes to adjust to the optimum focal length. It made sense so, when I went out to bat, I tried to see whether it would help. As it happened, Geoff was the bowler and, having beaten me a couple of times outside off stump, he shouted from the other end: "It's Duncan Fearnley, if you can't read it!"

After a couple of years without the constant net practice available when a professional, it was not easy to move my feet quickly and, when Wasim Akram was bowling, I managed, after a couple of plays and misses to the swinging deliveries, to get a leading edge towards the covers. I called immediately and set off for a single. My partner was quick but, if the throw had hit the stumps, he would have been well short. Fortunately the ball missed and sped to the boundary for four overthrows. I don't suppose many batsmen have hit Wasim for five to get off the mark. As wickets continued to fall to the pace men, Roger Harper was brought on at one end, and I saw it as my responsibility to fend him off!

At the start of September, with the international matches behind us, there was still time for one of my favourite games when I was at Lord's. The Village Cricket Final was played on a Sunday between Sessay from North Yorkshire and Sibton Park from Kent. It was a day to remember for Simon Mason who scored 138 and took Sessay to 307 for five, both of which were record scores for the competition.

On Wednesday 6 September the match between the MCC Schools team and the English Schools Cricket Association was played at Lord's. It was my birthday, and we celebrated with a Box of friends during the match. In my short speech of thanks for their being present, I made it clear that, in my mind, 70 was nothing more than 21 degrees Celsius, so it was an occasion for warm celebrations.

The season was nearly over as September drew to an end, but there were still meetings to attend, a pavilion to open at Wells Cathedral School and the box to host for the Royal London One-Day Cup (RL50), the successor to the Gillette Cup and the NatWest Trophy, which was between Surrey and Warwickshire. A repeat of the 1982 NatWest Trophy result was too much to ask for. This time Surrey batted first and Warwickshire went on to win comfortably, but it was still a most enjoyable day in the President's Box.

What a year it was! Chris and I have so many happy memories of all that happened. The year sped past, and then it was time to return to the delights of Oxford and a more normal retirement.

Part Three

Looking Back in Retirement

10

Cricket Now and Then – Reflections on the Game

I have always tried to avoid starting any conversation with 'In my day'. This is partly because I think I am still having my day but mainly because younger generations do not want to hear from someone living through 'all his yesterdays'.

It is easy as former players to write off new formats and changes to the cricket that we enjoyed in our playing days. We all do it. Whilst I shall always think that the multi-day matches, whether of three, four or five days, give players the best opportunity to test their skills and compete at the highest level, the limited-over matches may well be more appropriate for the present-day spectators. A preference may depend on whether a person is attracted to cricket more as a player or a spectator.

As a player I took part in 15-over evening matches for school staff teams, 40-over matches in the John Player League on Sundays, 55-over matches in the Benson & Hedges tournaments, 60-over matches in the Gillette Cup or NatWest Trophy, two-day games in the Minor County competition, three-day county championship matches, a four-day game in South Africa for the Derrick Robins XI and a five-day game as the Bengal Golden Jubilee Match in Calcutta. In 1981 I even played in the Lambert & Butler Cup, which was a contest of 10 overs for each team of seven players on a matting pitch under floodlights at the Chelsea football ground, where there was little future in elegantly straight-driving through the V along the well-grassed pitch towards the goals, so all batsmen tried to slog it over the very short midwicket or cover boundary. There was also one experiment where professional tennis players served at us as Surrey batsmen, and we tried to create a competitive match in an indoor arena. They all demanded different kinds of batting, bowling and fielding skills and approaches and, in some respect, they were all cricket.

As a spectator I feel relaxed about the length of the game, though I still prefer the longer format. Captains have more decisions to make, and there are more moments for batsmen to change from defence to attack and bowlers to take wickets or contain. The shorter the match, the greater the pressure on batsmen to get the bat on every ball, the fielders to stop every run and the bowlers to bowl 'dot balls'. Possibly the perfect bowling analysis in a JPL 40-over match was provided by Brian Langford in 1969, playing for Somerset against Essex at Yeovil, when he returned figures of 8-8-0-0, bowling at Brian Ward, who presumably thought he had identified the off-spinner as the main threat to his team!

Who knows whether the Hundred, the new competition imagined by ECB in conjunction with the television companies, will be a success? The move away from county teams was copied from the Australian Big Bash, but it also suited ECB in their wish to oversee the competition and limit the venues rather than leaving the 18 first-class counties to stage the matches and take the revenue themselves.

The concept was initially met with scorn from players, some administrators, some ground owners and the older supporters of cricket, who have barely come to terms with T20 matches, but the county chairmen and chief executives voted in favour of the competition. Perhaps the promise of additional funds from the centre was persuasive. We shall see whether it differs much from T20, which England pioneered and then watched as others developed it. This has proved a welcome source of income for the counties and has proved immensely popular round the world. MCC has embraced the concept of the Hundred and will welcome younger guests into the Pavilion. Without doubt it is in the game's interest to encourage the love of cricket amongst the younger generation.

It makes sense to bring the world's best players together in England for a short limited-over competition shown on terrestrial television, but whether a fourth format is necessary is very debatable. ECB would like to attract a new group of people to the matches, but that risks alienating the current spectators who watch the T20 matches and support their home team.

The Hundred will be played at eight grounds by players chosen by ballot, in teams with no link by name to a county, but it is slightly ironic that the competition was scheduled to begin in 2020. Did the marketing department miss a trick? Will the crowds actually be the same spectators who filled the T20 matches at the Test match grounds such as Lord's and the Oval? Why will the Hundred attract people to the grounds as opposed to a tried and tested format such as T20, or is the TV audience more important for revenue? Will spectators from Somerset, Devon or Cornwall travel to Cardiff, their nearest venue, to watch such a short game? We shall see.

Over the years priorities have changed as the marketing men and women, in conjunction with administrators, sponsors and the television companies, have attempted to make cricket more appealing to today's spectators. Television-viewing numbers have become increasingly important, though crowds at the grounds are still necessary to create an atmosphere for the players, who change from one format to the other as competitors or performers. Prices have increased hugely in the longer-format games, relying on corporate attendance but, sadly, discouraging families who may be considering introducing youngsters to the game. Games have become shorter to help the reduced attention spans of the screen-orientated generations. There is little time in a busy world for spectators, except for the retired, the unemployed, those on holiday or children playing truant, to sit through a whole day of cricket without a win or a loss at the end.

Crowd participation has been encouraged in most grounds; music and fireworks have been introduced. Counties have decreased their use of out-grounds because of the upkeep costs, have concentrated on selling tickets for the T20 matches, which have provided the best returns and have looked to other sources of income to supplement or replace the dwindling cricket gate receipts. This has not made it easy for spectators in outlying areas to watch the games live and, in the eyes of the traditionalists, has deprived us of the charm of so many smaller grounds. Added to the lack of cricket on terrestrial television for some years, numbers playing the game have dwindled.

There is little doubt that T20 competitions such as the IPL in India and the Big Bash in Australia, which have been copied in other countries, have attracted the top players because of the additional income they can generate from the franchises, the wealthy owners, the sponsors and the television companies. These are lucrative tournaments and the Hundred aims to be another. In some ways it is totally understandable that professional cricketers often prefer to play in these much shorter matches, bowl a maximum of four overs in a day and receive huge sums of money. Professional sportsmen and women have a short time in which to ply their skills and market their ability. Fitness cannot be guaranteed and opportunities that arise have to be seriously considered. As is often pointed out: 'You are a long time retired!'

Ultimately, it will be the players and the spectators who decide how cricket will continue. Will it be the short form of the game with its numerous sixes and fours over ever-shorter boundaries or will this become repetitive and monotonous? Will bowling develop new approaches as batting has already done more quickly? Will Tests and multi-day formats disappear for lack of spectators? Will cricket become an Olympic Sport, in which case it will have to be in the shortest possible format? Traditionalists hope that the longer format, with its infinite swings and its moments of high excitement occurring throughout a day, will prove to be resilient to the challenge from the shorter more easily marketable formats, but is that just wishful thinking?

There have been fantastic World Cup matches recently and pulsating Test matches. These and exciting players are what will encourage the younger generations to follow the game. Will it be possible to persuade them to take up playing at a time when there are so many other competing attractions? Covid-19 has not helped at all. Cricket is a complex game at its best, and spectating is easier to follow for those who have played. In its simplest form, though, there are still plenty of aspects to encourage youngsters and those unfamiliar with the game to take an interest. It is still unclear whether playing cricket encourages spectators to attend matches or whether spectating leads to more people playing.

I started writing this book in 2019, a year when we had seen some extraordinary cricket matches and exploits. Many former cricketers will still say that the sport was better when they played, but it is extremely hard to think of a World Cup Final and an Ashes Test series, which have been more entertaining and produced more exciting, nail-biting results. The matches have shown the brilliance of individual players, the spirit of cricket at its best and the strange decisions that governing bodies can sometimes make.

At the start of the year the lengthy bans on three Australian players, caught using sandpaper to rough up the ball and encourage reverse swing, were coming to an end. For a while they were the pantomime villains at English grounds, but slowly their performances were accepted and rightly applauded. They had served their punishment, apologised, brought down quite a few others within Cricket Australia and moved on. The Australian team, under their new manager, Justin Langer, was determined to show that their morally deficient, win-at-all-costs attitude of the past few years was behind them, but that their competitive spirit remained strong.

The World Cup was an excellent limited-over tournament, with India and Australia close to qualifying for the final at Lord's, but ultimately losing to New Zealand and England. Some of the shots played by batsmen would have been unthinkable in earlier decades. Helmets have changed the approach, but so has the T20 way of batting without fear. Bowlers bowled slower deliveries and adherence to line and length, so highly regarded in the past, was often punished. Bats were definitely improved, batsmen stronger, boundaries shorter and pitches flatter, although there was, as always in England, movement under cloudy skies and the pitches did take spin. All of this led to matches where there was a reasonable balance between the bat and the ball and made for exciting cricket.

The World Cup Final between England and New Zealand was an absolute highlight of the year. After the two teams had finished on the same number of runs after 50 overs, a 'super over' was played, which again could not separate the two teams by runs scored. In those two games there were two wonderful examples of cricketers understanding the Spirit of Cricket and showing their true character as players. Trent Boult caught the ball on the boundary but, as he threw the ball infield before stepping out of the field of play, he touched the boundary rope and Martin Guptill, who was close by and finished the catch, immediately signalled a six. Many players might not have been so instantly honest, but it was a real sign of a cricketer being prepared to act with integrity.

The other cricketer to show the right spirit was Ben Stokes, who, batting at a time when England were falling behind the run rate, was struck by a throw from the outfield and watched as the ball ricocheted over the boundary for four overthrows. At that stage England required nine runs off three deliveries to win and the overthrows were possibly crucial. He immediately apologised and even suggested that the runs should not count, although the Laws are clear that the umpire has no option but to signal four more runs for the batting team. Both were admirable reactions in vital moments of a closely contested and very tight match between two teams who clearly respected each other.

There were, on the other hand, two examples of what can be wrong with cricket. First, in that same incident, the umpires wrongly signalled that the four overthrows should be added to the two runs that they believed the batsmen had scored. In fact when the ball was thrown, the time when the completed runs are counted, the two England batsmen had not crossed for the second time, so the total number of runs for that ball should have been five and not six. With the third umpire watching everything on a television screen, that should have been picked up either by him or the umpires on the field. The protocols for the use of the third umpire apparently did not allow for any intervention, which seems to contradict the idea that the replays are to correct obviously wrong decisions. As it happens, there was still time for Ben Stokes to score the runs required, so it might not have altered the result of the match. With two needed to win off the last ball, instead of three, Stokes blocked the ball and one run was scored, after Mark Wood was run out in attempting a second, bringing the scores level.

The second example was the way that the match was eventually decided after the 'Super overs' of six deliveries from Trent Boult and then Jofra Archer, which also ended with the scores level. Instead of further 'super overs' or a contest of more skill by the players, the game was deemed won by the team scoring more boundaries. It is hard to see how a boundary is worth more than four or even six singles, but ICC had opted for deciding a winner in this way. It was extremely hard on New Zealand, who lost having taken more wickets in the match and having scored as many runs in both innings. Nevertheless, we witnessed a marvellous reaction from what must have been an extremely disappointed captain whose team had competed hard and fairly throughout the tournament and especially in the final.

The Ashes Test series saw some incredibly consistent batting by Steve Smith, who looked almost invincible with his method of moving around in the crease and making the bowlers bowl where he wanted the ball. He was supported really well by Marnus Labuschagne, who might not have been selected for any match if Steve Smith had not been hit on the head and suffered concussion in the second match of the series.

It saw top-class fast bowling as a pack by the Australians, Pat Cummins, Josh Hazlewood, James Pattinson, Mitchell Starc and Peter Siddle, and England's rejuvenated Stuart Broad benefitting from the newly-found pace and aggression of Jofra Archer at the other end for England. Ben Stokes played an extraordinary innings to rescue the series at Headingley, accompanied by England's number eleven, Jack Leach, who became a cult hero. Earlier in the year against Ireland at Lord's, as a night watchman, Leach had scored 92, but his single run in a 74-run last-wicket partnership allowed Ben Stokes to plunder the Australian bowling and win a match that to all intents and purposes had gone beyond England's reach. That the series ended at two wins apiece was a fair reflection of the sides and Australia kept the Ashes.

In many ways cricket has improved since my playing days. The batsmen are stronger and can play shots through 360 degrees, making field setting almost impossible. They bat fearlessly in limited-over cricket, often staying outside the line of the ball and clearing their front leg and side to allow their arms to come through and hit the ball wherever they choose. The fielding is athletic, skilful and innovative as fitter fielders combine to bring off astonishing catches near the boundary and dive to take spectacular one-handed catches inches from the turf. The bowlers have found ways to bowl slower deliveries and vary their pace, length and direction. Some aspects of the game may have been better in the past, but overall it is hard to argue that cricket is not at least as good as it has ever been.

The Spirit of Cricket

There have been many changes to cricket since 1967 when I first played at first-class level. Helmets have protected and given greater confidence to batsmen, fielders and wicket-keepers. Equipment has improved, formats have changed. New countries have embraced the game. Floodlit cricket, drop-in and hybrid pitches, hover-covers and technology have brought many advantages. Coaches and directors of cricket have become more knowledgeable and more aware of what technology can do to monitor performance and provide a clue to the strengths and weaknesses of their own and opposition players. Recreation time has become more limited. Attitudes in life have changed.

It is perhaps inevitable that attitudes towards the Spirit of Cricket have been challenged. It has been suggested that it would be simpler to play cricket according to the Laws without worrying about an ethical code which is not universally accepted or applied. The Spirit of Cricket has always been a thorny question. Is it woolly idealism or, as Michael Atherton, the former England captain, once put it, 'a load of well-meaning guff'? Is it pointless to attempt to retain a Corinthian concept like the Spirit of Cricket in what is essentially a cut-throat, professional business, which is about winning and avoiding losing. It is clearly aspirational, and yet it is something that impacts on all players, officials, coaches, teachers, administrators, parents and spectators. To MCC, as the lawmakers, it is a key element of the way the game should be played, and I believe passionately in the importance of it.

When MCC produced a new code of the Laws in 2000, Colin Cowdrey and Ted Dexter, both past Presidents and former England captains, were concerned that reports from the Club's out-matches against clubs and schools were becoming increasingly critical about the behaviour of players. The recreational game often takes its lead from the top international players, and the broadcasters had made much of the gladiatorial approach of Test teams and incidents of sledging, cheating and sharp practice to gain an advantage. The many cameras and stump microphones picked these up, and commentators referred to them, sometimes critically but sometimes with an acceptance that controversial episodes made for good television.

In many respects, over the years, international cricket appeared to have moved from being a game where players competed to an entertainment where spectators were treated to a 'spiced up' event, particularly in limited-over matches. Supporters at the grounds, with the replay screens, were encouraged to participate, with local competitions to win a prize by catching a six hit into the crowd. Cameras showed people in the crowd, who reacted to being on the screen at the ground or in homes. Fancy dress was encouraged and made competitive, and crowds became more unruly, with spectators in certain stands at some grounds proud of their negative booing of the opposition players. Gone was the humour of the barracking and now, at times, there was a more unpleasant atmosphere.

Part of a changing world in schools, clubs and counties was the greater influence of the professional coach. When schoolteachers ran the teams, they interacted with their pupils on the sports field and also in the classroom, so they wanted to bring out the best in them in every way. They were also aware of and keen to promote the wider aspects of education and social behaviour. Cricket coaches, who felt that their job depended on the success of the team and pressurised especially by some independent school head teachers, who were becoming increasingly keen to show prospective parents that their school was better than a rival establishment, worked rather more on results than the manner in which they were achieved. Society was also changing in its approach. Success was sought, applauded and rewarded by clubs seeking promotion in the leagues and counties chasing lucrative prize money. This, as well as the constant challenge of authority, was questioning and loosening the traditional moral standards in many different walks of life, including sport.

The Laws Working Party believed that it was important to include a preamble to the Laws to attempt to define the essence of the Spirit of Cricket. We discussed at length whether to introduce red and yellow cards for umpires to brandish in the event of bad behaviour. Cricket had always maintained in the Laws that umpires were 'the sole judges of fair and unfair play', but that captains were 'responsible at all times for ensuring that play was conducted within the Spirit of Cricket as well as within the Laws'.

Cards were not seen as the answer, though, mainly because the new code of the Laws was intended for all levels of cricket matches and, in many cases, the umpires might be members of the teams involved, either the numbers ten or eleven in the batting order or batsmen after they had been dismissed. Everyone agreed that captains should retain their responsibilities as that was something which made cricket different from other team sports, where a referee had a whistle and control of the game.

We consulted widely, but it was easier to say what should not be acceptable, and we were faced with a list of 'Thou shalt nots'. It was David Richards, the Chief Executive of ICC, who said that we were being too negative. He emphasised, absolutely rightly, that we needed a positive set of aspirational guidelines and so we concentrated on the word 'Respect'. Respect for one's own captain and team is generally accepted. Respect for opponents was more difficult but needed to be emphasised. Respect for the role of the umpires was clearly essential but, as in life generally, there was less deference to authority. Respect for the game and its traditional values was not helpful without further definition and clarification, but it was included nevertheless without further explanation.

There would undoubtedly continue to be disagreements about fair play even if we all decided to play solely to the letter of the Laws, because all cricketers accept the mantra 'Play Hard, Play Fair'. The question, as Rod Marsh put it, is "What is hard and what is fair"? As the Vice Chancellor of the University of Buckingham, Sir Anthony Seldon, once said, quoting Plato: "Good people do not need laws to tell them to act responsibly, while bad people will always find a way around the laws."

There is always a particular difficulty when trying to codify and put into succinct wording a proposed set of principles, guidelines and intentions as opposed to rules. For everything that is included, there will always be important points excluded, which competitive, hard-bitten professionals and amateurs will exploit.

There are, however, many aspects of the Spirit of Cricket which should be, and generally are, globally accepted. The game should be open to all regardless of race, nationality, gender, colour, caste or creed. Physical violence should be totally unacceptable. Acceptance of an umpire's decision is a fundamental requirement, and decency, respect and trust are very important for everyone involved in the game. Cricket is for players, officials and spectators, and they all have a part to play in maintaining the integrity of the game. Primarily it must be enjoyable, fun even, and an opportunity for players and officials to challenge themselves fully and fairly in a competitive atmosphere enjoyed by those watching.

The Spirit of Cricket branches into so many different areas, all of which need consideration. When do humour and banter become sledging and personal abuse? Where does the referral system in televised cricket fit with Law 2.12 that states that the umpire's decision, once made, is final and with the statement in the preamble which exhorts players to 'accept the umpire's decision'? Should the home team be able to benefit by having complete say in preparation of the pitch? Where does cheating differ from deliberate deception of the umpires or other players? Where does an appeal to an umpire or aggressive fielding become unacceptable intimidation? Ball tampering contravenes the Laws of Cricket; spot or match fixing is a crime. Regulations and guidance often go hand in hand and can be easily confused. The Laws of Cricket (Regulations) and the Spirit of Cricket (Guidance) are closely interlinked and sometimes overlap, but they are both important in the way the game is played and perceived.

Ball tampering is something that umpires at international and county level have been asked to watch closely. Those umpires who were bowlers know that players have always worked on the ball. Legally any player can clean, maintain or improve the condition of the ball within certain parameters, but the moment anyone attempts to worsen its condition there is uproar. There is very little difference between cleaning mud out of the seam and lifting the seam to gain advantage so, in the past, most umpires in county cricket accepted that bowlers would pick and raise the seam. Equally, although sun cream was sometimes illegally used to enhance the shine on the ball, most umpires understood that it was impossible to distinguish between that and the sweat from a bowler's brow that was deemed acceptable before covid-19 intervened. Vaseline and saliva from sticky sweets were thought to be unacceptable. What changed it all and brought it more into consideration was the introduction of bottle tops, dirt in the pocket and, recently, sandpaper. The Australians caught using sandpaper in the Test match in 2018, so that the ball might reverse swing earlier, were probably doing nothing much worse than others before them, but they were naïve to think that they would not be spotted by one or more of the many television cameras that surround a cricket ground nowadays. What is a surprise to many is that no bowlers were seemingly implicated in what became a national scandal and was condemned by the Australian Prime Minister. They were, after all, the beneficiaries of the ball tampering, which was clearly a premeditated action. Australia was the team that was caught, but there were probably others that were happy to cast criticism and hide behind Australian embarrassment. The outcome was that everyone believed that this was a breach of the Spirit of Cricket as well as of the Laws and the culprits were severely punished by lengthy suspensions.

There is a narrow dividing line between cheating and attempting to deceive. It is clearly cheating to hold up a ball that a fielder knows has reached him or her on the half-volley. Although not a fool-proof way to judge, I believe, if the ball has bounced first, the fielder's hands will usually come up with the ball, whereas fingers will stay down squashed to the ground if the ball has just carried. This is generally apparent in slow-motion replays, though the camera can foreshorten the view and not be clear whether the ball has touched the ground. There may be occasional times when there is doubt in the fielder's mind, but these are, in my view, very few and far between.

One of the areas that causes more antagonism and more negative vibes on the field of play than almost anything is when a batsman knowingly nicks the ball to the keeper and stands his ground, hoping not to be given out. This is not necessarily cheating, but there is sometimes the intent to deceive the umpire by additionally rubbing a forearm. The vitriol that is thrown by bowlers and fielders is always heartfelt. Often, however, the most vitriolic are those who would not 'walk' themselves.

Law 33.1 (Out Caught), which should be absolutely self-explanatory in the vast majority of cases, states:

> The striker is out Caught if a ball delivered by the bowler, not being a No ball, touches his/her bat without having previously been in contact with any fielder, and is subsequently held by a fielder as a fair catch, as described in 33.2 and 33.3, before it touches the ground.

Some say that the batsman should immediately walk off once it is clear the ball has been caught, as he would almost certainly do if caught away from the wicket. Others will say that the umpire should make the decision because there has inevitably been an appeal and, as umpires make mistakes, standing one's ground on an appeal might even up the mistakes.

Attitudes have changed. In county cricket in my playing days, but not always in international cricket, the majority of batsmen 'walked' if they knew they had touched the ball and it had been fairly caught. Umpires, usually former players, knew those who did not and often evened things up by giving them out at the next opportunity. When I started my professional career at Gloucestershire the captain, Tony Brown, made his views clear and said that, although it was an individual decision, a batsman had to look in a mirror when shaving the next day and know whether the person staring back at him had acted with personal integrity. Most county captains then believed the same thing, although I am aware of one instance of a former county captain moving counties when his successor said that he expected all of his batsmen to wait for the umpire's decision.

I remember Alec Stewart, in a very early match in his career at Surrey under my captaincy, waiting to be given out when caught behind. When I questioned and criticised him in the dressing room later, he was very surprised and explained that he had been playing in Western Australia for the last two winters and that was how he had been taught to react. I must have made my point, though, because he still refers to this episode, whether or not he agrees with it.

The Spirit of Cricket is silent on this issue of 'walking', because of the differing opinions around the world. However, I believe a batsman should walk off if caught anywhere on the field. Garry Sobers always makes that point when he speaks about the game and, when the greatest all-rounder the world has ever seen says batsmen should walk, it is good enough for me. I should hope that all schoolteachers and coaches would encourage younger cricketers to walk. There is the counter-argument that everyone should wait for the umpire's decision, because it would be easier if all players reacted in the same way. It would eradicate the suspicion that some batsmen walk on most but not all occasions, which has always been a temptation and has been a criticism aimed at some of the top players. Whatever the agreed norm, the most important thing is to be consistent in always accepting the umpire's decision without showing dissent.

In all televised cricket matches technology has become increasingly involved and mainly, but not always, helpful. Line decisions for stumpings, run-outs and no-balls are more accurately made by cameras, although, in the last case, the cameras are not consulted unless there is a wicket. This has led to inconsistency. Nobody wants a delay after every ball to check the position of the bowler's feet. However, the batsman is denied a chance of an extra run and a free hit, if a no-ball is not called. Perhaps there is a way to monitor every delivery in real time and for a call of no-ball to be made automatically. It would allow the umpires at the bowler's end to concentrate on the business end of the pitch, which is what they are now encouraged to do anyway. ICC is introducing such a protocol to see whether it can work.

Two further comments from Sir Anthony Seldon's excellent book, entitled 'Trust', seem particularly relevant to cricket: 'A presumption of trust is better than a presumption of distrust' and 'For trust to be built up, predictability and agreed norms of behaviour are fundamental.'

The Spirit of Cricket needs players to trust each other and to accept that they should act within agreed norms. The question to ask is how we arrive at these agreed norms.

I don't think the Decision Review System (DRS) is the complete answer, but aspects of it help. The intention, to improve decision-making, avoid obvious howlers by on-field umpires and give the players more confidence in the officials, is a worthy one. I believe strongly that the third umpire, watching all the action on a screen, should be included in the decision-making, but that this official, along with the on-field umpires, should make the decision when to employ the replays. Whether one, two or three reviews are available to a team there is no guarantee that unsafe decisions will always be corrected. In one Ashes Test the match ended with the use of DRS when England successfully reviewed a not-out decision to confirm their view that the batsman was caught behind. Conversely, if the umpire had given the batsman out, despite his being not out, Australia could not have reviewed the decision, as they had already used up their two reviews. Although brought about by the Australian captain's earlier unsuccessful challenges, surely this would have been a travesty.

Another problem with DRS was exposed in the same match when the broadcaster was replaying the nick to the wicket-keeper down the leg-side, which saw the end of Joe Root, and therefore could not produce any hotshot film of the next ball when Jonathan Trott may or may not have edged the ball into his pad. This was a time when intervention by the third umpire with control of the technologies available should have brought about a correct decision. The broadcaster's role is to bring live and replayed action to spectators as part of the entertainment, and Sky TV was right to show the dismissal on several occasions, although their timing might be questionable. The job of the officials and the administrators is to do their best to ensure that correct decisions are made. If ICC paid for its own cameras and other technological devices in key positions, it would be in a position to counter the claims of some countries that they cannot afford the

DRS system. National governing bodies have certain requirements from their international grounds, and the installation of all these technological aids should be universal.

In this same Test spectators saw the best and worst of the DRS system. The decision at the end of the match was an example of the best. Stuart Broad's decision not to walk off when he had clearly and knowingly hit the ball to slip was perhaps the worst. Australia had no reviews left, and there was no way that the wrong decision could be reversed. The TV commentators showed the incident regularly. There has always been considerable debate in the media about the morality of 'walking' or 'standing' and waiting for an umpire's decision. The knowledge that there can be intervention by a third umpire might lead to more people 'walking', which ultimately makes for a more pleasant, but not necessarily any less competitive, atmosphere between players. It would certainly make the job of the umpires easier and might help with the idealistic, but nonetheless desirable, aspirations of the Spirit of Cricket.

I believe that the decision to review should be entirely the responsibility of the umpires. The Laws or Regulations do not need to be changed drastically to include the possibility of a television umpire being consulted. The Laws already state that an umpire may consult his colleague on a point of fact, and this could be extended to the third umpire, if available. I also think that the third umpire should intervene whenever there may have been a wrong decision. Although this may lead to more delays in a game that has slowed over the last few decades, correct decisions are vitally important and must be the aim of all officials. I hope that the DRS protocols will be changed. It has always struck me that a second appeal by the fielding team, when the real-time appeal has failed, is contrary to the Spirit of Cricket, where players are expected to accept the umpire's decision.

Alain Rolland, one of the best rugby union referees, recently said: "We have worked very hard to ensure that the on-field official takes the majority of the decisions." He also disclosed that World Rugby would be taking responsibility for the use of TV cameras used in decisions. "A TMO [Television Match Official] will intervene when there is serious foul play or when a clear action has been missed in the act of scoring."

I like the fact that the referee has two calls that he can make to the television referee. He can say: "Is there any reason why I cannot award a try?" or "The on-field decision is a try", showing that he and his assistant referees are fairly confident that they have seen everything. The alternative call is: "Try or no try?" or "I have no clear sight of a touchdown, so the on-field decision is no try."

Each year the advice provided by the on-field referee to the TMO improves. Cricket could learn from this. Good umpires would probably be happy to say: "Is there any reason why I should not give the batsman out?" and await confirmation. Umpires are already giving a 'soft signal' as guidance to the third umpire, which is moving things in a better direction. With the advance of technology, the speed of availability of slow-motion replays needs to be quicker to avoid lengthy delays.

Golf is a better example to follow than most other sports in the way that the top professionals and most recreational golfers police themselves and usually own up to small errors on their part, such as coming into contact when addressing the ball. Cricketers, from WG Grace onwards, may never have been fully committed to playing with such values. However, the advent of close-up filming and the other technological advances has shown catches, lbws and near misses. It is up to administrators and officials to persuade players, especially at the top of the game, that a professional approach does not necessarily mean that sharp practice, deception, cynical exploitation of the weaknesses of an official or cheating are in the best interest of the game or the individual. If attitudes at the top of the game can be changed, the younger generation of cricketers will follow suit.

As a former member and chairman of the MCC Laws Working Party, I have never been convinced that the game of cricket is better for batsmen trying to deceive the umpire. Individuals may benefit, teams may prosper because of it, but the game of cricket loses some of its claimed charm of being different from other team sports.

The essence of cricket has always been the balance between bat and ball, so that batsmen and bowlers, both fast and slow, can compete equally. There are, of course, pitches which favour batting and those which give assistance to the bowlers. Limited-over cricket has led to pitches being prepared with more emphasis on batting and, in a shorter, one-day match, there is much less time for the pitch to change. In a Test at Lord's we always tried to prepare a pitch that would provide a fair balance. The aim of Mick Hunt and the cricket department for a Test match was to produce a dry pitch with pace, consistent bounce, an even covering of grass and hard enough to help the batsmen for the first three days, once any early movement, which would test the opening batsmen's technique against swing and seam, had ceased. It was always hoped that the pitch would wear and begin to take spin on the fourth and fifth days. The objective, of course, was to produce the ideal pitch, but much always depended on the weather conditions during the match and how hot or wet the days before the Test match had been, both of which might have necessitated the pitch being covered for lengthy periods. Batsmen, faster bowlers and slower bowlers should all feel they have a chance at some stage in a match, so that team selection prepares for all eventualities, as was often the case on uncovered pitches.

There is always pressure on the ground staff, because the ground authority ideally wants a match to last five days to optimise revenue, the home team and Board want a pitch that will favour their selected team or negate the strengths of the opposition, and the spectators want an exciting spectacle, which encourages them to pay the very high price of tickets. Mick Hunt was an excellent groundsman for many years at Lord's, knew the vagaries of the soil at the ground, was a close watcher of the weather patterns and always extremely nervous before the first ball of a major match. I was keen to support him despite attempts, usually from the England manager or captain or from an ECB representative, to dictate how they wanted the Test pitch prepared. It was his life's work and his career was at stake if it went wrong, so that any outside influence was usually ignored, though it was not easy for him. This was sometimes seen as unpatriotic and there was criticism that we were preparing pitches more suited to the opposition, which was nonsense, but the reason behind this apparent intransigence was an attempt to put into practice Law 6.3.

Law 6.3 Selection and preparation

Before the match, the Ground Authority shall be responsible for the selection and preparation of the pitch. During the match, the umpires shall control its use and maintenance.

The advantage of Lord's is that MCC is the ground authority and not directly responsible for either of the international or county teams participating. There have often been complaints of pitches elsewhere being prepared with a bias towards the home team, which is sad, but in a professional sport that will always remain a temptation.

As one cricket supporter once memorably wrote, 'Once banter and humour became sledging, it was all downhill from there!' There must be room for humour, for the letting off of steam and for comments in a cricket match, otherwise the whole atmosphere becomes sterile. Disappointment when the ball misses the bat and wicket or when a fielder drops a catch will always be expressed, often audibly and often captured avariciously by the stump microphones in a televised match. Bitter comments, criticism and complaints about one's own lack of luck have always been the preserve of bowlers. It is inevitable that fielders will show their support, encourage and sympathise with their bowler. However, when comments, initially generalised but increasingly more personal, become abusive or orchestrated attempts to drive a player on the opposition team towards 'mental disintegration', as Steve Waugh, the former Australian captain put it, things have gone too far.

Sledging has become an art form for some players and teams. It is usually loud, often unpleasant and would not be acceptable in another workplace. It can be a form of bullying, designed to annoy, intimidate, destroy concentration or make an opponent feel uncomfortable. It certainly goes against the Spirit of Cricket's exhortation to respect your opponent.

Nobody wants to make cricket a less exciting contest between hard, uncompromising contestants, but it is another area of the game which arouses intense aggravation and pushes players towards an over-aggressive attitude, which on occasions has even led, in club matches, to physical violence on the pitch. Experienced umpires see the signs at an early stage, and the best are able to diffuse the situation before it really leads to a full confrontation. Weak umpires are less able to do this, and this is where the behaviour of players worsens unless the captain stands up and takes responsibility, as required in the Laws.

It is all too easy for anyone trying to extol the virtues of playing within the Spirit of Cricket to be laughed off as someone who still believes in fairy tales. Ultimately it is up to the players, officials and administrators in the era in which they are playing to decide how they want to play their cricket. Attitudes change through the years, and moral standards which were once thought of as absolute are now sometimes regarded as relative. Is cheating acceptable if the person involved is not discovered? Does being a professional mean that winning at all costs is required? Has cricket at international level changed from being a game, a competitive contest between two teams, to an entertainment, a spectacle which needs to be presented to spectators with confrontation and controversy? I hope not.

Although cricket originated as a game on which wagers could be placed, administrators must be on their guard constantly nowadays for illegal betting, match and spot fixing. It has brought shame on a few players and prison sentences; it has links with organised crime and has purportedly led to more than one murder. It has cast doubt on the integrity of our game and put vulnerable players under pressure. It has no doubt brought wealth to some, who have not been caught, and has provided illegal bookmakers and their agents with a stream of business.

Cricket is certainly not the only sport having to deal with this threat, but that is little consolation. Education programmes have been introduced by ICC and the Full Members' Boards, but spot fixing such as deliberately bowling a no-ball or a wide on a given delivery, in particular, remains very difficult to detect. It is universally agreed that match fixing should have no place in cricket but it is an endless challenge to the sport's administrators.

The International Cricket Council's vision for cricket is that it should captivate and inspire people of every age, gender, background and ability while building bridges between continents, countries and communities. Central to this ambition is promoting the Spirit of Cricket, an ethos on how the game should be played and viewed both on and off the field.

It is easy to argue that the umpires are present to make decisions and therefore everything should be left to them. It can also be argued that batsmen may receive correct and incorrect decisions against them and therefore they should not do anything until the umpire's decision has been given. There is no doubt that many players believe this, if we are to judge by watching some batsmen at all levels of the game. Is this what we believe to be the Spirit of the Game? Is this showing respect for the umpires and our opponents? Is this approach engendering the atmosphere in which we want to play our cricket? Will this make cricket a better game? I firmly believe not, but the game is in the hands of those who play, officiate and coach it today. We should include with these three groups of participants the cricket writers and the media, who also have a huge influence over spectators, readers and followers of cricket.

Mike Brearley, in his recent book, entitled 'Spirit of Cricket', makes the very valid point that 'the Preamble sits as a preface to, a context for, the Laws, reminding us of the game's broad context, highlighting the informal contract that underlies the necessity for laws that express values such as positivity, safety, balance and equality.' He believes the Preamble should be as brief as possible and reminds us that 'the Laws can't cover everything.' He says: 'We do look to cricket for qualities such as generosity, courtesy and respect for the Laws and the officials who interpret them. I am at least tempted by the belief that we cricket lovers have some special hopes and expectations for the way the game is to be, and often is, played and promoted.'

His own suggested version would be: 'All those involved in cricket should respect the integrity of the game. On the field and off it, the spirit of cricket asks us to "play hard but fair". And let's not lose the essence of the word "play"!'

We all have our own thoughts on the Spirit of Cricket and what it means to us. The more the topic is aired, the more chance we have of reaching the agreed norms so necessary for the game to flourish among future generations of players, officials and spectators.

11

In Retirement

'Little did I think' is not one of my end-of-term reports, but it could easily describe how some of my teachers at Dulwich or supervisors at Cambridge might have thought. I should have worked harder at both educational establishments on the academic subjects although, in hindsight, I am not sure what better A Levels or a more distinguished degree would have done to help me in my three careers.

This expression sums up why I often pinch myself. Little did I think that I would gain a place at Cambridge, that I would play first-class rugby and cricket for the university, that I would captain a county cricket team, that I would become a headmaster, that I would live at Lord's as Secretary & Chief Executive of MCC, that I would have the opportunity to visit so many fascinating countries and meet so many interesting people, that I would build a house in New Zealand, that I would be so fortunate to meet and marry Chris and to produce two successful children and that I would write a book. Finally, as a Cambridge man, little did I think that I would love living in Oxford, which is where we have been since 2014. I am extremely grateful for all the opportunities.

Looking back on three careers, professional cricket as a player, teaching in schools and cricket as an administrator, I know I have been extremely fortunate, and I can't think of anything that I would rather have done. In earlier times I might have played cricket as an amateur as and when employment allowed. Now it would be absolutely impossible to play at a high level without giving total commitment as a professional to the exclusion of any other career. Equally, I would nowadays be hard pressed to find two schools so prepared to release me for the summer term. I loved both teaching and playing cricket, and I share the view of Neville Cardus, who wrote about his job as a cricket writer as 'something you would never give up – even if tomorrow you came into money'. I would have played cricket for nothing, just for the fun and experience and as a challenge, but to have been able to earn a living doing two things that I love was a joy.

Numerous books have been written on leadership and management. So how did I deal with my three distinctly different roles? To be a captain of a cricket team, a head of a school or a chief executive all need leadership. The governance structures are different, the manner of leadership may be different, but there are common values which apply.

Trust and integrity are vital. The ability to listen and to create a strong relationship with the Cricket Manager and Cricket Committee, with the Chairman and Board of Governors, and with the President or Club Chairman and Committee, in whose hands one's future employment may lie, obviously matters greatly. However, real leadership is seen in the respect and rapport that is developed between the captain and the team, the head and the teaching and support staff, and the chief executive and the executive staff. Nobody follows a leader nowadays unless there is an element of respect and confidence that the strategy has been thoroughly thought through and is being implemented and managed with calm, clear decisions. If not enough thought has been put in or the right people not sufficiently consulted, there is little to fall back on when trying to justify a decision. Gone are the days when the Sussex cricketers said that they followed their captain out of curiosity, to see where he would lead them.

There will nearly always be detractors or subordinates who doubt the wisdom of a decision-maker, but clarity of purpose and understanding why and from whom there will be opposition are essential starting points. It is inevitable that a leader cannot please everyone affected by a decision, and there are always 'stakeholders' with clear ideas and agendas of their own. With a cricket team there are players, both those selected and those left out, selectors, coaches and backroom staff, supporters, sponsors and the media. In a school there are pupils, staff, parents, governing body and alumni. At MCC there are members, committees, staff, spectators, home and visiting teams, sponsors and the media. The local community also needs consideration in all three cases.

In retirement, which started in 2006, I was able to continue to pursue the two strands of what had been my occupation for 36 years. It seemed a seamless transition from the world of employment to life as a non-executive. Before retirement I had been invited to join the governing bodies of Lincoln Cathedral School (1991-95), Rendcomb College (1994-99), Dulwich College in 2004 and King's Hall and King's College, Taunton in 1998. I joined the Millfield School governors in 2008 but stood down to avoid any possibility of a conflict of interest when I was invited to be

Chairman of Governors (Custos) of the King's Schools, Taunton in 2010, having chaired their Education Committee for six years. I finally severed my official links with education in 2016, when I retired from that position. Education still remains a real interest, and it is always stimulating to visit the school where our daughter, Katie, is chaplain, not to mention watching our grandchildren in their sports fixtures, plays or concerts.

I have always felt a commitment to Dulwich College Preparatory School and Dulwich College, so it was particularly gratifying to be elected as President of both Old Boys' Associations, the Alleyn Club (2009) and the DPSOB (2015-16).

After retirement I was invited to be President of Surrey CCC (2008), of Cambridge University Cricket Club (2009) and of MCC (2015), producing a kind of symmetry amongst three cricket clubs where I spent a good deal of time as a player or administrator. As Chairman of the Association of Cricket Umpires and Scorers and a Trustee of the MCC Foundation, my links remained as strong with cricket as with education. CUCC and the MCC Foundation still occupy my thoughts and my time and provide opportunities to return to Fenner's and to Lord's.

I still enjoy visiting cricket societies and reminiscing as well as discussing cricket today. There is much to be learnt from the stories of older people who attend the meetings and still retain a passion for the game. It would be very worthwhile for young players to attend occasionally and hear the stories of the older generation. Former players all speak of the enjoyment of the game when they played, and it reminds us all that winning and losing are not the be-all and end-all of a sport. Camaraderie is an essential aspect of the fun of playing. Cricket remains a marvellous game, and the people involved all benefit from it whether players, spectators, officials or statisticians.

One of the highlights of retirement has been fully exploring New Zealand. Chris and I attended the Wellington and Christchurch Tests in February 1997 on behalf of MCC. We were captivated by the beauty and variety of the country and the friendliness and straightforward approach of New Zealanders. In the three weeks we were there, we only stayed in a hotel for five nights. Everywhere else we were hosted by friends or relatives of friends. We arrived, were made to feel very welcome and were told that our hosts had arranged a dinner party for us to meet others. We loved it all and kept in touch with many of them, meeting them again when we took a holiday there in 2004. This was a year when we had just sold a small two-bedroomed apartment in Tenerife, which had served as a family winter holiday retreat for twenty years, so we had some money available. We had never considered a house in New Zealand but, led by an estate agent, we drove round Waiheke Island, where Warren and Lyn Lincoln, our very close friends from Cranleigh and Worksop teaching days, lived. There were some wonderful houses with expansive coastal views, which were well beyond our means, and some decent houses lower down surrounded by bush, more in our price range, which did not appeal to us.

On the last day of our trip it was raining and the estate agent made one last attempt to interest us, although we were still not set on buying anything. He drove to a hillside section, the only one of fifteen plots where there was no house but merely a double garage. The rest of the section was overgrown but had a few fruit trees. He explained that the owner had decided to build elsewhere and was keen to sell. Chris had remained in the car on the main road while I walked round the site and looked at the outstanding views. I was captivated. Chris was astonished when I got back in the car and said I thought that we should buy the land. We agreed a price with the agent and he said we would never regret buying. The flight home on the following day was twenty-four hours of anxiety and self-questioning. What on earth had we done by buying half an acre of land 12,000 miles away from the UK? Admittedly the price was similar to what we had in our pocket after the sale of the Tenerife property, but there was nothing left with which to build a house.

For six years we did nothing except pay a local gardener to keep the grass down. We travelled out once in 2006 to stay with the Lincolns and realised what a stunning position we had, despite the fact that we could still not afford to build. Then in 2010, when we were there again, we went to see the same agent, Clive Lonergan, who said that the land had appreciated. If we sold it, we would make a reasonable profit. Excited, we then spent a week in Christchurch with our other very close New Zealand friends, Richard and Jill Bromley, who said that, with that amount of money, we could buy a townhouse in Christchurch. We looked at some lovely properties, but there was not the same attraction in living in a city as being on an island in Auckland harbour.

On our return to Auckland we went for a walk along Muriwai beach near Kumeu. When we returned to the car someone had broken the back quarter light window and stolen Chris' handbag. Fortunately there was little of value in it, but we decided that we should report it to the police in Kumeu. On the way to the police station we drove past a ready-made house that was for sale and available to be transported to any site, as so often happens in

232

New Zealand. After reporting the loss of the handbag, we went back and walked round the two-storey house, which was on sale for NZ$250,000 (about £120,000 at the exchange rate then). Although that was a figure that we might be able to borrow, the house was not quite right. Amazingly there was a design-and-build company next door. We met the owner. It turned out that he had been a policeman on Waiheke Island, so he knew the area well.

Over the years I had attempted to design a floorplan bearing in mind the dimensions of the site; just in case ... ! I dug this out on my laptop and we were prepared for his visit the following day. As we wandered round the section, it became apparent that my single-storey plan needed to change to two storeys, to benefit more from the views and because it was cheaper to build up rather than out. From then on we were gripped with the idea of building a home on this island. Perhaps we were both looking for a new challenge.

After about ten drafts of the contract we agreed a final version and a price. To avoid additional expense through variations to the contract, we visited electricians regarding power points, lighting shops, painters for internal and external colours, kitchen and bathroom equipment stores for fittings, which were all to be included in the cost. We discussed the size of water tanks, because there was no mains water. We looked into the septic tank options, because there was no mains drainage, and investigated access for broadband, which would become an essential part of keeping in contact with the UK while we planned to be away. It was all new to us because not many British people build their own house and certainly not at such a distance. It became a really enjoyable project, and we have never regretted the decision.

There is a huge difference between seeing a new building being installed at a cricket ground and taking responsibility for your own new home. It is not easy to deal with a project manager from a distance of 12,000 miles with telephone conversations late at night and countless emails. However, we were sent photographs of progress, which seemed very slow at first, mainly because Christmas and the southern hemisphere summer holidays intervened. When we arrived back on the island, it was clear that we would not be able to move in before leaving in April. We lived in the double garage for three weeks so as to monitor progress from rather closer.

We bought essential items: a barbecue, bed, fridge and an outdoor table and chairs. We used water off the roof collected in a small tank and washed from a bucket. We had the builders' portable lavatory, which was not pleasant, but it served its purpose. We managed to give a supper party in front of the garage, quite an achievement in the circumstances. And so we came home to the UK with the house unfinished. The company promised to complete it by December when we intended to return. There had been some frustrating moments but, ultimately, we ended with a terrific home on Waiheke Island, which provides a welcome break from the UK winter.

It was a wonderful place to be marooned for three months when the covid-19 virus shut down the world. We went into lockdown for four weeks along with the whole of New Zealand. Our flights were cancelled, and we had to self-isolate and keep a social distance from everyone else. We were able to speak to neighbours from garden to garden or from driveway to balcony. We also stopped to chat, two metres apart, with friends whom we passed on the beach or on the wonderful coastal walkways. There was not a single case of the virus on the island, and New Zealand, with its smaller population, handled the pandemic efficiently and articulated clearly what each level of lockdown entailed.

During the construction period we soon came to realise that, although New Zealand was twelve hours ahead of Greenwich Mean Time, Waiheke Island was another timescale altogether. On one of the days when our local builder was on site, he asked whether he could take a couple of hours off at lunchtime to deliver his boat to be repaired. He did not reappear that afternoon but in the morning arrived with a couple of snapper for us, saying that it had been such a lovely day for fishing. We accepted his apology, as he was a first-class builder and certainly enjoyed our fish that evening on the barbecue. We had already seen the large notice that greets drivers arriving on the vehicular ferry to the island, which says 'Slow down you're here', so we should have been prepared for the speed of the lifestyle.

We have made many new friends there, volunteering as guides for 'Sculpture on the Gulf', a biennial exhibition of sculptures set up round a beautiful promontory, and the Waiheke House Tour, where there are a number of architect-designed 'Open Homes'. I drive visitors, Chris is based at one of the homes to greet people. The island has tennis courts, a golf course, a tiny 40-seater cinema, where everyone sits on second-hand sofas, beautiful beaches, very good restaurants and 27 wineries, two of which are within easy walking distance. We are situated at the top of our section, ten minutes' walk from the main village on the island, Oneroa, and twenty minutes' walk down a path through the bush to the ferry terminal, where the boats leave every half hour during the summer for a 35-minute crossing to Auckland city business district. Lots of friends from the UK, from elsewhere in New Zealand and from Australia have stayed with us. We entertained the MCC World Cricket Committee to a drink at Cable Bay Winery and then a barbecue at our home.

We organised our Ruby Wedding celebrations in 2011 as a three-day event on Waiheke. A barbecue on Saturday evening, drinks and speeches at the house with lunch at the Cable Bay restaurant on Sunday and activities on Monday, ranging from a walk round the headland, golf, a visit to a private sculpture exhibition to wine-tasting. Friends provided beds. We had six staying with us. What is so marvellous about New Zealanders is that they are a 'can do' nation. Our neighbours joined in the celebrations, and everyone contributed to a memorable occasion for Chris and me.

It might originally have seemed strange to buy a plot of land on the other side of the world on a whim, but it has turned out to be a fantastic decision.

We started married life by sharing our time between Eastbourne in the winter and Bristol in the summer. We had the split year based on education and cricket from 1971 until 1984 and now we spend several months during the UK winter in the southern hemisphere, whilst our main home remains Oxford.

The downside is that we miss children and grandchildren, but Skype, FaceTime, WhatsApp and Zoom compensate for that and allow us to communicate. There are so many upsides. We look forward to arriving in New Zealand for the southern hemisphere summer and to arriving back in the UK for spring and summer. We see friends in both places and have different routines. There is always a new challenge when we arrive on Waiheke Island and we have usually managed to organise house swaps in Australia or elsewhere in New Zealand en route to Auckland, so we keep in touch with other friends and see different places.

The advantage of Oxford is that it is easily accessible. It is a wonderful city in which to have a base. We live fifteen minutes away from Radley College, where the Real Tennis club is an attraction. From Oxford the transport system works well. Trains from the station, which is only ten minutes' walk away from our home, take an hour to Paddington or Marylebone. We can catch buses to London, Heathrow or Gatwick at a stop five minutes from the house. The motorway network via the M40, M4 or M5 takes us north, south, east or west. The city centre is walkable in ten minutes.

Dorset was a welcome eight years away from the hectic schedules in St John's Wood and London, where the slower pace of life gave us both the chance to recharge batteries and come to terms with retirement. Oxford now provides the proximity of shops and public transport, plenty of cultural activities and restaurants and good walks along the towpath or further afield.

My contract of employment with MCC prevented me from writing a book about the Club or my role within it for two years after my retirement date. In any case I did not want to publish my thoughts or record my memories while I was 'yesterday's man'. It was important to move on and allow my successor and the Committee the chance to take the Club in a new direction.

However, now that I am past that deadline, it is time to put some details down about my thoughts on the years at the helm of MCC. Now that there have been two successors, Keith Bradshaw and Derek Brewer, and Guy Lavender has become the sixteenth Secretary of MCC, I am the 'predecessor of the-day-before-yesterday's man'.

Why have I wanted to write? It is so that I can recall what have been key moments in my life, to regale my family and friends with my memories and to give others who may read the book an insight into the pleasures and challenges of my life in my twin passions of cricket and education.

My motivation is not unlike the words of Marilyn Monroe in the documentary, 'Love, Marilyn':

From time to time I
make it rhyme but
don't hold that kind
of thing
against me –
Oh well, what the hell,
so it won't sell.
What I want to tell – is
what's on my mind:
'taint Dishes,
'taint Wishes,
it's thoughts flinging by
before I die –
and to think in ink.

Others will write with differing views about the topics in the book, there will be minutes of some of the meetings or discussions mentioned, but I have wanted to write down my own recollections, as I was there. Although memories fade and recollections can vary over time, I kept diaries and copious notes throughout my time at Lord's, and I have referred to them in setting out some of the episodes in this book.

One of the things that I have learnt over the years is that it is important constantly to look at the present and forward to the future. The past has gone and, whilst it is vital to retain memories and learn from what has gone before, one must not keep hankering over a return to a former existence. Each of the moves that I have made has been after deliberation and then looking forward to something new rather than escaping or wistfully looking back. Retirement to Dorset came at the right moment after a full-on existence in London. The decision to leave the relative isolation of the West Country after eight years to move to Oxford to live in closer proximity to our children and grandchildren had the added advantage of moving to a city where public transport, museums, restaurants and shops were within easy walking distance. We always knew that a small city or large town would be essential as we grew older.

When we moved, Katie was chaplain at a girls' day school in Abingdon and Graeme lived in south-west London, practising as a criminal barrister. That Katie and her family moved a year later from a village just outside Oxford to take up her new post in the West Country has not made us regret our move in any way. From the sitting room window in Corscombe in West Dorset there was not a house in sight and an uninterrupted view for forty miles towards Glastonbury Tor. As Chris said, though, if there are no houses, there are few people. My sister and her husband and some very close friends lived within half an hour, but friends did not call in often. We made a small new group of friends, but there are more opportunities in Oxford to see and meet people.

12

A Christian Upbringing and Faith

Slowly through my life, and with hesitancy at times, I have become clearer about my faith as a Christian. A number of milestones along the way have guided my thoughts and confirmed my beliefs.

As a junior boy at Dulwich, I sang in the Chapel choir and went to church on Sundays. What persuaded me first to consider faith more seriously was a trip, as a school prefect, to hear the evangelist Billy Graham speak in London. A couple of coachloads of boys travelled to hear the inspirational speaker, and he was powerful and impressive. At the end of his presentation he asked anyone who felt suitably inspired to come down to the stage, and quite a few people went forward. I did not feel ready to do that, though there was a strong urge to join the group congregating in front of me. Although I left the choir when my voice broke, I continued to go to the College chapel each Sunday with my parents and the boarders.

The St Catharine's College chaplain, Rev David Sparrow, challenged me and made me think during the years at Cambridge, though I was not a regular chapel attendee. In the first teaching appointment at Eastbourne College, where I was a tutor in Gonville House, I teamed up with another tutor, Euan Clarke, and we held house prayers when we were on duty. We discussed and sought views from the boys, but it also gave me the chance to consider my own beliefs about Christianity and ethics, challenged by sensible questions from the boarders.

There were other factors in my spiritual growth. I was invited by Rev Andrew Wingfield Digby, director of Christians in Sport, to take part in a cricket tour to India. I could only go for the week of half term, whereas the tour lasted three weeks, but it was another insight into the good work done by that organisation. Before we left for India every member of the tour party was asked to write a few words, to be included on a personal card, which we would carry with us. It was slightly embarrassing that there was a misprint on my card. I had intended to say: "I could not think of a more worthwhile trip than one which encompassed cricket and Christianity." Sadly the printer had included an extra 'e' at the end of 'trip', so I kept most of my cards to myself.

On the tour we coached youngsters at cricket, and various members of the team, but not I, preached. I remember, after one of the matches, when Andrew was given the microphone as we all sat out on the cricket square, being surprised to see how many spectators had stayed on to hear the speeches. There was an amazingly colourful stand of women in their saris, and everyone was keen to hear what Andrew had to say. It was as he said, "Although we are in India to play cricket, the main point of the tour is to spread the word of Jesus Christ", that my neighbour on the line of chairs, one of the opposition players, turned to me and asked whether Andrew was aware that all the crowd were Hindus. Nevertheless we were welcomed, the words of wisdom went down well, and it was a marvellous experience to visit the country where cricket is the top sport.

As a result of the link with Christians in Sport, I was invited to give a testimony in front of about three hundred professional footballers after a dinner. The Christian tennis commentator, Gerald Williams, was to put questions to a scout from Manchester United, the Swindon Town goalkeeper and me, about our faith. Cliff Richard was the last man on the agenda, so we were all delighted to be on the same bill as the great singer. As the dinner drew to a close, I began to wonder how any comments about faith would be received by a group of professional footballers and whether what we said would be greeted with cynicism.

My concern grew even more when the Swindon Town goalkeeper went to join Gerald Williams on stage, and the opening question was; "What part does faith play in your life?" The goalkeeper took the microphone and said with great enthusiasm that whenever he went up to gather a high ball he knew that Jesus was behind him. The reaction was muted from the footballers, and I realised that I would not be able to make a statement such as that.

What part did faith play in my life? I read the Bible each day and, as I said when it was my turn, the words of the Bible helped me to keep a balance as a professional sportsman. It was all too easy to be on a high after one game and then down after a bad day. Reading the Bible gave me perspective and helped me to focus on other things more important than the immediate successes or failures that were bound to come along in a professional career where consistency was extremely difficult. I do not recall the response to what I said, but I felt that I had been honest and had not made any claims that might have given rise to a cynical reaction. Listening to Cliff Richard sing and then give his own testimony was a much easier task.

I realised then how difficult I found it to speak about my faith, something which has never really changed. I wish I had read then a recent quote by Sonny Bill Williams, the New Zealander who reached the top in rugby union, rugby league and boxing, when he was speaking to the *New Zealand Herald* about his faith. He had turned to Islam, but what he said was heartfelt and reminded me of very similar sentiments as a Christian. "It enables me to take a step back and look at my blessings," he explained. "But then it also allows me to be a fierce competitor, to know that my opportunities don't come too often."

As a housemaster and then a headmaster, there were always invitations to give a talk or preach a sermon at preparatory schools, which were an opportunity to communicate ideas and also encourage the boys and girls to consider coming on to my schools. On one occasion I was invited by Stuart Morris, the headmaster of Papplewick Prep School, to speak to his boys at a Sunday Service. I had decided to make use of the acronym JOY and recommend that the way to live one's life was first to put Jesus, second to consider Others and finally to think about Yourself. I had been impressed by the simplicity of the message when I first heard it in a sermon. We were sitting in Stuart's drawing room just before the service was due to start when the doorbell rang, and he ushered in one of the parents. I felt that I recognised the man but could not place him or think where I might have met him. However, it all became clear when Stuart introduced me to King Hussein of Jordan, whose son had recently joined the school. I do not think that I have ever preached to a king since that day, but it was certainly a new experience.

Some years later, in 2005, I was due to speak in Sherborne Abbey to the boys' school's boarders one Sunday when the chaplain rang me and asked whether I could be available on the following Sunday rather than the date which had been in my diary for some months. The occasion was one of the several memorial services, organised after the death of Bishop David Sheppard, an Old Shirburnian, and the headmaster thought it would be appropriate for me to speak at this Service, which would be attended by David's widow. I had met Grace at Lord's when she donated one or two items of the great man's official clothing to MCC's museum, and it was a privilege to accept the invitation.

It led to much greater preparation than usual, but that gave me enormous pleasure, as I researched what he had done as a Cambridge University, Sussex and England cricketer as well as his many strengths as Bishop of

Liverpool. I recalled how the groundsman and coach at Fenner's, Cyril Coote, had spoken glowingly of the early 50s, when Cambridge University had four outstanding batsmen in the same team. Hubert Doggart, John Dewes, Peter May and David Sheppard were all England cricketers and, in Cyril Coote's view, the best of them all was David Sheppard.

Both Chris and I were thrilled when our daughter Katie was ordained into the Church of England. She had veered in that direction after teaching English in a prep school, where the headmaster was the same Euan Clarke, who had inspired me to launch into house prayers at Eastbourne College. She was encouraged by her husband, Roy, who was also a committed Christian and who often played the organ in church, as well as improvising on the piano and entertaining customers for hours on end in Brown's Restaurant in Cambridge. We were more than pleased to take communion from her in her church in Bath, where she was briefly the vicar of Widcombe.

The impending arrival of twins rather cut short that career, though she is now expanding both her teaching and her pastoral strengths as chaplain in a boarding school. When Graeme, our son, married Meredith, his American fiancée, in Plymouth, Massachusetts, Katie was asked to officiate. The local vicar, a rather austere woman priest who had to be in attendance to oversee one formal part of the ceremony, was surprised, perhaps even shocked, when Katie started her address by saying that she would never have expected to be in a church marrying her own brother. The wedding was a lovely ceremony.

As Headmaster of Worksop College and later as Chairman of Governors of King's College, Taunton, I was heavily involved with two Woodard Schools, Anglican foundations with leanings towards a high-church approach. In both cases I thoroughly enjoyed being in chapel, taking part in serving the communion wine, preaching a sermon or reading a lesson. I always thought it was a central part of the education in those schools, and I was fortunate to have inspiring chaplains and Woodard provosts who showed real interest in the spiritual growth of the boys, girls and staff. I did notice, though, as headmaster that the pupils often only bowed their heads when the sermon was in full swing and then sat upright, in minor rebellious mood, when the prayers were announced. That had almost certainly been the same when I was a sixth former at Dulwich, and I accepted it as the way teenagers react to being expected to attend a chapel service. It is noticeable, though, how often they readily recall their services when they return as former pupils and then ask to be married in the chapel. Something must have rubbed off on them during their schooldays.

I believe in the power of prayer and try to say a few words of thanks each day as well as reading a passage from the Bible. Undoubtedly, I am like many others and tend to focus my prayers when real concerns emerge, as I did when Chris learned from a specialist in Southampton that she had an acoustic neuroma, a non-malignant tumour close to her ear and her brain. It came as a real bolt out of the blue to be told that she had two options: to do nothing and risk having a heart attack, a stroke or facial palsy, or to undergo surgery, which, being so close to the brain, carried a risk of a heart attack, a stroke or facial palsy and certain loss of hearing in that ear. The options seemed appalling and we came away shattered.

I did pray harder than ever for the next few days, and then we were both reminded that one of the surgeons in Harley Street, with whom Chris had worked as a practice manager, was an Ear, Nose and Throat specialist. We contacted Jonny Harcourt and went to see him, with his recommended neurologist, in London. The consultation and examination could not have been more encouraging. Jonny said that there was an alternative method of treating these acoustic neuromas, provided the tumour was limited in size, which Chris's was, though it was close to the upper limit. There were only five hospitals in the UK which had the right machine and, fortunately, his neurosurgeon had access to one of them.

The result was that, a few weeks later, she had gamma knife surgery, which is a non-invasive radio therapy treatment using gamma rays. It was certainly not pleasant, and the after effects were destabilising and caused nausea and a lack of balance and confidence for months, but the treatment worked wonderfully well and reduced over time the size of the tumour. Chris took some time to recover her full confidence and I continued to pray, convinced that my prayers had been heard and were being answered.

I still find difficulty in expressing with clarity and confidence my true religious beliefs, but attending a small midweek Fellowship Group linked to our church in Oxford, St Ebbe's, has helped as we have discussed and studied the Bible in greater depth. Chris and I attend St Ebbe's church in Oxford, where Vaughan Roberts is an inspiring leader, where sermons are based on the Bible reading and where there is a cross-section of younger and older worshippers amongst whom we feel comfortable.

One of the songs that we have sung in the church was written by Bob Kauflin in 2006 and is called 'O Great God', which I believe is appropriate as a prayer as I come towards the end of this chapter.

O great God of highest heav'n,
Occupy my lowly heart,
Own it all and reign supreme,
Conquer every rebel pow'r.
Let no vice or sin remain
That resists Your holy war;
You have loved and purchased me;
Make me Yours for evermore.

I was blinded by my sin,
Had no ears to hear your voice,
Did not know Your love within,
Had no taste for heaven's joys.
Then Your Spirit gave me life,
Opened up Your word to me,
Through the gospel of Your Son
Gave me endless hope and peace.

Help me now to live a life
That's dependent on Your grace;
Keep my heart and guard my soul
From the evils that I face.
You are worthy to be praised
With my ev'ry thought and deed;
O great God of highest heav'n,
Glorify Your Name through me.

Rather than stating my faith openly or evangelising, I have often alluded to it by delivering Grace at dinners. That all began at Eastbourne College when I was master in charge of rugby and thought that the team should start their end-of-season dinner with a few words of thanks for the meal. They had not been accustomed to that, so I decided that I had to make the Grace topical and particularly relevant to them and use words to which they might listen. It began a regular habit of delivering Grace in rhyme, which continued at Cranleigh, Worksop and Lord's.

It was extremely flattering, but always felt wrong, when diners applauded the Grace. However, it did attract their attention and perhaps they listened to the words of gratitude to the Lord. It was an honour and especially pleasing, though, when one of these Graces, from a dinner in May 1997,

243

was included in 'A Breathless Hush – The MCC Anthology of Cricket Verse' by the editors, Hubert Doggart and David Rayvern Allen.

As usual, after the AGM, the Club held the annual Anniversary Dinner of that year in the Long Room. The Australians had arrived. They were a formidable team and always played the game in an uncompromising way. England won the first Test at Edgbaston and, after a draw in the Lord's Test, went to Old Trafford still one up in the series. The series of six Tests was eventually lost 3-2, as Australia won the third, fourth and fifth Tests before losing the last Test at the Oval. It was the first time for some years that England had been ahead in an Ashes series. It was close but in the end still a defeat. There had been optimism after England had won all three ODIs and as Taylor, the Australian captain, was put under pressure by criticism of his captaincy. In the end McGrath, Gillespie and Kasprowicz, supported by Warne, were too much for the England batsmen. England had not won at Lord's since 1934, and the rain-affected draw extended a sequence that only ended in 2009. This was the Grace.

We give thanks for our guests from Australia
And the pleasure their visit affords.
As there's no Ashes Tour that's a failure
We look forward to matches at Lord's.
As we all look ahead to the cricket
And we pray for a summer of sun,
Though we know that it's tough at the wicket,
May we hope that the players have fun?
Bless us all at this MCC dinner
Every cricketer present or past.
Bless each batsman, each keeper each spinner
And those fortunate men who bowl fast.
Make this evening one more for our treasures
Bless the food that we eat and the wine
Make us grateful for all cricket's pleasures
As we sit down together to dine.

One of the most satisfying aspects of starting a meal with a rhyming Grace is that people listen and sit down to eat in a good mood. It is most encouraging that Keith Bradshaw continued to deliver such a Grace, as did Derek Brewer, and now more often than not it is the custom for a rhyming Grace by the Secretary & Chief Executive to be delivered in the

Long Room. Guy Lavender is probably the best of us all with his words. It is strange to see how small traditions are created.

There is a collection of Graces in the next chapter. Looking through the collection of all the Graces it became clear that they were a good historical record, providing memories of dinners, events, people and evenings enjoyed. They all reflected the mood and specific happenings of the time, and now they remind me of some memorable occasions. There are, perhaps inevitably, similar themes which recur and rhymes which are repeated. Whilst making no claims to being a poet, I have enjoyed writing, and at times struggling at the last minute to produce, meaningful Graces with suitable and relevant words.

In each instance in the next chapter I have described, briefly, the background to the date and the dinner at which the Grace was delivered. On occasions I have also been reminded of other poignant memories and branched off into a short digression. These Graces have brought back to me emotions and moments from the past in the same way as the music on the radio programme, Desert Island Discs, does to the guests who have chosen their favourite records.

13

The Dinner Graces

There were many Graces that could have been included here, but these all hold particularly happy memories for me. In each case there is a topical relevance which influenced my choice of words.

Dinner in Honour of Doug Insole

A dinner in honour of Doug Insole following an MCC Committee meeting. Doug had been cricket captain of Cambridge University and went on to captain Essex for many years. He was one of the Wisden Cricketers of the Year in 1956. He was chairman of selectors for England in the 1960s. For his many services to cricket, he was appointed a CBE in 1979. He was an England tour manager, highly influential within Essex, the TCCB and ICC. He later became chairman of the European Cricket Council and helped to build the number of cricket-playing countries in Europe to thirty.

Doug had, for years, turned down invitations by outgoing Presidents to become MCC President. He was eventually persuaded by Robin Marlar, my last President, to accept in 2006-07 and, although sadly it was not during my time as Secretary & Chief Executive, it was thoroughly deserved and a popular decision. I would have relished working closely with Doug. He and Norma, Chris and I used to go to Pizza Express in Dean Street to listen to the jazz. He had been at St Catharine's College, Cambridge with Peter Boizot, the founder and owner of the chain of restaurants and, whenever we went, Doug would point out and introduce us to the musicians and diners who were MCC members, of whom there were several.

Bless the game which brings us together
Throughout the world in every weather.
As England play in climes much warmer
We come to dine with Doug and Norma.
Help our team to play their best,
Especially in the coming Test.
Thanks for the food we shall all soon be eating
Now the Committee has finished its Meeting.
As we now sit down to dine,
LORD, our thanks for food and wine.

Pakistan Touring Team Dinner – 1996

MCC always used to invite the touring party to a lunch or dinner at Lord's around the time of the Lord's Test. It was not always welcomed by the players, but it was very much enjoyed by the members and the Committee who attended. It was a tradition that the Club wished to continue. Some teams were less gracious in accepting the invitation, but the Pakistan team of 1996 were delightful, attended in full touring dress of blazers and contributed thoroughly to the dinner in the Long Room, including a fine speech from their captain who introduced the players.

All you men from Islamabad and from Lahore,
From Karachi, Rawalpindi, here dining once more,
May we welcome you here as our guests for this week.
Let our Lord bless our food and the words that we speak.
May we wish that both teams can produce of their best?
When, on Thursday, we come back to Lord's for the Test.
When your team and the English set out on this match
Make your runs, take your wickets and catch every catch.

Long Room Dinner – 1997

Lord Alexander, then an influential Committee member, was keen on bringing together members, committee members and the staff, and we held this dinner in the Long Room in 1997. It was an Ashes year and England had not played well against the Australians for some years, so there was hope but not expectation for the season. The England team had just returned from Zimbabwe, the first time that the team had visited that country. They played and lost the three one-day internationals and drew both Tests. The leading Zimbabwean wicket-taker in the ODIs was Eddo Brandes, who was a chicken farmer, which became a joke in the media and made the defeats galling to the professional set-up under the newly-formed ECB.

David Lloyd, the coach, was frustrated that his team could not pull off a victory in either Test and both were drawn. He was quoted as saying to the media: "We murdered them. We got on top and steamrollered them. We have flipping hammered them. One more ball and we'd have walked it. We murdered them, and they know it. To work so hard and get so close, there is no praise too high. We have had some stick off your lads. We flipping hammered them."

The dinner was welcomed by staff and members.

As we come to the start of the season
And we gather to talk of the past,
We look forward to greeting the Aussies,
In the hope that we'll beat them at last.
May we all put this winter behind us,
And the comments we've read in the press.
One-Day games have been quite disappointing,
Though we murdered the team in the Tests!
Bless the Lord Alexander of Weedon
And the Treasurer here in the chair.
May their words give us all inspiration,
When we've tasted the caterers' fare?
Bless our food and the wine on our tables,
Make us grateful for what we receive.
Bless the staff and the members attending;
Guide them home when they finally leave.

Dinner in Honour of EW (Jim) Swanton

There have been many dinners to celebrate and honour individuals in the Long Room, probably the most famous room in cricket. The dinner for EW (Jim) Swanton evokes several memories from my links with a man who was an extensive writer and broadcaster, summarising Test matches for years, and who had just celebrated his 90th birthday. He was a member of the Arts & Library Sub-Committee of MCC and never short of advice.

He had acted as one of my referees when I was being interviewed for the position at Lord's and when Chris and I moved into the Secretary's House, which had been Sir Gubby Allen's home before his death, there was a message on John Stephenson's answerphone, which, as his successor, I had inherited. It was a gruff message from Jim, asking whether he could stay the night. He came to stay with us, as he had in our Cranleigh boarding house, when he attended a dinner there to speak as an Old Cranleighan.

When I attended one of my early Arts & Library meetings they were discussing the positioning of the portraits and paintings in the Pavilion. Everyone on that sub-committee had views on what should be where. I was, though, momentarily thrown when Jim asked me whether I was joining the 'hanging committee'. I was aware that Lord's was sometimes seen as an intimidating place, but I did not think it had that sort of power over life and death!

One of the most fascinating conversations that I have heard was in 1998 when Jim was asked to interview Mrs Primrose Worthington, the 93-year-old granddaughter of WG Grace, at the launch of an exhibition to celebrate the 150th anniversary of the great cricketer's birth. She recalled travelling between Beckenham and Croydon to visit him and sitting on his knee plaiting his beard. When asked how she had travelled, she replied that it was by bus. Jim immediately asked whether it was the number 13, horse-drawn, and she seemed to think it was. It was wonderful to hear two 90-year-old characters chatting.

Bless us all as we sit down this evening,
Here to celebrate ninety great years.
As a batsman approaches his century
He's assailed by a number of fears:
Should he pace himself throughout the nineties?
Should he look for a six and a four?
Should he take fewer risks than his partner?
We know Jim will go on as before!
May the Lord bless our food at this dinner,
As we show that we're grateful to Him?
Make us welcoming, charming companions;
And especially for Ann and for Jim.

Melbourne CC Dinner at Lord's – 1997

After the Ashes Test match at Lord's or at the MCG we had instituted a match between the two MCCs, Marylebone Cricket Club and Melbourne Cricket Club. This was always a competitive match, although it was mutually accepted that neither team would be boosted by 'ringers' brought in to steal a march on the visiting opposition. On this occasion the match was ruined by rain, as the Test match had been. There had been a problem with intruders on the ground at some matches that season, and all sorts of measures were put in place to catch and eject them. It was proposed by some uncharitable spectators that they should be ejected from the ground without allowing them to return to their clothes, which were generally left with a friend from where they made their dash. We decided that this was definitely not right and would only draw more attention to them, however embarrassing it might be for them to catch a bus or tube to get home.

Lord, bless the Melbourne team, who came
To seek success or failure.
But found the weather spoilt the game
As England and Australia.
Lord, bless us all from MCC
As we sit down to dinner.
We'll play again at MCG,
With one of us the winner.
We say our thanks for friendships made
Through tours abroad and cricket.
We pray these links will never fade
In bars and at the wicket.
Lord, bless our food and bless the words
We'll hear from both the speakers.
Lord, bless our cricket ground at Lord's,
And keep it free from streakers!

Cricket Writers' Club Dinner – 1997

The NatWest Final had been scheduled to be played on Saturday 6 September in 1997, but Princess Diana had died in a car crash on 31 August and her public funeral service was to be held on that day. Out of respect the match was postponed until Sunday 7 September. The Cricket Writers held their dinner on what should have been the eve of the match, and John Woodcock, Wendy Wimbush and Patrick Eagar were present in their positions of President, Secretary and Chairman.

> At this time of deepest sorrow,
> And the lack of Match tomorrow,
> May we still enjoy this meal,
> Whilst reflecting how we feel.
> At the Writers' annual meeting,
> Where there's drinking and good eating,
> We give thanks for food and wine,
> As we now sit down to dine.
> Wooders, Wendy, Chairman Patrick:
> What a most impressive hat trick!
> Thank you, Lord, for all these winners,
> And the Cricket Writers' dinners.

Princess Diana Memorial Ball – 1998

In 1998 MCC celebrated the 150th anniversary of WG Grace's birthday, but the Club decided to stage this match for an additional, very sad reason – the untimely death of Princess Diana, as mentioned in the previous Grace. On the evening before the match we organised a dinner and dance in the Nursery Pavilion in an attempt to increase the amount of money that the match itself would raise for charity. The two teams were present, captained by Michael Atherton and Sachin Tendulkar. The world's best players had shown great support and were pleased to have been invited.

The match was a huge success and raised over £1 million for the Princess Diana Memorial Fund. Michael Atherton's MCC XI scored 261 for four in their 50 overs, Shivnarine Chanderpaul scoring 127 and Mohammad Azharuddin 61 off the bowling of Wasim Akram, Ian Bishop, Chris Cairns, Mushtaq Ahmed and Tom Moody.

In reply, Sachin Tendulkar's Rest of the World XI scored 262 for four with six overs to spare. Sachin himself, who sadly never scored a Test century at Lord's and therefore missed out on his name being included on the honours board in the dressing rooms, made a magnificent 125 and Aravinda de Silva scored 82 off a star-studded bowling attack of Glenn McGrath, Javagal Srinath, Allan Donald, Brian McMillan, Anil Kumble, Aamir Sohail and Sourav Ganguly. Their presence at the Ball did not seem to affect the performance of the batsmen on the pitch the following day.

We give thanks for the great Grace of cricket,
Who was loathe to surrender his wicket.
We give thanks for the Princess Diana,
Who appealed to the world by her manner.
Now we stand in the Nursery Pavilion
And we aim to raise close to a million.
Bless our food as we offer our prayers,
Joined today by the world's finest players.
God bless Lord's where we've fitted this match in.
Bless the captains, both Athers and Sachin,
May our game, which for some brings employment,
Bring to all those involved great enjoyment.

West Indies Touring Team Lunch – June 2000

This was the 100th Test match played at Lord's and, to celebrate, MCC invited a number of former West Indies cricketers to join the teams a couple of days before the match for lunch. It made us all realise how many outstanding quick bowlers had made up their teams over the years.

Lord, bless all these great men from West Indies,
Who are here for the hundredth Lord's Test.
Now the players at Lord's from those islands
Have a chance to show why they're the best.
Bowlers Ambrose, Walsh, Marshall and Holding,
Garner, Roberts, Croft, Sobers and Hall,
Gibbs and Griffith are names that bring fear.
We give thanks they're not holding a ball.
We give thanks for Weekes, Worrell and Walcott,
Lara, Kanhai and Greenidge and Haynes.
As we thank you for food at our table,
We are glad that great friendship remains.

MCC Spirit of Cricket Cowdrey Lecture Dinner – 2001

The MCC Spirit of Cricket Cowdrey Lecture was first delivered in 2001. Held in the Nursery Pavilion, Richie Benaud was invited to be the first person to share his views on the game as it is, as it was and how he thought it should be. He was given a broad brief as has been the case in all subsequent lectures. He was outstanding, as one might expect from a former Test captain who became one of the best-loved commentators.

The dinner afterwards in the Long Room was also a great success. Several generations of the Cowdrey family were there at the occasion, which had been initiated in memory of Colin who had died on 4 December 2000. I had, for some time, wanted to create cricket's equivalent of the Reith Lectures, and this MCC Spirit of Cricket Cowdrey Lecture has become a traditional annual event at Lord's.

One of the guests at the Lecture and dinner was Jimmy Adams, the West Indies captain on the tour to England in 2000 and the first recipient of a Spirit of Cricket award presented by MCC. Apart from the way he handled himself and his team on the pitch, Jimmy had set a marvellous example when caught low to the ground at cover when playing well. The moment that the fielder said he had caught the ball, Jimmy walked off, accepting his word and not waiting for the umpires to make a decision. MCC wanted to use this as an example of the Spirit of Cricket and respect for an opponent's word.

God bless our food and bless our wine, at this our Special Dinner,
The Spirit of the Game award and Jimmy, our first winner.
Please bless the Cowdrey family and our friends, who've been invited.
Bless Richie and the words he spoke, by which we were delighted.
We give our thanks for all the fun within the game of cricket;
For bowlers and the fielding side, for batsmen at the wicket.
We all await the match this week of England v Australia.
We hope they'll play both hard and fair, without the fear of failure.
We thank you for the friends we make when playing cricket matches.
As older men we talk again of wickets, runs and catches.
We'll spread the Spirit of the Game and try not to betray it.
We'll hope that youngsters learn the game and love to watch and play it.

Members' Long Room Dinner – 2004

Every President has a number of decisions to make as soon as the appointment is named by his predecessor. There are five winter dinners, monthly from October to February in the Committee Dining Room and another dinner in the Long Room in March. For all of these the President is asked to choose and invite a speaker. Other decisions are to choose a prominent person to deliver the MCC Spirit of Cricket Cowdrey Lecture. Not quite so urgent, but the most important decision, which needs immense thought, is to nominate at the AGM yet another successor for the role of President.

On the occasion of the Long Room dinner in March 2004 the invited speaker was Sir Richard Stilgoe. I was delighted, because Richard had spoken at one of my Benefit Year events at the Oval in 1984, writing the words in the afternoon to a couple of songs which he performed that evening. He is a brilliant lyricist and songwriter and a man who has spent much of his time helping and raising money for disadvantaged children.

I felt that my Grace had to mention Warne and Muralitharan, if not by name at least by their deeds as the world's top spin bowlers. We had just witnessed Test matches between India and Pakistan, sadly a rare and therefore newsworthy event. I also wanted to mention England's performances in the West Indies. Michael Vaughan's team had won three out of the four Test matches and thus already won the Wisden Trophy. Soon after this dinner at Lord's, I was privileged to be at the Antigua Recreation Ground in St John's to witness a marathon of concentration, Brian Lara's innings of 400 not out in Antigua, in the final Test.

As we stand to give thanks for our dinners,
We reflect on the most recent cricket.
We've admired both the world's greatest spinners
Who've each taken their five hundredth wicket.
We've seen India and Pakistan playing
At Karachi's great ground and Rawalpindi's.
And on England's behalf we're now praying
They can build on their start in West Indies.
There is always a rhyme for these Graces
As the regular members will well know,
So before we sit down at our places
Let's all welcome our guest, Richard Stilgoe.

Anniversary Dinner – 2004

John Barclay was the speaker at the Anniversary Dinner which followed the AGM in 2004. A staunch Sussex and MCC man, who always embraced the Spirit of Cricket and enjoyed discussing the game on any occasion, John and I played together for my two years at Hove. Although a keen fisherman, his nickname, Trout, actually stems from his third given name of Troutbeck. He was born in Bonn in Germany, once played internationally for Hong Kong, captained Sussex successfully and was unfortunate not to have gone further into the England team as a player. He later became a tour manager and supported Ray Illingworth when he was manager of the England team.

As usual the AGM had given rise to a number of questions from the membership, and the President, Charles Fry, had handled them all with the support of the MCC staff and his fellow Committee members. During the dinner Charles spoke of his choice of successor: Tom Graveney, the first former professional cricketer to be nominated as President.

Plans were in place for a complete restoration of the Pavilion which, as a listed building, fulfils different functions besides being a stand for members to watch cricket, with several catering facilities and dressing rooms for players and officials. The Long Room, probably the most famous room in any sport, is a marvellous venue for dinners, lunches, receptions, concerts and lectures. The whole Pavilion is an art gallery, housing many valuable paintings. There are meeting rooms for committees and offices for some senior MCC executives. There are the Members' Bar and the Bowlers' Bar, both overlooking the ground, the Members' Lounge and, since the renovation, there is a wonderful terrace where members can sit or stand to watch the game near to one of the two turrets where there are bars. It is an important part of the Lord's Tour for all the many visitors who enjoy a trip round the ground, being shown the dressing rooms and the honours boards, where they see the names inscribed of all players, England and visiting teams, who have scored a century or taken five wickets in an innings at Lord's. Until recently they were only included if the feat was achieved in the Test match, but, rightly, One-Day International matches are now included.

We've expressed many views at our meeting
And we've argued each point till we're dry.
So before we sit down and start eating
We say thank you to President Fry.
At this Club Anniversary Dinner,
In the Long Room we're soon to restore,
We're delighted that Vaughan's team's a winner
And comes home with three wins out of four.
We give thanks for our friends made through cricket,
Which the Spirit of Cricket's about.
We'll recall all our runs and each wicket,
Then we'll settle to listen to Trout.

Members' Winter Dinner – October 2004

The winter dinners in 2004 had to be held in another venue, as the Pavilion was undergoing its complete renovation. The members present stood to remember Keith Miller, who had died on 11 October that year. One of the great Australian team of 1948, Keith was a real friend of Lord's and MCC. He visited whenever he could, particularly when the Ashes series were being played.

Several of the survivors of the 'Invincibles' arrived for these matches at Lord's, generously paid for by a New Zealander philanthropist, who had settled in Sydney but never wanted his name to be mentioned as the sponsor of the trip for Neil Harvey, Keith Miller, Alan Davidson, Arthur Morris, Bill Johnston and Peggy Lindwall, Ray's widow.

On one of the Australian tours to England, when Richie Benaud was making his early appearances for his country, Keith is said to have taken the young player into the Long Room and said: "Take a look at the greatest cricket ground in the world." Apparently, Richie's response, on looking out of the large Long Room windows at the square and the Compton and Edrich Stands, was that it wasn't flat. The Lord's slope has been mentioned countless times throughout the history of cricket, and it has always required a slight readjustment from batsmen and bowlers, who both have their favourite ends.

Keith Miller's death was a particularly poignant moment for me. I was introduced to Keith by Denis Compton at the Paul Getty cricket ground at Wormsley in August 1993, just before I took up the position at Lord's. He told me that Lord's was a special place for him and for other cricketers and wished me luck. When I moved into my new office on 4 January 1994 there was a letter from him on my desk. He said that he knew that I would enjoy the role and was confident I would do a good job. What is more, two days later he telephoned from Australia to wish me luck again. What a man!

At this dinner the speaker was David Kendix, the Middlesex scorer, who went on to become advisor to ECB and ICC on the application of the Duckworth/Lewis method of determining the winner in the event of a rain-affected or delayed match.

As we meet with our numbers diminished,
And a very long season just finished,
We give thanks for this different location
To allow all our redecoration.
Bless our Club and all those who've attended.
Bless Keith Miller whose life sadly ended.
For the food and the wine make us grateful,
As we sit and devour every plateful.
When it rains and the scorers say "who is
The best man to decide Duckworth/Lewis?"
They're delighted to see whom the Board picks.
Bless our speaker tonight, David Kendix.

Members' Winter Dinner – November 2004

The following month Alec and Eric Bedser were the guest speakers. There was much talk in the media about the number of meaningless one-day matches without any context that were being played. Also there was a good deal of ongoing speculation about Murali's action when bowling the doosra, which cast a shadow over his extraordinary performances. It led to ICC defining an illegal delivery as being where the player's elbow extends by an amount of more than 15 degrees between their arm reaching the horizontal and the ball being released.

Once again the dinner was held in the Warner Stand restaurant. Linda Le Ker was the catering manager in the Players' and Committee Dining Rooms. She took over from Nancy Doyle who was a legend in the way she handled players who dared to come into her dining room improperly dressed. Nancy once threw Philippe Edmonds out, during a county match, for not wearing socks and shoes. Linda and her husband, Alain, a proud and welcoming Frenchman, who was the maître d'hôtel in the two dining rooms, were an excellent couple.

When Linda started, the Middlesex physiotherapist came straight up and suggested that the Middlesex team would like a light healthy lunch during matches. He was followed almost immediately by the Middlesex captain, Mike Gatting, to tell her to ignore the physio's advice and continue with the full lunches to which he and the other players had become accustomed. As county players, we all recognised that lunches at Lord's were the best on the circuit, though not necessarily conducive to running around in the field afterwards. Usually batsmen preferred to eat a roll or salad in the dressing room, unless they could have managed to find a way to get out just before lunch, as some invariably seemed to do.

As we gather again in November
And discuss all the games we remember,
Let us all spare a thought for our players
Who have gone through some pointless one-dayers.
There's been much in the press about throwing,
And an off-spinner seems to be crowing,
As we look through our "tolerance" glasses
May we hope that this crisis soon passes!
It's a year when we seek a new corner,
(And tonight we shall dine with Plum Warner)
As we strive to update the Pavilion
In a project that costs several million.
Lord, we thank you for all you've provided:
For the menu that Linda decided;
For the members attending this dinner;
For Sir Alec and Eric, the spinner.

Members' Winter Dinner – January 2005

On Boxing Day in 2004 Asia suffered from the tsunami, and Sri Lanka amongst other countries was badly hit. The world was shocked, and in the 2005 season MCC staged an exhibition match between two top teams of the world's best players to raise funds in support of the survivors. The idea had taken root by the time of the January Winter Dinner and, later in 2005, I travelled out to Colombo to see where our money could most helpfully be spent.

England were struggling in South Africa, although the members of the Barmy Army were loud in their support of the team. For this dinner Nigel Plews, one of the Test match umpires, was the speaker. I was delighted that several Old Alleynians, who, like me were former Dulwich College boys, came as a group to hear the speech and enjoy a get-together.

As members of the greatest Club, we're standing here for Grace.
We give our thanks for food and drink and friendship in this place.
Our hearts go out for all the lands that suffered from the wave.
We pray for all survivors and for those they could not save.
Our thanks for health and fitness as we start another year.
Please bless all those less fortunate who live both far and near.
Although it's now the winter months, we follow every match.
We watch each run, each wicket lost and every well-held catch.
The team's moved on from Cape Town where we've seen another loss.
Please help our captain, Michael Vaughan, who cannot win the toss.
The Barmy Army did their best and gave the team support.
Please teach our batsmen how to hook; they're always getting caught!
Please bless the group of Dulwich boys who've gathered as OAs.
We've come to meet and reminisce about our schoolboy days.
At MCC we love the game of cricket, win or lose.
Lord, bless the umpires here tonight, especially Nigel Plews.

Farewell Dinner for Stephanie Lawrence – 6 April 2006

This was a special dinner for a special member of MCC staff. Stephanie Lawrence became my PA when I arrived in 1994 and guided me through so many situations where her experience was hugely helpful. She was a key figure at Lord's for 39 years, was PA to three Secretaries, and her knowledge of Lord's and MCC was always invaluable. Alongside the MCC Secretary, Steph was the main person in the secretariat which administered the ICC for many years, taking minutes and getting to know so many of the leading officials from overseas. This was extremely important to me at a time when MCC was attempting to find its new role, and Chris and I learned who should be entertained at our home at 4 Grove End Road as well as in the Secretary's hospitality box. When we travelled overseas Steph always knew whom we should contact.

She retired a few months before I did, but she had schooled Rachel Lee, her successor, and my administrative support continued well. As all senior executives will know, the right Personal Assistant is a vitally important member of staff and support, keeping an eye on all correspondence, making sure that all papers are produced and sent out in a timely manner, acting as gatekeeper to the Secretary & Chief Executive's office and generally keeping everyone informed. Steph did all this and much more.

We give thanks for the meal that we've come here to eat
In the Long Room at Lord's, which is where great friends meet
To enjoy all the food and the MCC wine.
But this evening's quite special. We've come here to dine,
Though we've mainly attended to honour our guest,
Who for thirty-nine years has been one of our best.
We give thanks for the loyalty Steph has displayed,
For her love of this ground and the effort she's made.
Steph's been PA to Jack, to the Colonel and me.
She's administered cricket within ICC.
Invitations to Boxes she's handled with ease
(It's a difficult task with so many to please!)
She has gained great experience and made many friends
And we pray that her love of this Club never ends.
She has worked here through good times and moments of strife
And it's right Steph's an Honorary Member for life.

Ode to My Wife on her 60th Birthday – 27 June 2006

I suspect that I was more nervous before delivering this Grace than usual. There were so many friends and family members present who had played a part in Chris's life, and there was a danger that I would miss some vitally important episode here and in what I was to say later. She has often been the unsung hero and allowed me and others to take the credit and praise for what she has done behind the scenes, preferring to position herself as the worker who rolls up her sleeves and gets on with a task without wanting to be up front.

Gina Buchanan, her school friend from very early days, Jane Timmis, who trained as a nurse with her, and Terri Rea, who worked with her as an air stewardess at BOAC, all had stories to tell. It was a lovely evening, and I really did want to start with what I called 'Ode to my wife on her 60th birthday' or, more appropriately, 'Owed to Chris – Everything'.

We have shared so many wonderful moments and experiences together in the roles we have had, the countries we have visited, and with the friends we have made all round the world, and this was a very good time to say how much I appreciated it all. Her support to me as Housemaster's wife, Headmaster's wife and MCC Secretary's wife was immense and, as well as bringing up our family and running the household, she managed to be a theatre nurse, an air stewardess, a practice manager in Harley Street, a fund raiser, director of a charity and a hostess.

Our children, Katie and Graeme, and their respective husband and wife, Roy and Meredith, were there amongst the many guests in the Long Room. There is a mention in the Grace of Sydney, our golden retriever, who regularly took the boarders' socks and biscuits at Loveday House, Cranleigh School, was taken for walks by the sixth-form girls at Worksop College and returned smelling of cigarette smoke and cheap perfume, used in an attempt to cover the smell of the smoke, and escaped on a couple of occasions into the kitchens at Lord's, where he managed to eat two large fish about to be served at a dinner. He was a character who survived until the age of seventeen and his ashes were buried in the garden of 4 Grove End Road, St John's Wood.

Now it's sixty whole years since the day of your birth,
It's the time for admirers to value your worth.
For the past thirty-five I've been part of your life,
Since that day of great joy we've been husband and wife.
But before then you moved several times after Sale.
Solihull was the first place: the start of your tale;
That's where Gina and you made the greatest of friends;
It's a friendship you both will ensure never ends.
Potters Bar was the next, after school on the coast,
Then Jane's Barbican flat, I remember the most.
The best home of them all was at Sunbury on Thames,
Where a friendship with Terri was one of your gems.
You were great as a stewardess and as a nurse;
Even work on the marketing could have been worse!
In both medical practices duties were wide
And the Worksop Appeal you just took in your stride.
As a wife and a mother, the best there can be,
You've looked after the children, and Sydney, and me!
Now it's time for us all to say thanks very much
For the love that you've shown and the practical touch,
Which has bound us and welcomed both Merry and Roy
To our family – two parents, a girl and a boy.
As you move to the phase, which will start a new life,
I'm so pleased we're together, as husband and wife!
We are lovers, great friends and each other's soul mate
And we've two lovely children in Graeme and Kate.

My Retirement Dinner – 11 September 2006

I retired at the end of September 2006 after twelve and a half years at Lord's. The dinner in the Long Room was a super event. The words spoken were extremely complimentary, and both Chris and I were grateful to the Club for hosting the many people present, some of whom were dining in another room and were taking part via a video link. Although, in some ways, a sad moment, it was the right moment for me to step down and hand over to the 14th Secretary (by now called Secretary & Chief Executive, as I had been for a number of years). Keith Bradshaw, a Tasmanian captain from Hobart, was to be my successor, and he had been working alongside me for the last few months. We got on well.

It had been pointed out to me a month or so earlier that the outgoing Secretary had traditionally played a match on the main ground at the end of his tenure. I was keen to uphold this tradition so I decided to get fitter. I had been going early on most mornings either to the gym in the indoor school or for a walk round Regent's Park. However, as part of the fitness regime, I ran round the park and was surprised how easily I had done it. The next day, on a lovely sunny morning, I repeated the exercise and, once again, I felt rather good afterwards. It was only on the following day that I could not move without a searing pain in the back of my leg. I went to the physio, who referred me to a specialist, who told me that I had ruptured my Achilles tendon and that if I were a cross country runner she would ban me from running for over a year.

Inevitably, I missed the match, but I was more concerned that the last Test match at which I would lead the staff was only a fortnight away. The medical specialist had recommended that I should keep my leg raised for several weeks to avoid pressure on the tendon, but I was determined not to miss this last Test match. Spectators cannot have missed the sight of the old Secretary limping round Lord's, accompanied by a very sprightly successor to the role. It summed it all up – the old and the new! The one upside to this injury was that it allowed Graeme, my son, to play a game at Lord's in my place.

We give thanks for the food on our table,
As we stand here together for Grace.
For us here and those watching on cable
The Lord's Long Room's a marvellous place.
We give thanks for the Club and its members;
Its traditions, its values, its aims.
As each cricketer always remembers,
MCC has the greatest of names.
We give thanks for the great game of cricket;
For the matches, the friendships, the fun.
We look back to each run and each wicket
And those glorious days in the sun.
We are now at the end of an era;
And it happens quite often in sport.
As one day of retirement draws nearer,
Let's give Sara and Keith full support.

Wisden Dinner – April 2016

The new edition of Wisden is always eagerly awaited. There is much speculation and then discussion about the choice of the Five Cricketers of the Year. As President of MCC in 2015/16 I was invited to the dinner in the Long Room and asked to deliver a Grace. The Almanack is the most complete summary of the past season and of so much cricket history, and each year there are some excellent articles produced, written by the best cricket writers. To hold the dinner at Lord's is both a privilege for the Club and a pleasure. England were playing a series in India.

We thank you, Good Lord, for our friends at this dinner;
Each batsman, each keeper, fast bowler or spinner.
We'll wait to hear what our main guests have to utter,
Describing the cricket just played in Calcutta.
This evening, which welcomes the start of the season,
We're here, in this Long Room, for very good reason.
The launch of a Wisden is always exciting,
With scores and reviews and some wonderful writing.
It mentions each year every run and each wicket.
No wonder it's known as the Bible of Cricket.
The Almanack was the first name it went under.
Its founder, John Wisden, they called Little Wonder.
We're gathered, at Lord's, for this annual meeting,
Please bless all our drinks and the food we'll be eating.

14

Final Thanks and Acknowledgements

Without the solid and loving base provided by a stable family background, little of this might have been possible, so first I shall express my gratitude to my parents, which, regrettably, I am not convinced I ever really did properly when they were alive. Chris, Katie and Graeme have given me the space to pursue my two passions of education and cricket and I have the chance here to say a heartfelt thank you to them. Chris and I celebrated our Golden Wedding in March 2021, Katie and her husband, Roy, have given us three grandchildren and Graeme and Meredith two. Anna, Danny, Jonah, Alex and Mariella continue to keep us young at heart and to give us opportunities to watch and encourage them in their sports, drama and musical activities.

This book was initially inspired by Des Wilson, who said that I should write down my memories and, in particular, to explain my thoughts to the outside world about cricket, MCC, Lord's, ECB and the ICC, which have all played a large part in what I have done. I have chosen to expand this advice and to link my careers in education, as a schoolmaster, and cricket, both as a player and as an administrator, which have brought so much happiness to me and led to countless experiences. Some readers may be more interested in my days of playing professional cricket, others in the complex issues that we faced at MCC, and even others interested to know how on earth I arrived in the positions that I held.

Des and I first met when MCC needed sound advice on dealing with the media and we have remained firm friends ever since. He acted as the Club's PR and Media advisor, subsequently joined the England and Wales Cricket Board as a director and was one of my first choices as a speaker at an MCC Members' Winter Dinner in 2015, during my year as President. He is an experienced author and a man of principle, who loves his cricket. He is also great company whenever we find time to get together. We have a regular commitment to dinner in London during the Lord's Test each year, when Jane and Des, Chris and I catch up on all the latest news and his newest challenge.

After an afternoon where I was the guest speaker of the Bath Cricket Society, Stephen Chalke, my host and interviewer, also encouraged me to go ahead and offered his assistance as a publisher and as an experienced cricket writer, which I gladly accepted.

Stephen has a wealth of experience as an author, editor, biographer and publisher. His help has focused my thoughts and assisted in decisions about what to include and what to omit from the years covered by these memoirs. Stephen gave me the final nudge to commit myself to putting down in writing anecdotes and memories that have emerged over many years in after-dinner speeches, talks at Cricket Societies and in general conversation. Where my memories of cricket matches may have become distorted in places, he has put me right by researching and finding the facts.

Other friends have, from time to time, suggested that I should embark on this exercise and I also took inspiration from my father who wrote his own book – DVK – Dulwich Man. I was tempted to call this book 'Aa**RDV**ar**K** – Cricketer and Schoolmaster' and use the only word in the English language that contains my initials in the right order. I also wondered whether to call it 'A Knight in the Oval Office and the House of Lord's', but I think they are better as chapter headings. I realised that my experience as a player, a captain, a coach, an umpire and, ultimately, an administrator with an office window overlooking Lord's had provided me with the 'best views of cricket', the game I love, so that was another possible title. Without planning a career path, I now see how well the diverse executive and non-executive positions have served me and helped me to develop in the various roles!

Ultimately, 'Boundaries' seemed to encompass every aspect of my life so far. Boundaries regarding how far to conform as an individual, how to set parameters for children and pupils to learn self-discipline, how to succeed as a batsman and how to understand and operate within the different roles of an executive or a non-executive.

I hope this book provides insights into the life in schools, professional cricket and MCC, which has occupied so much of my time and which Chris has shared with me. As in batting, so in life, timing is everything and we are most fortunate to have been in the right places at the right time to enjoy all the opportunities, challenges and wonderful moments that have come our way.

Appendices

Cricket career statistics

Scorecards of two Lord's finals

Cricket teams, tours and appointments

Educational, charitable and other appointments

Initiatives and building work at Lord's 1994-2006

Events of my year as MCC President

FIRST-CLASS CRICKET

Cambridge University (1967-70), Surrey (1968-70), Gloucestershire (1971-75),
Sussex (1976-77), Surrey (1978-84, *captain 1978-83*)

BATTING AND FIELDING

	M	I	NO	Runs	HS	Ave	100	50	Ct
Cambridge Univ	48	90	5	2428	164*	28.56	2	17	27
Gloucestershire	105	186	13	5610	144	32.42	11	29	93
Sussex	43	75	6	2112	165*	30.60	2	13	24
Surrey	174	290	32	8712	142	33.76	15	52	138
Other	17	31	5	696	100*	26.76	1	3	14
TOTAL	**387**	**672**	**61**	**19558**	**165***	**32.00**	**31**	**114**	**296**

*Other Matches for Combined Universities, England Under-25, MCC,
Test Trial, Overseas XI (Bengal Golden Jubilee), DH Robins XI*

1000 runs in a season
13 times, highest 1350 in 1974

Centuries (31)
Derbyshire, Essex (3), Glamorgan (3), Gloucestershire, Hampshire (2),
Kent, Lancashire (2), Middlesex (2), Northamptonshire, Nottinghamshire,
Somerset (2), Surrey (2), Sussex, Warwickshire (2), Worcestershire (3),
Cambridge University, Oxford University (2) & Pakistanis.

Scores of 150+ (2)

165*	Sussex v Middlesex	Hove	1976
164*	Cambridge University v Essex	Fenner's	1970

BOWLING

	Overs	Mdns	Runs	Wkts	Best	Ave	5wi
Cambridge Univ	737.1	184	2084	60	6-65	34.73	1
Gloucestershire	1182.4	226	3561	100	6-44	35.61	1
Sussex	411.3	78	1405	29	4-46	48.44	-
Surrey	2041.5	514	5549	163	5-44	34.04	2
Other	242.4	57	736	17	4-38	43.29	-
TOTAL	**4615.5**	**1059**	**13335**	**369**	**6-44**	**36.13**	**4**

Six wickets in an innings (2)

18	9	44	6	Gloucestershire v Northamptonshire	Northampton	1974
30	10	65	6	Cambridge University v Essex	Fenner's	1970

ONE-DAY (LIST A) CRICKET

BATTING AND FIELDING

	M	I	NO	Runs	HS	Ave	100	50	Ct
Gloucestershire	102	100	8	2086	96	22.67	-	13	29
Sussex	44	44	8	1628	127	45.22	4	9	11
Surrey	161	149	15	3121	92*	23.29	-	18	45
Other	3	3	-	74	38	24.66	-	-	-
TOTAL	**310**	**296**	**31**	**6909**	**127**	**26.07**	**4**	**40**	**85**

Other Matches for Minor Counties, DH Robins XI

Centuries (4)

127	Sussex v Hampshire	Hove	JPL	1976
117	Sussex v Surrey	The Oval	B&H	1977
109*	Sussex v Worcestershire	Hove	JPL	1976
109	Sussex v Leicestershire	Eastbourne	JPL	1976

BOWLING

	Overs	Mdns	Runs	Wkts	Best	Ave	4wi
Gloucestershire	758	88	3132	112	5-39	27.96	3
Sussex	162.4	7	774	35	5-42	22.11	2
Surrey	976	93	3889	147	4-19	34.04	2
Other	26	3	96	3	1-22	32.00	-
TOTAL	**1922.4**	**191**	**7891**	**297**	**5-39**	**26.56**	**7**

Five wickets in an innings (2)

10	1	39	5	Gloucestershire v Surrey *(Gillette)*	Bristol	1971
7.2	0	42	5	Sussex v Nottinghamshire *(JPL)*	Trent Bridge	1977

Trophies (2)

Gloucestershire	Gillette Cup	1973
Surrey *(captain)*	NatWest Bank Trophy	1982

Man of the Match Awards (10)

Gillette Cup (5): Gloucestershire v Surrey (1971), Glamorgan (1973), Essex (1973); Surrey v Gloucestershire (1980), Yorkshire (1980).

Benson & Hedges Cup (5): Gloucestershire v Middlesex (1972), Minor Counties South (1973); Sussex v Surrey (1977); Surrey v Northamptonshire (1979), Nottinghamshire (1981).

Gloucestershire won by 40 runs

 LORD'S GROUND

GILLETTE CUP - FINAL
GLOUCESTERSHIRE v. SUSSEX
‡ Saturday, 1st September, 1973

GLOUCESTERSHIRE — Innings

1	Sadiq Mohammad	l b w b Buss	9
2	R. D. V. Knight	b Snow	2
3	Zaheer Abbas	b Buss	9
4	M. J. Procter	c Morley b Buss	94
5	D. R. Shepherd	c Griffith b Marshall ...	11
*6	A. W. Stovold	c Griffith b Snow	10
†7	A. S. Brown	not out	77
8	J. C. Foat	b Snow	7
9	D. A. Graveney	run out	6
10	J. B. Mortimore	-----------------------------	
11	J. Davey	-----------------------------	
		B 4, l-b 10, w , n-b 9,	23
		Total	248

FALL OF THE WICKETS
1—5   2—22   3—27   4—74   5—106   6—180   7—229   8—248   9—   10—

ANALYSIS OF BOWLING

Name	O.	M.	R.	W.	Wd.	N-b.
Snow	12	4	31	3	...	2
Greig	12	1	53	0	...	2
Buss	12	5	46	3	...	...
Marshall	12	3	29	1	...	5
Spencer	12	0	66	0	...	...
	...	...	...	...	...	...
	...	...	...	...	...	...

SUSSEX — Innings

1	G. A. Greenidge	b Knight	76
2	J. D. Morley	c Zaheer b Brown	31
3	R. M. Prideaux	b Davey	28
4	P. J. Graves	not out	36
†5	A. W. Greig	run out	0
6	M. A. Buss	c Graveney b Knight ...	5
*7	M. G. Griffith	b Knight	3
8	M. J. J. Faber	run out	9
9	J. A. Snow	b Procter	4
10	J. Spencer	b Knight	2
11	R. P. T. Marshall	b Procter	0
		B 5, l-b 9, w , n-b ,	14
		Total	208

FALL OF THE WICKETS
1—52   2—121   3—155   4—156   5—173   6—180   7—195   8—204   9—207   10—208

ANALYSIS OF BOWLING

Name	O.	M.	R.	W.	Wd.	N-b.
Procter	10.5	1	27	2	...	...
Davey	10	1	37	1	...	...
Mortimore	12	3	32	0	...	...
Brown	12	1	33	1	...	...
Graveney	2	0	18	0	...	...
Knight	10	0	47	4	...	...
	...	...	...	...	...	...

Umpires—A. E. Fagg & T. W. Spencer   Scorers—A. G. Avery & W. S. Denman

† Captain   * Wicket-keeper

Play begins at 10.45 a.m.   Stumps drawn at 7.30 p.m.

Luncheon Interval—12.45 p.m. to 1.15 p.m.

Tea Interval 4.15 p.m.—4.30 p.m. (may be varied according to state of game)

‡This match is intended to be completed in one day, but three days have been allocated in case of weather interference

Gloucestershire won the toss

National Westminster Bank Trophy 1982

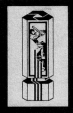

The County winning the Trophy will receive a prize of £12,000, the losing Finalist £5,500, the losing Semi-finalists £3,250 each and the losing Quarter-finalists £1,600 each.

MARYLEBONE CRICKET CLUB

NatWest Bank Trophy Final

15p   ## SURREY v. WARWICKSHIRE   **15p**

at Lord's Ground, †Saturday, September 4th, 1982

SURREY

1 A. R. Butcher	not out	86
2 G. P. Howarth	c Oliver b Lethbridge	31
3 D. M. Smith	not out	28
†4 R. D. V. Knight		
5 M. A. Lynch		
*6 C. J. Richards		
7 D. J. Thomas		
8 G. A. Monkhouse		
9 S. T. Clarke		
10 R. D. Jackman		
11 K. S. Mackintosh		
	B , l-b 4, w , n-b 10,	14
	Total...	159

FALL OF THE WICKETS

1...80 2... 3... 4... 5... 6... 7... 8... 9... 10...

Bowling Analysis	O.	M.	R.	W.	Wd.	N-b
Willis	7	0	23	0	...	7
Small	8	0	60	0	...	3
Ferreira	6	0	16	0	...	...
Lethbridge	6	1	23	1	...	...
Kallicharran	6.4	1	23	0	...	...
	...	...	...	...	...	...
	...	...	...	...	...	...

WARWICKSHIRE

1 K. D. Smith	hit wicket b Thomas	12
2 T. A. Lloyd	l b w b Jackman	2
3 A. I. Kallicharran	c Howarth b Knight	19
4 D. L. Amiss	b Thomas	0
*5 G. W. Humpage	c Richards b Thomas	0
6 P. R. Oliver	run out	2
7 M. Asif Din	l b w b Jackman	45
8 A. M. Ferreira	l b w b Clarke	8
9 C. Lethbridge	c Howarth b Knight	4
10 G. C. Small	c Richards b Clarke	33
†11 R. G. D. Willis	not out	8
	B 8, l-b 11, w , n-b 6,	25
	Total...	158

FALL OF THE WICKETS

1...3 2...32 3...42 4...48 5...51 6...52 7...67 8...74 9...136 10...158

Bowling Analysis	O.	M.	R.	W.	Wd.	N-b
Clarke	11.2	5	17	2	...	1
Jackman	12	2	27	2	...	...
Thomas	11	1	26	3	...	3
Monkhouse	8	0	36	0	...	...
Knight	12	3	14	2	...	...
Mackintosh	3	0	13	0	...	2
	...	...	...	...	...	...

Any alterations to teams will be announced over the loud speaker system

RULES—1 The Match will consist of one innings per side and each innings is limited to 60 overs.
     2 No one bowler may bowl more than 12 overs in an innings.
     3 Hours of play: 10.00 a.m. to 7.00 p.m. In certain circumstances the Umpires may order extra time.

Luncheon Interval 12.30 p.m.—1.10 p.m.   Tea Interval 20 minutes (time according to state of game).
     ‡Captain   *Wicket-keeper
Umpires—H. D. Bird & B. J. Meyer   Scorers—J. Hill, S. P. Austin & E. Solomon
†This match is intended to be completed in one day, but three days have been allocated in case of weather interference

Surrey won the toss and elected to field

Surrey won by 9 wickets

Total runs scored at end of each over:

First Innings	1	2	3	4	5	6	7	8	9	10	11	12	13	14	15	16	17	18	19	20
	21	22	23	24	25	26	27	28	29	30	31	32	33	34	35	36	37	38	39	40
	41	42	43	44	45	46	47	48	49	50	51	52	53	54	55	56	57	58	59	60

Second Innings	1	2	3	4	5	6	7	8	9	10	11	12	13	14	15	16	17	18	19	20
	21	22	23	24	25	26	27	28	29	30	31	32	33	34	35	36	37	38	39	40
	41	42	43	44	45	46	47	48	49	50	51	52	53	54	55	56	57	58	59	60

CRICKET TEAMS REPRESENTED

1963-66	Dulwich College 1st XI (Captain 1966)
1967-70	Cambridge University (Secretary 1970)
1968-70	Surrey CCC
1970-98	MCC
1971-75	Gloucestershire CCC
1976-77	Sussex CCC
1978-84	Surrey CCC (Captain 1978-83)
1987-88	Bedfordshire CCC (Captain 1988)
1988	Combined Minor Counties XI

CRICKET TOURS

1972/73	South Africa – DH Robins XI
1973/74	East Africa – MCC
1975	West Africa – MCC
1979	Far East – Surrey CCC
1980	Bengal Golden Jubilee Match
1985	India – Christians in Sport
1989	France (Bicentenary) – MCC
1993	Kenya – MCC

APPOINTMENTS IN CRICKET

1982	NCA Advanced Coach
1987-90	Surrey Cricket Committee
1988-90, 1992	MCC Committee
1992-97	President, European Cricket Federation
1994-2006	MCC Secretary/MCC Secretary & Chief Executive
1994-2006	President, Cross Arrows
1996-2010	ICC Development Committee
1997-2006	ECB Management Board
2003	Chairman, ECB Interface Review Group
2004-06	Chairman, MCC Laws Working Party
2006-10	Chairman, European Cricket Council
2008-17	Chairman, ECB Association of Cricket Officials
2008/09	President, Surrey CCC
2009-	President, Cambridge University CC
2015/16	President, MCC

EDUCATIONAL APPOINTMENTS

1970-78	Assistant Master & House Tutor, Eastbourne College
1978-83	Assistant Master, Dulwich College
1983-90	Housemaster, Cranleigh School
1990-93	Headmaster, Worksop College
1991-93	HMC Sports Sub-Committee
1992-94	Boarding Schools Association Executive Committee
1994-99	Governor, Rendcomb School
1998-2018	Governor, King's Schools, Taunton
2004-10	Chairman, KST Education Committee
2004-10	Governor, Dulwich College
2008-09	Governor, Millfield School
2009/10	President, Alleyn Club
2010-18	Chairman of Governors (Custos) – KST
2015-16	President, Dulwich Prep School Old Boys

CHARITABLE APPOINTMENTS

1987-92	Trustee, TVS Trust
1994-2006	Chairman, Hornsby Trust
1994-2021	Trustee, MCC Foundation
1997-2001	Director, London Playing Fields Society

OTHER APPOINTMENTS

1985-90	Vice Chairman, SE Region of Sports Council
1987-90	Chairman, SE & London Regions Centres of Excellence Management Committee

INITIATIVES AT LORD'S 1994–2006

Opening the MCC membership to Women

Rewriting the MCC Club Rules

Setting up a Marketing Department

Setting up a Communications Department

Setting up an IT Department

Initiating the Members' Bridge Club

Initiating the Members' Chess Club

Initiating the Members' Golf Society

Initiating the Members' Film Evenings

Initiating the Members' History Society

Initiating the Long Room Concerts

Initiating the MCC Spirit of Cricket Cowdrey Lectures

Initiating the MCC Carol Concerts

Rebranding Lord's

Securing the 2012 Olympic Bid for archery

Staging the Inaugural European Indoor Tournament

Initiating the European Young Cricketers at Lord's

Initiating the MCC Spirit of Cricket Challenge

Staging ICC World Cup

Taking catering in-house at Lord's

Negotiating Staging Agreements with ECB from 1999 to 2009

Revising the Laws of Cricket – 2000 Edition

BUILDING WORK AT LORD'S 1994–2006

1994	New Indoor School
1995	ECB Offices and Lord's Shop
1998	Grand Stand
1999	Media Centre
1999	Updating Electronic Scoreboards
2000	Scorers' Box
2001	Relaying the Outfield
2004	Refurbishing the Pavilion
2005	Replacing the roof of the Mound Stand

EVENTS OF MY YEAR AS MCC PRESIDENT

Some of the many Dinners, Lunches and Receptions as a Host or a Guest

Farewell to the outgoing Club Chairman, Oliver Stocken

The Centenary of the death of WG

The Combined Services

European Real Tennis Final held at Lord's

Burns Night

MCC West Country Members

MCC Anniversary Dinner

MCC Tennis Finals

MCC World Cricket committee at Lord's

MCC North of England Members

MCC Playing Members

MCC Trustees

MCC Candidates

The 80th birthday of Garry Sobers and also the Barbados Golden Jubilee

40th Anniversary of first women's match at Lord's

Guest at presentation of the Walter Lawrence Trophy for fastest century of the year

Guest of Odgers Berndtson with Heads of schools and their Chairmen of Governors

MCC Golf Society

Cross Arrows Cricket Club

The XL Club

South Australia Cricket Association Gala Dinner in Adelaide

Sheffield Cricket Lovers' Society

MCC Tennis Weekend

Sri Lankan Airways, hosted by the chairman, Ajith Dias

The launch of the Wisden Almanack

Surrey Past Presidents

All-Party Parliamentary Cricket Group

The Cricket Society

High Table at St Peter's College, Oxford

Cranleigh Scholars

Surrey Dining Club

Surrey Youth Trust

The Hamilton-Russell Chess Cup

Six MCC Members' Club Winter Dinners

33 meals at cricket matches, 27 other lunches and 14 receptions

Memorial or Thanksgiving Services

Memorial Service for Mark Williams

Memorial Service for Lord Griffiths

Thanksgiving Service to commemorate WG Grace's life

Memorial Service for Tom Graveney

Thanksgiving Service for Donald Carr

Memorial Service for David Emms

Other Highlights

MCC AGM

ECB ACO AGM

Cambridge University CC AGM

Visit to Adelaide for Test Match

Two MCC World Cricket committee meetings

Choral Eucharist in Adelaide Cathedral

Visit to Durban for Test Match

Visit to Cape Town for Test Match

Visit to the MCC Centre of Excellence in Seenigama, Sri Lanka

Dinner and Compline at Lambeth Palace

Opening of the Blavatnik building for the Oxford Department of Government

Play in MCC Tennis Weekend

Commonwealth Garden Party

Guest in the Royal Box at Wimbledon

Cranleigh Scholars' Lecture

Play in Annual Tennis Mixed Doubles Charity Tournament at Little Bredy, Dorset

Read a lesson in Worcester Cathedral at Tom Graveney's memorial service

MCC Spirit of Cricket Cowdrey Lecture

First Lord's Test Match – England v Sri Lanka

Second Lord's Test Match – England v Pakistan

Lord's ODI – England v Pakistan

Hosting in the MCC Committee Room after matches

Visits to other Test Match grounds

Hosting in the Surrey Committee Room at the Oval Test Match

Visit to Wells Cathedral School to open a new pavilion

Visit to Scarborough Festival

INDEX

(close family are omitted)

286